INTRODUCTION

This book, *Arabic Reading Lessons,* is a new and modified version of the book, *Arabic Learning Lessons* by the famous author Duncan Forbes. The aim of taking up some nip and tuck was to make this book more user-friendly valuable and practical. With stet changes, this book surely looks more contemporary and becomes more handy for the learners.

According to the original preface of the book at the time of its first publication, "this was a kind of a book that had long been very much needed, as there had never been anything of the kind for the use of the learners of Arabic language". However, this book still retains the same usefulness for the learners of Arabic language. It is as much needed today as it was at the time of its first publication. The importance of this book lies in the value of the lessons that it contains, which include matters extracted from classics of Arabic literature. To have a mastery over a language, it is often said, one has to read its classics. This book truly gives the pleasure and joy of learning the language from its original sources. It has many reading lessons which are taken from the Quran, the masterpiece of classical Arabic.

Besides, this volume has vast and rich vocabulary. This will help enrich the learner's own vocabulary. This book also has annotations which have been specially included with a view to drawing the attention of the learners towards the grammar of Arabic language in a very easy-to-understand language.

The orthographical symbols have been strictly and very meticulously given in this book. This has been done very painstakingly knowing the importance of vowel points in Arabic language. The publisher wishes to convey readers that they have put the orthographical symbols in the book as correctly as possible, and if somebody finds any mistake, the publisher would feel obliged if they would bring it to the publisher's notice.

New Delhi   Khalid Pervez
April 2005

Arabic READING Lessons

DUNCAN FORBES

GOODWORD

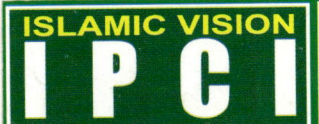

Goodword Books Pvt. Ltd.
1, Nizamuddin West Market, New Delhi-110 013
E-mail: info@goodwordbooks.com
First published 2005
Printed in India
© Goodword Books 2005

VOCABULARY

ARABIC AND ENGLISH

As a general rule, the words in the following Vocabulary are to be looked for under their appropriate triliteral roots. At the same time such words as involve a little irregularity, or more strictly speaking, a little peculiarity, are given in their appropriate place in the alphabetical order, together with a reference to the triliteral root from which they emanate. For example, a mere beginner might feel at a loss where to look for the word اِتَّـضَـعَ. Well, that word I have given in its regular place together with a reference both to its root وَضَـعَ. The same remark applies to اِزْدَرَيْتُ, اِزْدَدْتُ, and many others. The vowels in italics, a, i, and u, included in parentheses, and appended to each triliteral verbal root, indicate respectively the middle vowel of the Aorist Active. Finally, the Roman numerals I. II. III. etc., indicate successively the various formations emanating from the primitive root.

أ

أ *(interr. particle)* what; whether; either; to which replies أَمْ (or); as, أَتَفْعَلُ ذَلِكَ أَمْ whether will you do that, or...?

آل race, family, people.

آلَةٌ an instrument, a tool.

أَبٌ (for أَبَوٌ) a father; (in construction) *nom.* أَبُو ; *gen.* أَبِي; *acc.* أَبَا.

أَبَدَ *(i.)* he was eternal; أَبَدٌ age, time to come, eternity without end; أَبَدًا eternally, for ever.

أَبْرَصُ leprous; a leper.

أَبْلَغُ *(comp.* of بَلِيغٌ) more or most eloquent; very eloquent.

إِبْلِيسُ *(pl.* أَبَالِسَةٌ or أَبَالِيسُ) the devil.

إِبْنٌ a son; إِبْنَةٌ a daughter. See بَنَى

أَبَى *(a. & i.)* he rejected, refused, was averse from.

إِتِّضَاعٌ humiliation, abasement, from وَضَعَ.

أَتَى *(i.)* he came; there passed; when construed with the *prep.* بِ it is equivalent to "he brought", as أَتَى بِكِتَابٍ he came with a book; i.e. he brought a book.

أَثَرَ *(i. & u.)* he alleged; he warned or reminded; أَثَرٌ *(pl.* آثَارٌ) a trace, vestige; أَثَرِهِ on his steps or track, after him, behind him.

أَثِمَ *(a.)* he was wicked, he sinned. إِثْمٌ sin, iniquity; آثِمٌ a sinner.

إِثْنَانِ and *fem.* إِثْنَتَانِ two, from ثَنَى he doubled.

أَجَرَ *(u. & i.)* he remunerated; أَجْرٌ remuneration, wages, hire; fare.

أَجَلَ *(u. & i.)* he appointed; fixed a term; أَجْلٌ a cause, reason; لِأَجْلِ ذَلِكَ on that account; أَجَلٌ the destined period of life; fate, death.

أَجْوَدُ better, best, most excellent See جَادَ

إِحْتِقَارٌ contempt. See حَقَرَ

أَحَدٌ *(fem.* إِحْدَى) one, any one See rt. وَحَدَ. أُحُدٌ the name of a mountain near Madinah.

أَحَدُّ more or most violent; sharper; sharpest. See حَدَّ.

أَحْمَدُ more or most laudable, highly praised, Ahmad, a man's name.

أَحْمَقُ very foolish, an egregious fool.

أَحْنَفُ bandy-legged; also a man's name.

أخ

أَخٌ‎ أَخوٌ‎ for a brother. (In construction) nom. أَخُو‎; gen. أَخِي‎; acc. أَخَا‎. إِخْوَانٌ‎ and إِخْوَةٌ‎ (pl.) brethren; أُخْتٌ‎ for أُخْوَةٌ‎ a sister.

أَخَذَ‎ (u.) he took; he began; vii. اِتَّخَذَ‎ he assumed, he adopted.

أَخِرَ‎ (i.) he was last; I. أَخَّرَ‎ he kept back, he retarded; تَأْخِيرٌ‎ delaying, postponing; IV. تَأَخَّرَ‎ he drew back, he delayed; آخَرُ‎ (fem. أُخْرَى‎) another, other; آخِرٌ‎ last, final; فِي آخِرِ الأَمْرِ‎ at length, in short; الآخِرَةُ‎ the world to come; (pl. أَوَاخِرُ‎) أَخِيرٌ‎ last, latter.

أَدُبَ‎ (u.) he was polished, and well informed; أَدَبٌ‎ good breeding, education, polite literature; (pl. أُدَبَاء‎) أَدِيبٌ‎ polite, accomplished, of good education.

أَدْرِ‎ aor. apoc. of دَرَى‎ he knew, q.v.

آدَمُ‎ Adam, the first man.

أَدْنَى‎ (comp. of دَنِيٌّ‎ q.v.) more or most base or vile

أَدَى‎ (i.) it was copious; I. أَدَّى‎ he paid, performed.

أسد

إِذْ‎ when, then, at that time; interj. lo! behold!

إِذَا‎ and إِذَاكَ‎ when; then.

أَذِنَ‎ (a.) he gave ear; he proclaimed the hour of prayer; he permitted, allowed; III. آذَنَ‎ he proclaimed, announced; IX. اِسْتَأْذَنَ‎ he asked leave; إِذْنٌ‎ permission, leave; أُذُنٌ‎ (pl. آذَانٌ‎) the ear.

أَذِيَ‎ (a.) he was hurt, injured; III. آذَى‎ he hurt, injured; مُوذٍ‎ noxious, injurious.

أَرْبَعَةٌ‎ (fem. أَرْبَعٌ‎) four; أَرْبَعُونَ‎ forty.

أَرَّخَ‎ and أَرَخَ‎ he dated (an epistle or book, etc.) تَأْرِيخٌ‎ (pl. تَوَارِيخ‎) dating, a date; history, annals.

أَرْضٌ‎ (pl. أَرَضُونَ‎ and أَرَاضِي‎) the earth; land; a country.

أَرْنَبٌ‎ (pl. أَرَانِبُ‎) a hare.

أَرِيكَةٌ‎ (pl. أَرَائِكُ‎) a couch; a throne.

اِزْدَدْتُ‎ VII. of زَادَ‎ q.v. he increased

اِزْدَرَيْتُ‎ VII. of زَرَا‎ q.v. he despised.

أَزِمَّةٌ‎ (pl. of زِمَامٌ‎) camel's halters or reins (rt. زَمَّ‎ q.v.).

أَسَدٌ‎ (pl. أُسْدٌ‎) a lion; also the name of an Arab tribe.

أسر

أَسَرَ (i.) he bound, took captive; أُسْرٌ a ligament, a joint; that by which one thing is fastened to another; a rein or bridle; بِأَسْرِهِ with his bridle; hence, the whole, entirely; أَسِيرٌ bound, a captive.

أَسِفَ (a.) he mourned, grieved; أَسَفٌ grief, sorrow.

إِسْلَامٌ Islām, the Muslim faith. See سَلِمَ

إِسْمٌ a name. See rt. سَمَا

أَسَى (a.) he felt grieved, he was sorry or sad, he regretted.

أَشِدَّآءُ (pl. of شَدِيدٌ from شَدَّ q.v.) intense; strong, violent, powerful.

أَشْرَفُ eminent, most noble; also man's name.

أَشْيَآءٌ (pl. of شَيْءٌ) things, affairs.

اِصْطِنَاعٌ inf. VII. of صَنَعَ q.v.

أَصُلَ (u.) it was firmly rooted; أَصْلٌ the foundation or base, root, origin, source or first principle of anything (opposed to فَرْعٌ); أَصِيلٌ the evening; a noble steed.

اِضْمَحَلَّ (quadrilit.) he vanished, disappeared (III. formation)

أَعْجَمِي . See عَجَمِيٌّ a barbarian, more especially a Persian.

8

أَلَا

إِعْطَاءٌ inf. III. of عَطَوَ (for عَطَى q.v.)

أَعْلَالٌ (pl. of عِلَّةٌ) diseases, infirmities.

اِعْوِجَاجٌ inf. VIII. of عَوِجَ he was crooked; wryness, curvature, obliquity.

أَعْيَانِي pret. of III. of عَيَّ (q.v.) with نِي the affixed pronoun 'me.'

أَغْنَى comp. & sup. of غَنِيٌّ rich, wealthy; richer, more or most wealthy; أَغْنِيَاءُ (pl. of غَنِيٌّ from غَنِيَ q.v.)

أَفْلَاطُونُ the philosopher Plato.

أَفَنَقْتَدِي 1st pers. pl. of VII. قَدَى (q.v.) with the interrogative أ and the particle ف prefixed.

إِقْوَاءٌ inf. of III. of قَوِيَ q.v. strengthening, etc.

أَقْوِيَاءُ pl. of قَوِيٌّ strong, very powerful.

أَكَّدَ See وَكَّدَ he confirmed.

أَكَلَ (u.) he ate; imp. كُلْ ; مَأْكَلٌ eating; أَكْلٌ whatever is eaten, food.

أَكْمَهُ blind from one's birth. See كَمِهَ

آلٌ (see rt. أَوَلَ) family, race, etc.

أَلْ the definite article The, indeclinable.

أَلَا verily, be assured; أَلَّا for أَنْ لَا that not; إِلَّا for إِنْ لَا if not, unless, except.

أَلَا (a.) he was deficient, he failed; III. آلَى he swore, he vowed; أَلِيَّةٌ an oath, a vow.

أَلْبَابٌ (pl. of لُبٍّ) hearts, intellects.

أَلَّذِي (pl. أَلَّذِينَ) he who, him whom.

أَلْسِنَةٌ (pl. of لِسَانٌ) tongues; languages.

آلَةٌ a tool, an instrument, implement.

أَلِفَ (a.) he frequented, resided in; اَلْوَطَنُ الْمَأْلُوفُ the land we live in, home; أَلْفٌ a thousand.

أَلِمَ (a.) he was in pain; أَلِيمٌ painful, grievous.

أَلَّهَ he adored, worshipped; إِلَهٌ a God, a divinity; اَللَّهُ the God, the true God; اَللَّهُ تَعَالَى God the Most High; اَللَّهُمَّ (in prayer) O God!

إِلَى (prep.) to, towards, up to.

أُمٌّ a mother; أُمُّ الْوَلَدِ the mother of children; a law term applied to the female slave who has borne children to her master.

أَمَّا but, yet; أَمَّا بَعْدُ but after; a form used by the Arabs in letter writing, signifying "these things being premised."

إِمَّا either, both.

إِمَامٌ a chief, generally means a chief priest, Imam; a sovereign; إِمَامَةٌ the office or dignity of chief priest.

أَمَرَ (u.) he ordered, commanded; V. تَوَامَرَ he determined, resolved; VII. اِئْتَمَرَ he submitted, obeyed; أَمْرٌ an affair, subject; an order, command; أَمِيرٌ (pl. أُمَرَاءُ) a commander; a prince; أَمِيرُ الْمُؤْمِنِينَ commander of the faithful (a title assumed by the Caliphs).

مَرْءٌ a man; إِمْرَأَةٌ a woman (rt. q.v.)

أَمْسِ the day before; بِالْأَمْسِ yesterday.

اِمْضِ go, march; imp. of مَضَى q.v.

أَمَلَ and أَمَّلَ hope, expectation.

أَمِنَ he confided, he trusted; آمَنَ (a.) he was secure, safe; III. he made safe or certain; he believed; مُؤْمِنٌ a true believer; أَمَانٌ safety, safeguard.

آنٌ time; اَلْآنَ now, at present.

أَنْ that, to the end that; إِنْ if; أَنَّ and; أَنَّهُ because, since; إِنَّ and; إِنَّهُ indeed, truly; إِنَّمَا certainly;

it is only this.
أَنَا (*1st pers. pron. com.*) I.
إِنَاءٌ (*pl.* آنِيَةٌ) a vessel, a *cup*.
أَنْتَ (*2nd pers. pron. masc.*) you; أَنْتِ (*fem.*).
اِنْتِقَامٌ (from نَقَمَ) revenge, retaliation.
أَنِسَ (*a.*) he became familiar; III. he associated with, he made friendship; إِنْسٌ the human race, mankind; إِنْسَانٌ a human being (as opposed to a brute); (*pl.* أُنَاسٌ generally contracted into نَاسٌ)
أَنِفَ (*a.*) he disdained, scorned; IX.
اِسْتَأْنَفَ he renewed; it recommenced; أَنْفٌ the nose.
أَنْفُسٌ (*pl.* of نَفْسٌ) souls; selves.
أَنُوشِيرْوَانْ name of a Persian king of the Sassanian Dynasty who reigned in the sixth century. He was famed for his justice.
أَنَى and *v.* تَوَانَى he delayed, tarried or lingered (by the way); اَلتَّأَنِّي tardiness, slowness.
أَنْيَابٌ (*pl.* of نَابٌ) teeth, especially those of a dog; canine teeth.
آنِيَةٌ (*pl.* of إِنَاءٌ) vases, vessels.

أَهَلَ (*u. & i.*) he married; أَهْلٌ people; a person; a master, lord; أَهْلُ الدَّارِ people of the house, domestics, attendants.
آلَ or أَوَلَ (*u.*) he returned; آلٌ a family, race, people; أَوَّلٌ first; the beginning. أَوَّلاً firstly.
أَوْ *conj.* or, either, whether.
أُولَئِكَ (*pl.* of ذَلِكَ) *demonst. pron.* those.
أَيْ that is to say; *i. e.;* أَيٌّ (*pron. com. gen.*) whosoever, whichsoever; *interrog.* who, which; أَيُّكُمْ which of you.
أَيَّا and إِيَّا (a pleonastic particle prefixed to pronouns of every gender and person); as إِيَّايِ I, or me; إِيَّاكِ thou, or thee, etc.; إِيَّاكَ take care, be on your guard; construed with مِنْ or وَ.
أَيَّامٌ (*pl.* of يَوْمٌ) days; times, seasons.
آيَةٌ (*pl.* آيَاتٌ) a sign; a miracle; a verse of the Qur'ān.
أَيِسَ (*a.*) he despaired.
أَيْضًا likewise, also; the same, ditto.
أَيْقَنُ (*comp.* and *sup.* of يَقِينٌ) more or most certain, truer, truest; quite sure.

أَيَّل

أَيَّل or أَيِّل (pl. أَيَائِلُ) a stag; a species of mountain goat, chamois, gazelle.

إِيْمَانٌ faith, religion. See أَمَنَ.

أَيْنَ where, whither, مِنْ أَيْنَ whence.

أَيُّهَا (interj.) O! hear! listen!

أَيْوَانٌ (Persian ايوان) a palace,

ب

ب (insep. prep.) in, to; by, with.

بَأَرَ (a.) he dug a well; بِئْرٌ a well.

بارِدٌ cold. See بَرَدَ.

بَاعَ for بَيَعَ (i.) he sold; also he bought; he trafficked.

بَانَ for بَيَنَ (i.) it was manifest, clear, or evident; I. بَيَّنَ he made manifest, shewed, or declared.

بَؤُسَ for بَأَسَ (u.) he was courageous; بَئِسَ (a.) he was miserable; بَأْسٌ valour, ardour, force, violence.

بَحْرٌ (pl. بُحُورٌ and بِحَارٌ) the sea.

بَخَرَ (a.) it exhaled; بَخُورٌ (pl. بَخُورَاتٌ) perfume, fumigation; بُخَارٌ exhalation, fume, steam, vapour.

بَذَلَ

بُخْلٌ (pl. بُخَلَاءُ) بَخِيلٌ avarice; avaricious; a miser.

بَدَّ (u.) he separated, disjoined; تَبَدُّدٌ being dispersed, being scattered; بُدٌّ separation, avoidance; لَا بُدَّ there is no avoidance or escape, it must be.

بَدَأَ (a.) he began, commenced; III. أَبْدَأَ he produced, he created; he shewed; VII. اِبْتَدَأَ he commenced, began; بَدْءٌ and بَدْوٌ beginning, origin; اِبْتِدَاءٌ a commencement.

بَدَرَ (u.) he hastened, he anticipated; II. بَادَرَ he hastened to perform (anything for another); III. أَبْدَرَ he did (anything) when the moon was full; بَدْرٌ the full moon; مُبَادَرَةٌ haste, precipitation.

بَدَلَ (a.) and I. بَدَّلَ he changed, exchanged; تَبْدِيلٌ and بَدَلٌ substitution, permutation, exchange.

بَدَنَ (u.) he was corpulent; بَدَنٌ (pl. أَبْدَانٌ) the body; strictly speaking, it means the trunk, independent of the head and feet.

بَذَلَ (i. & u.) he bestowed,

expended, lavished, squandered.

بَرَّ (*a.*) for بَرَرَ he was just, virtuous; بَرٌّ dry land, earth (as opposed to بَحْرٌ sea); أَبْرَارٌ (*pl.*) just, righteous, holy men; بَرِّيَّةٌ the country, the open plain, a desert; بَرِّيٌّ of or belonging to the desert.

بَرَأَ (*a.*) he recovered from sickness; he was cured; III. أَبْرَأَ he cured, healed, or restored to health.

بَرُدَ (*u.*) it was cold; بَرْدٌ the cold; بَارِدٌ cold; بَرِيدٌ a courier, post, messenger; مِبْرَدٌ a file.

بَرَقَ (*u.*) it glittered, it shone; بُرُوقٌ (*pl.*) lightning, the thunderbolt; إِبْرِيقٌ an ewer, a water-jug; إِسْتَبْرَقٌ a rich silken robe, brocade.

بَرَكَ (*u.*) he stood firm; he kneeled, bent the knee; II. بَارَكَ he blessed; مُبَارَكٌ blest, prosperous, thriving.

بَرْمَك the name of a noble family who flourished at Baghdād under the caliphate of Harūn-al-Rashīd; بَرْمَكِيٌّ belonging to the Barmakī family; a Barmecide.

بُسْتَانٌ (from the Persian بوستان) a garden, a pleasure-ground; بُسْتَانِيٌّ a gardener, a florist.

بَسَطَ (*u.*) he expanded, stretched out, it was wide; بِسَاطٌ a cushion, carpet, rug, or mat; anything spread out for a seat.

بَسَمَ (*i.*) تَبَسَّمَ he smiled.

بَشَرَ (*u.*) and I. بَشَّرَ he announced glad tidings, he greeted; بَشَرٌ a human being, man.

بَصَرَ (*u.*) he saw, he beheld; بَصَرٌ (*pl.* أَبْصَارٌ) the eyesight, the eye; بَصِيرٌ a seer, one possessed of sight; بَصِيرَةٌ inward perception, penetration.

بَضَعَ (*a.*) he cut off (a portion); بَضْعَةٌ a piece, a morsel.

بَطَحَ (*a.*) he cast down, fell down; VI. إِنْبَطَحَ he fell prostrate.

بَطِرَ (*a.*) he was mirthful, he bore himself haughtily or insolently; III. أَبْطَرَ he annoyed, made insolent.

بَطَلَ (*u.*) it was abortive, void, of no effect; I. بَطَّلَ he abolished, caused to cease, made void.

بَطَنَ (*u.*) it was hid, it lay

بَعَثَ

concealed; بَطْنٌ (pl. بُطُونٌ) the belly, interior.

بَعَثَ (a.) he sent; he raised (from the dead).

بَعُدَ (u.) he was remote, distant, IV. بَعَّدَ and V. تَبَاعَدَ he went to a distance, he withdrew; بَعْدُ after; بَعِيدٌ far, distant; بُعْدٌ distance.

بَعْضٌ (pl. أَبْعَاضٌ) a certain one, someone; بَعُوضٌ and (noun of unity) بَعُوضَةٌ a small fly, gnat, mosquito.

بَغْدَادُ the city of Baghdād.

بَغُضَ (u.) he was hateful, he hated; بُغْضٌ hatred, maliciousness.

بَغْلٌ (pl. بِغَالٌ) a mule.

بَغَى (i.) he transgressed, he sought; بَغْيٌ injustice, mutiny, rebellion.

بَقَرٌ (pl. بُقُورٌ) an ox. (collectively) cattle; بَقَرَةٌ a cow.

بَقِيَ (i.) he remained; III. أَبْقَى he caused to remain; he preserved, saved; بَقَاءٌ duration, continuation;

بَكَرَ (u.) he rose at dawn, he did (anything) betimes; بِكْرٌ (pl.

بَلَا

أَبْكَارٌ) a virgin; بُكْرَةٌ the time of dawn, morning; بُكُورٌ hastening, a doing of anything betimes, diligence.

بَكَى (i.) he wept; V. تَبَاكَى he was moved to tears, he joined (others) in weeping; بُكَاءٌ weeping.

بَلْ but, yet; بِلَا without.

بَلَّ (u.) he wet or moistened.

بَلَدَ he sojourned, he abode; he was stupid; بَلْدَةٌ and (pl. بِلَادٌ) a country, district; a town; بَلِيدٌ stupid, stolid, dull, obtuse.

بَلِعَ (a.) he swallowed.

بَلَغَ (u.) he reached, attained; came; (used impersonally) it came to one's knowledge; بَلَاغٌ that which comes or is brought to any one; بَلِيغٌ fluent, eloquent بُلُوغٌ maturity, perfection.

he was silly; أَبْلَهُ foolish, a simpleton.

بَلَا for بَلَوَ (u.) he tried, he tempted, he afflicted; VII. إِبْتَلَى he was involved in trouble, he suffered adversity; بَلَاءٌ proof, experience; evil, trouble, adversity; بَلِيَّةٌ an experiment,

بَنَى

trial; also sorrow, affliction by which men are tried; بَلَى yes, verily.

بَنَى (i) he built, founded; بِنْتٌ a daughter; اِبْنٌ a son (pl. بَنُونَ obj. case بَنِينَ); (in construction) بَنُو and بَنِي; بُنَيَّ (dimin.) a little son; يَابُنَيَّ O my (dear) little son; بَنَّاءٌ a builder, an architect; بُنْيَانٌ building; بِنْيَةٌ or بُنْيَةٌ an edifice.

بَهَجَ (a.) and VII. اِبْتَهَجَ he was glad or delighted.

بَهَا for بَهَوَ (u.) it was beautiful, it shone; بَهِيٌّ beautiful, good, fair.

بَهِيمَةٌ (pl. بَهَائِمُ) a beast of burden; a brute; an animal.

بَابٌ (pl. أَبْوَابٌ) a door, a gate; a chapter بَابُ الْأَبْوَابِ the gate of gates; the name given by the Arabs to the strait called Porte Caspiae by the Romans, and دَرْبَنْد by the Persians; between the Caspian Sea and Mount Caucasus.

بَاتَ for بَيَتَ (a. & i.) he abode during the night, he passed the night; بَيْتٌ (pl. بُيُوتٌ) a house, a tent; (pl. أَبْيَاتٌ) a verse

or couplet.

بَاسَ (from the Persian بوسه) he kissed, embraced; بُوسٌ a kiss.

بَاضَ for بَيَضَ (i.) it was white; بَاضَتْ (the hen, etc.) laid eggs; بَيَاضٌ whiteness; أَبْيَضُ (pl. بِيضٌ) white; بَيْضَةٌ an egg.

بَاعَ for بَيَعَ (i.) he sold; VII. he purchased; بَيْعٌ act of selling; اِبْتِيَاعٌ purchasing.

بَانَ (u. & i.) it appeared; it was clear and distinct; I. بَيَّنَ he elucidated, he explained, related; III. أَبَانَ he revealed, manifested; IV. تَبَيَّنَ it was evident; it appeared; بَيْنَ between, among, in the midst of; بَيْنَا and بَيْنَمَا whilst; بَيَانٌ explanation, relation, eloquence, expression; بَيِّنَةٌ anything manifest and clear, convincing; demonstration; مُبِينٌ manifest, clear.

ت

تَارٌ and تَارَةٌ a time, a turn; once, one time; تَارَةً at one time, one while.

تَأَم (i.) he had a twin; تَوْأَم (du. تَوْأَمَان) a twin, twins.

تَبِعَ (a.) and VII. اِتَّبَعَ he followed; تَابِع a follower, a sectary.

تِبْن straw, hay, fodder.

تَجَرَ (u.) he traded, trafficked; تَاجِر (pl. تِجَار and تُجَّار) a merchant, a trader; تِجَارَة commerce, traffic, merchandise.

تَحْتَ (prep.) under, beneath.

تَرِبَ (a.) it was earthy; تُرْبَة soil, earth, clay; تُرَاب (pl. تِرْبَان and أَتْرِبَة) dust, soil, earth.

تَرْجَمَ quadril. he translated one language into another; تَرْجُمَان, تَرْجَمَان or تُرْجُمَان an interpreter.

تَرَكَ (u.) he left, abandoned; he made or deemed.

تِسْع (masc. تِسْعَة) nine.

تَعِبَ (a.) he was fatigued; تَعْبَان fatigue, labour, pain; wearied, oppressed.

تِقَن nature; skilful, perfect; III. أَتْقَنَ he perfected; he made skilfully and judiciously.

تِلْك (dem. pron. fem.) that.

تَمَّ (i.) it was complete, concluded; تَمَام the whole, completion.

تَابَ (u.) he turned back, reformed, repented; he changed; I. تَوَّبَ he caused to repent or change.

تَوَانِي (rt. وَنَى q.v.) delay, slowness.

ث

ثَبَتَ (u.) it was firm, it remained, was permanent; ثَابِت firm, fixed.

ثُعْبَان (pl. ثَعَابِين) a dragon, a large species of serpent.

ثَعْلَب (pl. ثَعَالِب) a fox.

ثَغْر (pl. ثُغُور) a row of teeth.

ثِقَة confiding, trusting (rt. وَثَقَ).

ثَقُلَ (u.) he was heavy; ثِقْل weight, heaviness; ثَقِيل heavy; grievous.

ثُلُث a (masc. ثَلَاثَة) three; ثَلَاث third.

ثَلَجَ (u.) it snowed; ثَلْج (pl. ثُلُوج) snow; ثَلْج ثَالِج heavy, thick snow.

ثُمَّ and ثُمَّتَ then, afterwards.

ثَمَرَ it was fruitful; ثَمَر and ثَمَرَة a (pl. أَثْمَار and ثُمُور and ثِمَار) fruit; single fruit.

ثَمَانِي (masc. ثَمَانِيَة) eight; ثَمَانٍ for

ثَمَن eighty; ثَمَانُونَ price.

ثَنَى (i.) he bent; he doubled; ثَانٍ second; أَثْنَاءٌ the midst; the middle; إِثْنَان (fem. إِثْنَتَان) two.

ثَابَ (u.) he turned, for changed; ثَوْبٌ (pl. ثِيَابٌ and أَثْوَابٌ clothes) a coat, a garment. ثَوَابٌ reward (in a future state) for good works done in this life.

ثَارَ (u.) it was stirred up for (dust, anger, a tumult, etc.) ثَوْرٌ (pl. ثِيرَانٌ) a bull; frenzy, madness; a fool.

ج

جُبٌّ (pl. جِبَابٌ) well, a pit, a cistern.

جَبَرَ (u.) he bound together, reunited; جَبَّارٌ powerful, haughty; a tyrant.

جَبَلَ (u. & i.) he formed, created; جَبَلٌ (pl. جِبَالٌ) a mountain.

جَدَّ (i.) he was great, powerful; it was new; I. جَدَّدَ he made new or renovated; جَدِيدٌ new; جِدًّا violently, exceedingly.

جَرَّ (u.) he drew, dragged.

جَرَحَ (a.) he wounded, tore up; جَوَارِحُ birds or beasts of prey; جَرَّاحٌ a surgeon, a phlebotomist.

جَرَدَ (u.) he took away, stripped off; I. جَرَّدَ he caused to be pulled off (his clothes; he unsheathed (his sword); جَرَادٌ (collective), جَرَادَةٌ (noun of unity) a locust.

جُرَذٌ (pl. جِرْذَانٌ) a species of field-rat.

جُرْزَةٌ a bundle (especially of hay, grass, or firewood).

جَرَى (i.) it flowed; it came to pass, occured; جَارِيَةٌ (pl. جَوَارِي) a girl, a female slave; جَارٍ flowing (water); جَرْيٌ running (a race).

جَزَرَ (i.) he slaughtered; جَزَّارٌ a butcher (especially of camels).

جَزَا he recompensed, repaid; II. جَازِي the same; جَازَاهُ خَيْرًا he prayed (God) to recompense him; جَزَاءُ recompensing; requital, reward.

جَسَرَ (u.) he passed over; he was bold, he ventured; جِسْرٌ a bridge.

جَسُمَ (u.) he was fat, large, or

جَعْدَ

bulky; جِسْمٌ (pl. أَجْسَامٌ) the body; جَسِيمٌ large, corpulent or portly.

جَعِدَ he had curling hair; جَعْدٌ curly-haired, crisp-haired, frizzle-haired.

جَعَلَ (a.) he placed; he made; he appointed; he feigned.

جَفْنٌ (pl. أَجْفَانٌ) an eyelid.

جَلَّ (i.) he was great; جَلِيلٌ (pl. أَجِلَّاءُ) great, illustrious.

جَلَدَ (i.) he flayed; he scourged; he flogged; جِلْدٌ (pl. جُلُودٌ) the skin, the hide.

جَلَسَ (i.) he sat down (on the ground in the Oriental manner,— قَعَدَ expressing the European fashion); مَجْلِسٌ (pl. مَجَالِسُ) the time or place of sitting, a sitting-room, an assembly, session; جُلُوسٌ an assembly, a sederant.

جَمَعَ he collected, united; II. جَامَعَ he had connection with; VII. اِجْتَمَعُوا they assembled, agreed; جَمْعٌ a number, multitude; أَجْمَعُ all, entire, whole; جَمِيعٌ collected, the whole; جَمِيعًا together, altogether, entirely; جَمَاعَةٌ a body, a band.

جَمُلَ (u.) he was comely, beautiful; جَمَلٌ a camel (especially when full-grown, and strong); جَمَالٌ beauty, comeliness; جَمِيلٌ handsome, graceful.

جَنَّ (u.) (the night) concealed or veiled; جِنٌّ a spirit, genie, demon (as being invisible); جَانٌّ genii, demons; جَنَّةٌ a garden, paradise.

جَنَبَ (i.) he shunned; جَنْبٌ and جَانِبٌ (pl. جَوَانِبُ) the side.

جَنَاحٌ (pl. أَجْنُحٌ) the human hand or arm; wing of a bird, fin of fish.

جُنْدٌ (pl. جُنُودٌ) an army, a legion.

جِنْسٌ (pl. أَجْنَاسٌ and جُنُوسٌ) genus, kindred, race.

جَنَقَ (i.) he shot (from a balista); مَنْجَنِيقٌ a balista or catapult for discharging missiles.

جَهَدَ (a.) he strove; he laboured; VII. اِجْتَهَدَ he took pains; he strove; بَذَلَ الْمَجْهُودَ he put forth every effort.

جَهَزَ (a.) he rushed on (a wounded foe to despatch him); I. جَهَّزَ he appointed, equipped, he

جَافَ for جَوَفَ (u.) it was hollow; جَوْفٌ the inside of anything, the belly, a concavity.

جَوِّيٌّ internal, (opposed to بَرِّيٌّ external).

جَاءَ for جَيْاً (i.) he came; جَاءَ بِكِتَابٍ he brought a book; مَجِيْئٌ arrival, coming.

جَيْشٌ (pl. جُيُوشٌ) an army, troops.

ح

حَبَّ (i.) and III. أَحَبَّ he loved, desired; حُبٌّ and مَحَبَّةٌ love, regard, affection.

حَبِرَ (a.) it (the field) flourished; حُبُورٌ joy, gladness; مَحْبُورٌ joyous, filled with joy, overjoyed.

حَبَسَ (i.) he confined, imprisoned; حَبْسٌ confinement, imprisonment.

حَتَّى unto, until (time or place).

حَجَّ (u.) he sought; he performed a pilgrimage to Makkah; VII. he argued, insisted that; حَجَّةٌ the pilgrimage to Makkah; حُجَّةٌ proof, argument.

حَجَرَ (u.) he interdicted, guarded;

---

despatched.

جَهِلَ (a.) he was ignorant, silly; جَاهِلٌ (pl. جُهَّالٌ) silly; an ignoramus.

جَابَ for جَوَبَ (u.) he cut, split; III. أَجَابَ he answered; he asserted; he granted. جَوَابٌ an answer, reply.

جَادَ for جَوَدَ (u.) he was generous, bountiful, good, or famous; جُودَةٌ goodness; جَيِّدٌ good, excellent; أَجْوَدُ best or most excellent.

جَارَ for جَوَرَ (u.) he transgressed; he erred; he was unjust (in his decision); he acted tyrannically as sovereign; III. جَاوَرَ he was neighbour to (one); he associated with (one); جَوْرٌ injustice, tyranny; جَارٌ a neighbour, a partner in trade; جَوْرَةٌ a pool or basin in a running stream.

جَازَ for جَوَزَ (u.) he went, passed by; also VII. إِجْتَازَ the same.

جَاعَ for جَوَعَ (u.) he hungered; I. جَوَّعَ he kept hungry; he famished; جَائِعٌ hungry, starving; جُوعٌ hunger; جُوعًا in a state of hunger, starving.

حِجْرٌ the bosom, the lap.

حَدَّ (*i.*) he limited; حَدٌّ (*pl.* حُدُودٌ) boundary, limit, goal; حَدِيدٌ sharp, pointed, violent; iron أَحَدُّ more or most sharp. حَدَّادٌ a worker in iron, a blacksmith.

حَدَثَ (*a.*) it happened, it came to pass; I. حَدَّثَ he related, narrated حَدِيثٌ a tale, tradition.

حَدَرَ (*u.*) and VI. اِنْحَدَرَ he descended.

حَدَقَ (*i.*) he was circumspect; حَادِقٌ acute, clever, skilful; أَحْدَقُ more or most skilful.

حَذِرَ (*a*) he bewared, was cautious; he shunned; حَذَرٌ caution, avoidance.

حَرَّ (*i.*) it was hot; it glowed; (*a.*) he was free, of noble race; حَرٌّ (*pl.* أَحَارِرُ and حُرُورٌ) heat, fervour; حَرِيرٌ silk.

حَرَبَ (*u.*) he waged war; حَرْبٌ (*pl.* حُرُوبٌ) war.

حَرَثَ (*u.*) he ploughed, cultivated; حَرْثٌ tillage, agriculture; مِحْرَاثٌ a plough, a coulter.

جِرْدَوْنٌ and جِرْذَوْنٌ a lizard. a land crocodile.

حَرَشَ (*i.*) (strife) was raised; III.

أَحْرَشَ he exasperated, he irritated, excited anger.

حَرِصَ (*a*) he was covetous; greedy, covetous.

حَرَقَ (*i. & u.*) it was burning; III. أَحْرَقَ he set on fire; he burnt; VII. اِحْتَرَقَ it caught fire; it was burnt.

حَرَكَ (*u.*) it was in motion; it shook; I. حَرَّكَ he moved; he set in motion. حَرَكَةٌ motion.

حَرُمَ (*i.*) it was forbidden, unlawful; حَرَامٌ and حُرْمَةٌ that which the law prohibits; مُحَرَّمٌ sacred, interdicted; name of the first month in the Arabian Calendar, during which, warfare was prohibited.

حَزَقَ (*i.*) he bound, restricted.

حَزْمٌ steadiness, vigilance, caution.

حَزَنَ (*a.*) he sorrowed, mourned; حُزْنٌ and حَزَنٌ (*pl.* أَحْزَانٌ) sorrow, grief.

حَسَّ for حَسِسَ (*u.*) he felt, he perceived, he thought, he knew.

حَسِبَ (*i.*) he reckoned, was of opinion, accounted.

حَسَدَ (*i. & u.*) he envied; حَسَدٌ

envy; مَحْسُودٌ envied; حَاسِدٌ and حَسُودٌ envious.

حَسُنَ (*u.*) he was good, handsome, excellent; III. أَحْسَنَ he made good; he did good; he was liberal; IX. إِسْتَحْسَنَ he accounted good; he approved; مُحْسِنٌ benevolent, good, virtuous; حُسْنٌ beauty; حَسَنٌ good, beautiful, splendid; أَحْسَنُ (*fem.* حُسْنَى) better, fairer, best; بِالْحُسْنَى in the best manner.

حَشَّ (*u.*) it (the grass) became dry; حَشِيشٌ forage, fodder, hay, straw.

حَشِمَ (*a.*) and VII. اِحْتَشَمَ and اِحْتِشَامٌ he had many attendants; حَشَمٌ and اِحْتِشَامٌ a retinue; a large establishment, servants and attendants.

حَصَدَ (*u. & i.*) he reaped; حَصْدٌ reaping.

حَصَلَ (*a.*) it happened, arrived, came to pass; I. حَصَّلَ he produced, made manifest; حَوْصَلَةٌ the stomach, maw, crop, craw.

حَصَنَ and حَصُنَ (*u.*) it was strong or fortified; حِصْنٌ a fortified place; حُصَيْنٌ a small fort, a redoubt.

حَصِيَ he understood, comprehended in his mind; III. he knew, he enumerated.

حَضَرَ (*u.*) he was present; he appeared; it was near at hand; III. أَحْضَرَ he made present; he produced; he summoned; حَضْرَةٌ presence, majesty; حَاضِرٌ present, at hand, ready; on the spot.

حَطَّ and III. أَحَطَّ (*u.*) he set down, he laid down; he alighted, settled. حَطَبَ (*i.*) and VII. اِحْتَطَبَ he collected wood for fuel; حَطَبٌ fuel, firewood.

حَظِيَ (*a.*) he lived in affluence and dignity; he was honoured; حَظِيَّةٌ a married man's concubine.

حَفَّ (*u. & i.*) he surrounded, carried round; حَافَّةٌ (*pl.* حَافَّاتٌ) a border, brink, margin.

حَفِيَ (*a.*) he walked barefoot, was sore in the feet by much marching.

حَقَّ (*i.*) it was right and proper; IV. تَحَقَّقَ it was proved true; حَقٌّ (*pl.* حُقُوقٌ) verification; تَحْقِيقٌ

حَقَرَ — truth; God; a right, a lawful claim; حَقِيقٌ real, proper, true; مُسْتَحِقٌّ حَقِيقَةٌ reality, truth; meriting, deserving, worthy of.

حَقَرَ (i.) he condemned, despised; VII. اِحْتَقَرَ he deemed contemptible; حَقِيرٌ despicable; اِحْتِقَارٌ and حِقَارَةٌ contempt.

حَكَمَ (u.) he exercised dominion; he passed judgement; he ordered; he was learned and wise; I. حَكَّمَ he gave (to another) power, control, or right (over his property); حُكْمٌ an order, a law; حِكْمَةٌ science, skill, art; حَكِيمٌ (pl. حُكَمَاءُ) a sage, a philosopher; a doctor, a physician.

حَكَى (i) he told, he related; حِكَايَةٌ a tale, a narration; a fable.

حَلَّ (u.) he loosened; he descended; it was due; حُلَلٌ striped garments, the vestments of the blessed in Paradise.

حَلِفَ (a.) he swore; he made oath; حِلْفٌ alliance, a sworn treaty of friendship.

حَلُمَ (u.) he was meek, and long suffering; V. تَحَالَمَ he feigned meekness; حَلِيمٌ meek, mild, long suffering, clement.

حَلَا for حَلَوَ (u.) it was sweet; حَلَاوَةٌ (pl. حَلَاوَاتٌ) sweetness, a sweetmeat (more especially that in which honey is freely used).

حَلَى (i.) and I. حَلَّى he adorned, he decked; حَلْيٌ (pl. حُلِيٌّ) an ornament, a female ornament.

حَمَّ (u.) he heated (the water); he became enraged; IX. اِسْتَحَمَّ he bathed; حَمَّامٌ a warm bath حَمَامَةٌ a dove, pigeon.

حِمَارٌ (pl. حَمِيرٌ) an ass.

حُمَةٌ (pl. حُمَاتٌ) venom of a scorpion, sting of a bee or wasp, etc.

حَمَدَ (a.) he praised; حَمْدٌ praise; مُحَمَّدٌ much praised; a proper name; حَمِيدٌ praised, praiseworthy.

حَمِقَ (a.) he was silly, foolish; أَحْمَقُ folly, silliness; حُمْقٌ a fool.

حَمَلَ (i.) he carried; he sent; he excited; he imputed; (a

female) was pregnant; I. حَمَّلَ he caused to carry or convey (a burden, epistle, etc.).

حَمَا (i.) he defended; he was modest; حِمَايَةٌ modesty, shame, a nice sense of honour; protection; حُمَةٌ (pl. حُمًى and حُمَاتٌ) venom; the sting of a serpent, wasp, or bee.

حَمِيَ (a.) it was hot or burning.

حِنْطَةٌ (pl. حِنَطٌ) wheat.

حَنِقَ (i.) he was inflamed with anger; حَنَقٌ rage, vehement anger, wrath.

حُوتٌ a whale or any large fish (in contrast with سَمَكٌ which denotes the smaller species of fish).

حَاجَ (u.) and VII. اِحْتَاجَ he was in want of, he needed, was necessitous; حَاجَةٌ (pl. حَوَائِجُ) anything necessary; necessity, want; مُحْتَاجٌ needy, indigent.

حَاطَ for حَوَطَ (u.) he guarded; he surrounded; he girded; حَائِطٌ (pl. حِيطَانٌ) a wall, an enclosure.

حَالَ (u.) it passed; it was turned or changed; he was crafty; VII. اِحْتَالَ he devised stratagems;

he laid snares; حَالٌ (pl. أَحْوَالٌ) a state, situation, or posture (of affairs); حَوْلَ around; حِيلَةٌ stratagem, deception, art, trick; مُحَالٌ impossible, absurd; لَا مَحَالَةَ guile, evasion; مَحَالَةٌ without evasion, undoubtedly, inevitably, certainly.

حَامَ for حَوَمَ (u.) (the bird) flew around, skimming in circles.

حَيِيَ for حَيَّ (a.) he felt ashamed; he lived; III. he restored to life; IX. اِسْتَحَى he preserved alive; he was ashamed, he had a sense of shame; حَيٌّ alive; an animal; حَيَاءٌ modesty, shame; حَيَاةٌ and حَيْوَةٌ life; bashfulness; حَيْوَانٌ (pl. حَيْوَانَاتٌ) a living creature, an animal; حَوَّاءُ Eve, the mother of mankind.

حَيَّةٌ a serpent; du. حَيَّتَانِ.

حَيْثُ where, in whatever place.

حَارَ for حَيِرَ (a.) and IV. تَحَيَّرَ he was confounded, amazed.

حَانَ for حَيَنَ (i.) the time arrived; حِينٌ time, a period; حِينَ at the time when.

خ

خَاقَانٌ an Emperor; the great Khān (this title is especially applied to the Emperor of China).

خَبَا and I. خَبًّا he concealed.

خَبُثَ (*u*.) he was depraved and wicked; خُبْثٌ and خَبَاثَةٌ malice, perfidy; خَبِيثٌ perfidious, wicked.

خَبَرَ (*u*.) he was acquainted with; I. خَبَّرَ and III. أَخْبَرَ he informed, acquainted, told; خَبَرٌ (*pl*. أَخْبَارٌ) news, information; خَبِيرٌ well informed, knowing, or conversant with (matters).

خَبَزَ (*i*.) he baked; خُبْزٌ baking; bread.

خَبَطَ (*i*.) and I. خَبَّطَ (a quadruped) pawed the ground with his forefeet.

خَتَمَ he sealed; خَاتِمٌ a seal; a seal ring.

خَجِلَ (*a*.) he was ashamed, abashed; خَجِلٌ modest, ashamed, abashed.

خَدَعَ (*a*.) he deceived; خَدِيعَةٌ and خِدَاعٌ fraud, deception; خِدَاعًا fraudulently, treacherously.

خَدَمَ (*u*.) he served, tended, waited on; خِدْمَةٌ service, duty; خَادِمٌ (*pl*. خَدَمٌ and خُدَّامٌ) a domestic servant, an attendant.

خَذَلَ (*a*.) he was disappointed, was destitute of aid or hope.

خَرَّ (*i*.) he fell prostrate (in adoration); he fell (dead).

خُرَاسَانُ the country bordering on the Oxus; خُرَاسَانِيٌّ a man of Khurāsān.

خَرَبَ (*a*.) and I. خَرَّبَ he laid waste, he devastated.

خَرَجَ (*u*.) he went out; he rebelled; III. أَخْرَجَ he sent out; he expelled; خَارِجِيٌّ an insurgent, a rebel.

خَرُوفٌ (*pl*. خِرْفَانٌ and أَخْرِفَةٌ) a lamb. خَرِيفٌ autumn, fall of the leaf.

خَزَنَ he stored, hoarded; مَخْزَنٌ (*pl*. مَخَازِنُ) a magazine; a store room; خِزَانَةٌ a treasury, a store-chamber.

خَشِيَ (*a*.) he feared, dreaded; خَشْيَةٌ fear, dread, awe.

خَصَفَ (*i*.) he sewed together; he clothed (himself) in leaves.

خَصْلَةٌ (*pl*. خِصَالٌ) condition, quality (good or bad).

خَصَم

خَصَم (i.) he disputed; V. تَخَاصَمَ he engaged in altercation; he disputed with.

إخْضَرَ (a.) and VIII. إخْضَرَّ it was green; أخْضَرُ (fem. خَضْرَاءُ) green.

خَطِئ for خَطَأ (a.) he erred, sinned; خَطَاءٌ errror, mistake, failure; خَطِيَّةٌ or خَطِيئَةٌ (pl. خَطَايَا) sin, crime.

خَطَب (u.) he made a discourse; he preached a sermon; II. خَاطَبَ he spoke to, he addressed, he accosted; خُطْبَةٌ a short formula of prayer or benediction offered up in the mosques on Fridays.

خَطَر (u.) he was in peril; II. خَاطَرَ he encountered or underwent danger; خَطَرٌ imminent danger, jeopardy; مُخَاطَرَةٌ mutual danger.

خَطَف (i.) VII. إخْتَطَفَ he snatched away, he carried off; III. أخْطَفَ it deviated from the mark; خَطَّافٌ a depredator; Satan; خُطَّافٌ a swallow.

خَطَا for خَطَوَ (u.) he stepped; خَطْوَةٌ (pl. خَطَوَاتٌ) a step, a pace.

خَفَّ (i.) it was of light weight; خِفَّةٌ lightness, agility, nimbleness; إسْتِخْفَافٌ holding light; contempt.

خَفِيَ (i.) and III. أخْفَى he concealed; خَفِيٌّ hidden, occult.

خَلَّ (u.) it was spoilt. corrupted; he was intimate with; خَلَلٌ disturbance, disorder, defect; خَلِيلٌ an intimate, chosen friend.

خَلَب (u.) he wounded, or carried off with his claws; مِخْلَبٌ (pl. مَخَالِبُ) a claw or talon.

خَلَد (u.) he was eternal; I. خَلَّدَ he immortalized, made eternal; خَالِدٌ eternal; مُخَلَّدٌ rendered immortal.

خَلَص (u.) he was free; it was pure and unadulterated; I. خَلَّصَ he set free, he saved from evil; VI. إنْخَلَصَ he was freed, delivered.

خَلَط (i.) he mixed; II. خَالَطَ he associated, connected himself with.

خَلَع (a.) he stripped off; he abdicated; he deposed; he bestowed a dress of honour; خَلْعٌ abdication; خِلْعَةٌ a dress of honour.

خَلَفَ he followed, succeeded (to another); II. خَالَفَ he opposed, rebelled against; خُلْفٌ opposition, hostility; خَلْفَ after, behind; خَلِيفَةٌ a successor; the Caliph; خِلَافَةٌ succession; rank or dignity of Caliph, the Caliphate; مُخَالَفَةٌ opposition, rebellion; مُخْتَلِفٌ various, different, diverse.

خَلَقَ (u.) he created, formed; خَلْقٌ all created beings (peculiarly) mankind; خُلُقٌ innate disposition (in a good sense).

(pl. خَلَاقِينُ) خَلْقِينٌ a large brass cauldron.

خَلَا for خَلَوَ (u.) it was empty, void; he was at leisure, disengaged; he was alone (with another); I. خَلَّى he let alone; he set free: he left at liberty; IV. تَخَلَّى he was set free or separated from.

خَمَرَ (u.) it fermented; خَمْرٌ wine; fermented liquor.

خَمْسٌ (masc. خَمْسَةٌ) five; خَمْسُونَ fifty.

خَمَلَ (u.) he was obscure, vile.

خِنْزِيرٌ (pl. خَنَازِيرُ) a hog, a pig.

خِنَّوْصٌ (pl. خَنَانِيصُ) a young or sucking pig.

خُنْفَسَةٌ (pl. خَنَافِسُ) the scarabaeus or black beetle.

خَنَقَ (u.) he strangled, throttled, suffocated; he overcame.

خَافَ for خَوِفَ (a.) he feared, he stood in fear; خَوْفٌ fear, dread.

خَابَ for خَيَبَ (i.) he was disappointed and balked; he failed in his object; I. خَيَّبَ he disappointed, frustrated, confounded.

خَارَ for خَيَرَ (i.) he was well, or well off, and in good circumstances; I. خَيَّرَ he gave the option; he offered the choice; VII. اِخْتَارَ he chose, he adopted; اِخْتِيَارٌ choice, free choice; election; أَخْيَرُ better or best; خَيْرٌ good; better; a good action.

خَيْزُرَانٌ a cane, a rattan.

خَاطَ for خَيَطَ (i.) he sewed; خِيَاطَةٌ sewing, stitching, needlework; خَيْطٌ thread, a string; خَيَّاطٌ a tailor; a shoemaker.

خَالَ for خَيَلَ (a.) he imagined;

دَاءٌ خَيَالٌ a shadow, a phantom, phantasm, dream, imagination; a vain fancy, empty notion.

د

دَاءٌ disease, sickness.

دَأَبَ (*a.*) he laboured, strove; دَأْبٌ state, habit, manner.

دَابَّةٌ (*pl.* دَوَابُّ) any living creature that moves on dry land (more especially cattle, sheep, horses camels, etc.; from the rt. دَبَّ (*u.*) he walked, he crept).

دَبَرَ it was behind, and in the rear; it passed; I. دَبَّرَ he disposed, arranged, managed; تَدْبِيرٌ managing, management; disposing, disposal; counsel, advice; prudence, good sense.

دِثَارٌ a cloak, an outer garment, one not worn next the skin.

دَجَاجَةٌ (*pl.* دَجَاجٌ) a domestic fowl; a hen.

دَخَلَ (*u.*) he entered; III. أَدْخَلَ he caused to enter; he introduced, inserted; دُخُولٌ entering, entrance, ingress.

دَخَنَ (*a. & u.*) it smoked; دُخَانٌ (*pl.* أَدْخِنَةٌ) smoke; fumigation.

دَرَّ (*i. & u.*) it flowed copiously; it streamed forth; دَرٌّ any good thing; an action; لِلَّهِ دَرُّكَ how bountiful hath God been to thee! (a form of praising equivalent to excellent! wonderful!) إِدْرَارٌ a causing to flow; a stipend, allowance, appointment, exhibition, or pension.

دَرْبَانٌ (*pl.* دَرَابِنَةٌ) a doorkeeper, a porter or janitor (Persian دَرْبان).

دَرَكَ he followed; he attained; overtook, reached; III. أَدْرَكَ he comprehended; he hunted (it) down; he understood; he attained the years of discretion; he lived sufficiently long to be contemporary with; V. تَدَارَكَ he reached, overtook; he repaired, mended.

دِرْهَمٌ (*pl.* دَرَاهِمُ) a dirham; a silver coin, or drachm.

دَرَا (*i.*) he knew, was acquainted.

دَعَا (*u.*) he called; he invited; he prayed; he invoked (a

دَغَلٌ

blessing); VII. اِدَّعَى he claimed; he arrogated, pretended to, he boasted; IX. اِسْتَدْعَى he invited, entreated; دَعْوَةٌ a feast; a call, an invitation.

دَغَلٌ fraud, vice, deception.

دَفَعَ (a.) he repelled; دَفْعَةٌ act of repulsion; دَفْعَةٌ once, one time; one turn or bout.

دَفَنَ (i.) he hid; he buried.

دَقَّ (i.) it was slim, slender, light, or graceful; دِقَّةٌ slimness; lightness, nimbleness.

دُكَّانٌ (pl. دَكَاكِينُ) a shop, warehouse.

دَلَّ (u.) he led the way, directed; pointed out, indicated; إِدْلَالٌ reliance, conviction; دَلِيلٌ proof, argument; دَلَّالٌ a broker, a salesman; a conductor, a guide.

دُلَامَةٌ darkness, blackness; أَبُو دُلَامَةٍ name of a celebrated poet.

دَلَا (u.) he let down (a bucket); III. أَدْلَى he let fall; he dropped; he allowed to hang; IV. تَدَلَّى he was let down; it hung downwards; دَلْوٌ a bucket; مُدْلٍ

دَارَ

(مُدْلِيٌّ for) a thrower down; allowed to hang down; loose, dishevelled.

دَمٌ for دَمَوٌ (pl. دِمَاءٌ) blood.

دِمْنَةٌ See كَلِيلَةْ وَ دِمْنَةْ.

دَنِسَ (a.) it was foul and dirty; دَنِسٌ filthy, nasty.

دَنَا (u.) he approached; it was low, base; III. he rendered vile, he abased; دُنْيَا the world; the present world (as being nigh to us); دَنِيٌّ base, ignoble; دَانٍ near, approaching.

دَنَانِيرُ (pl. of دِينَارٌ or دِنَّارٌ q.v.)

دَهَرَ (a.) it befell; it occured; دَهْرٌ (pl. دُهُورٌ) time, age, period.

دِهْلِيزٌ a court, an area; the open space between the outer gate and the main building.

دَهَنَ (u.) he anointed, greased; دُهْنٌ (pl. أَدْهَانٌ) oil, butter, grease, ointment, unguent.

دَوَاةٌ an inkstand, inkhorn.

دَاخَ (u.) he was low, base, and abject; he subdued, he subjugated; I. دَوَّخَ he made base and abject; he overcame, subdued, and subjugated.

دَارَ for دَوَرَ (u.) he encircled; he went round, made a circuit, moved in a circle; دَارٌ (pl. دِيَارٌ) a house, habitation, dwelling; دَوْرٌ a cycle; a period: a revolution.

دَاسَ for دَوَسَ (u.) he trod out corn; دِيَاسَةٌ treading out corn (by means of oxen).

دَالَ for دَوَلَ (u.) it revolved; دَوْلَةٌ (pl. دُوَلٌ) a cycle or revolution of years; a period; dominion; a dynasty.

دَامَ for دَوَمَ (u.) he remained, he continued or persevered (in any course); دَائِمًا always, perpetually; مَادَامَ as long as endureth; whilst, during.

دَانَ for دَوَنَ (u.) he was base, low; دُونَ under, short of, near, before.

دِيَةٌ the price of blood, or mulet for homicide. See rt. وَدَى.

دِيكٌ (pl. دُيُوكٌ) a cock; a male bird.

دَانَ for دَيَنَ (i.) he was indebted; he submitted, obeyed; دِينٌ religion, religious, observance.

دِينَارٌ (pl. دَنَانِيرُ) a dīnār, a gold or silver coin used as money in some Arabian countries.

ذ

ذَا (demonst. pron.) this; ذَلِكَ that; لِمَاذَا or مَاذَا why, wherefore, for what.

ذِئْبٌ (pl. ذِئَابٌ) a wolf.

ذَبَّ (u.) he guarded, defended; ذَبٌّ guarding, protecting; keeping off.

ذَبَحَ (a.) he sacrificed; he slaughtered; ذَبِيحَةٌ a sacrifice, a victim.

ذَبَلَ (u.) it was withered, flaccid, or dried up (a plant, etc.); ذُبُولٌ act or state of withering.

ذَخَرَ (a.) he stored up (for future use); ذُخْرٌ and ذَخِرَةٌ a store, a hoard.

ذَرَّ (u.) he scattered, strewed, sprinkled; ذُرِّيَّةٌ progeny, offspring.

ذَكَرَ (u.) he remembered, recollected; he related, mentioned; ذِكْرٌ and ذُكْرٌ memory, mentioning, record; ذَكُورٌ mindful, of good memory; تَذْكِرَةٌ reminding; a remembrancer, anything which recalls to the memory;

ذَلَّ admonition; مَذْكُورٌ mentioned; worthy of note.

ذَلَّ (i.) he was base, abject; he was humble and submissive; I. أَذَلَّ he brought low; III. ذَلَّلَ he humbled, subdued; تَذْلِيلٌ a lowering, a bringing down.

ذٰلِك that; same as ذَالِك q.v.

ذَمَّ (u.) he reviled; ذَمٌّ reviling, reproach; ذِمَّةٌ subjection, clientelage, protection.

ذَنَبَ (i. & u.) he followed; ذَنَبٌ (pl. أَذْنَابٌ) the tail; ذَنْبٌ (pl. ذُنُوبٌ) a fault, an offence.

ذَهَبَ (a.) he went; he passed; I. ذَهَّبَ he gilded, he ornamented with gold; ذَهَبٌ gold; money.

ذُو possessed of, endowed with; ذَاتٌ (fem.) nature, essence, reality.

ذَابَ for ذَوَبَ (a.) it melted, became liquified.

ذَاقَ for ذَوَقَ (u.) he tasted.

ذَيْلٌ the train, skirt, or border of a robe; the extremity of anything.

ر

رَأَسَ (a.) he was chief, he governed; رَأْسٌ (pl. رُؤُوسٌ) the head, the summit; the source; رَئِيسٌ a chief, captain, leader, principal; رِئَاسَةٌ superiority, headship, authority.

رَأَى (a.) he saw, he deemed; رَأْيٌ an opinion, judgement, wisdom.

رَبٌّ a master, lord; a possessor.

رِبْحٌ profit, gain, advantage (rt. رَبَحَ).

رَبَضَ (i.) (cattle) rested, reposed, lay down with the feet tucked under them; رَبَضٌ any place wherein cattle are kept; a cowhouse, sheepfold, etc.

رَبَطَ (a. & u.) he bound, tied, fastened.

رَبَعَ (a.) he was fourth; he took one quarter; I. رَبَّعَ he quartered; أَرْبَعٌ (masc. أَرْبَعَةٌ) four; أَرْبَعُونَ forty.

رُبَّمَا often, sometimes, occasionally.

رَبَا (i.) he grew up, was educated; I. رَبَّى he brought up, educated;

رَجَعَ

تَرْبِيَةٌ also تَرَبٌ education, rearing.

رَجَعَ (*a.*) he returned; he repeated; II. رَاجَعَ he returned, or caused to be returned; he replied; he conversed with; V. تَرَاجَعُوا they returned together; رُجُوعٌ returning, return.

رَجَلَ (*u.*) he tied the feet; رِجْلٌ (*pl.* أَرْجُلٌ) the foot; رَجُلٌ (*pl.* رِجَالٌ) a man; رِجَالٌ attendants, footmen, people.

رَجَا for رَجَوَ (*u.*) he hoped, he confided in.

رَحِبَ (*a.*) it was wide, roomy, ample, spacious, convenient; I. رَحَّبَ he greeted with the salutation مَرْحَبًا welcome; all hail! make yourself easy, there is plenty of room.

رَحَلَ (*a.*) he departed, he marched; رِحْلَةٌ a journey, departure.

رَحِمَ (*a.*) he pitied; he was compassionate; رَحْمَةٌ pity, compassion; رَحْمَانٌ (often written رَحْمٰنُ) and رَحِيمٌ merciful, pitiful, clement, compassionate.

رَدَّ (*u.*) he returned; he returned an answer; he sent back; VII. اِرْتَدَّ he returned; he apostatized; رَدٌّ returning, drawing back.

رَدَعَ (*a.*) he prohibited; he rejected, drove off, pushed away.

رَزَقَ (*u.*) he bestowed (what was needful for subsistence); رِزْقٌ whatever is necessary for the support of life; stipend; pension; رَزَّاقٌ a bestower; God (as the Giver of daily bread).

رَسَلَ (*u.*) he sent intelligence; he announced; III. أَرْسَلَ he despatched, sent; IX. اِسْتَرْسَلَ he let down; made use of رَسُولٌ (*pl.* رُسُلٌ) an ambassador, an envoy; an apostle; a messenger; a prophet; رِسَالَةٌ anything sent (a letter, missive, tract, etc.)

رَسَمَ (*u.*) he marked, stamped, impressed; رَسْمٌ (*pl.* رُسُومٌ) character, manner, custom, stamp.

رَشَّ (*u.*) he sprinkled, he watered.

رَشَدَ (*u.*) he was in the right way; he was well directed; رَشَدٌ the right path; the straight way to

رَضِيَ

salvation; direction; رَشِيدٌ a sure and trusty guide, director, or conductor.

رَضِيَ (*a*.) he was satisfied, pleased, content; III. أَرْضَى he satisfied, gratified, pleased.

رَعَبَ (*a*.) he frightened, terrified.

رَعَدَ (*a*. & *u*.) it thundered; VII. اِرْتَعَدَ he was confounded, alarmed; he trembled, quaked.

رَعَى (*a*.) (cattle etc.) grazed, pastured; مَرْعًى pasture-ground; رَعِيَّةٌ a flock; subjects, people; a ryot.

رَغِبَ (*a*.) he desired; he liked; I. رَغَّبَ he rendered desirous; he incited; مَرْغُوبٌ liked, desired.

رَغِدَ (*a*.) he was in affluence, he led an easy and comfortable life; رَغْدٌ affluence, plenty, abundance; ease, comfort.

رَفَسَ (*u*. & *i*.) he struck the ground with his feet; he pawed.

رَفَعَ (*a*.) he raised; he removed; he left off; VII. اِرْتَفَعَ it raised itself; he was raised; مُرْتَفِعٌ raised, elevated, lofty, sublime; أَرْفَعُ more or most lofty, elevated, or powerful

رَمَى

(from رَفِيعٌ lofty).

رَفَقَ (*i*.) he was kind, he aided, benefited; he associated with; رَفِيقٌ a traveller, a companion, associate.

رَقَبَ (*u*.) he fastened by the neck; رَقَبَةٌ the neck.

رَقَعَ (*a*.) he patched (a garment); رُقْعَةٌ a piece of paper on which anything is written; a tablet on which anything is drawn.

رَقِيَ (*a*.) he ascended, mounted; he enchanted; VII. اِرْتَقَى he ascended; رُقْيَةٌ (*pl*. رُقًى) magic, enchantment, philter, charm.

رَكِبَ (*a*.) he rode; he mounted; رَاكِبٌ one who rides (on horseback, etc.) or is conveyed (in a boat, etc.); I. رَكَّبَ he arranged, he disposed, he placed.

رَكَعَ (*a*.) he bowed himself; رَكْعَةٌ an inclination or bowing of the head or body (as an act of worship).

رَمَضَ it was sun-burnt, رَمْضَاءُ land scorched by the sun.

رَمَى (*i*.) and III. أَرْمَى he cast, threw; he shot, he hit; مَرْمِيٌّ thrown or fallen down.

رَهِبَ (a.) he feared, he reverenced: IV. تَرَهَّبَ he devoted himself to the service of God; he became devout, he feared greatly.

رَاحَ for رَوَحَ (u.) he rested; he went; he smelt; III. أَرْوَحَ he caused to rest or repose; IX. اِسْتِرَاحَ he took rest; he reposed himself رُوحٌ (pl. أَرْوَاحٌ) soul, spirit, life; رِيحٌ (pl. أَرْيَاحٌ and رِيَاحٌ) the wind, air, vapour; odour, smell; رَاحَةٌ rest, repose; رَيْحَانٌ (pl. رَيَاحِينُ) an odoriferous herb; رَائِحَةٌ (pl. رَوَائِحُ) smell, odour.

رَادَ for رَوَدَ (u.) he sought; III. أَرَادَ he wished, willed, desired, intended; he pursued.

رَاضَ for رَوَضَ (u.) he trained or broke in (a colt); رَوْضَةٌ (pl. رِيَاضٌ) a garden; a meadow, a flowery mead.

رُومٌ Rome, Greece, the Turkish Empire (generally applied to Asiatic Turkey); رُومِيٌّ a Turk, or Grecian.

رَامَ for رَوَمَ (u.) he was desirous, he wished or intended.

رَوَى (i.) he related, told, recorded.

رِيَاءٌ desiring to be seen; hence, hypocrisy, dissimulation, fraud (rt. رَأَى).

ز

زَجَرَ (u.) he replied; he chode; he drove away (fowls); he scared away (sheep) by crying 'shoo' or something similar; he forced; زَجْرٌ repelling, driving off.

زَرَعَ (a.) he sowed; زَرْعٌ sowing, agriculture; زَرَّاعٌ a sower, labourer, cultivator, husbandman.

زَرَى (a.) and VII. اِزْدَرَى he despised, scorned, condemned, or undervalued.

زَعَجَ (a.) he moved, disturbed; VI. اِنْزَعَجَ he was disturbed, moved, alarmed; اِنْزِعَاجٌ confusion, alarm.

زَعْزَعَ quadril. (the wind) shook, disturbed, or violently agitated (the trees).

زَعَمَ (u.) he was of opinion; he supposed; زَعِيمٌ (pl. زُعَمَاءُ) a spokesman; a leader; a chief.

زَكَا for زَكَوَ (*a.*) he was pure, holy; I. زَكَّى he deemed pure; he justified; he rendered pure; زَكْوَةٌ and زَكَاةٌ alms, purification. According to the Islamic law, it is incumbent on every individual to give, for pious purposes, a certain portion of his property in nature of tithes, not less however than a fifth, by way of purifying and securing a blessing on the remainder.

زَمَّ (*u.*) he bound, he fastened, or restrained; زِمَامٌ a (camel's) bridle, or halter.

زَمْرٌ (*pl.* زُمُورٌ) a song accompanied with instrumental music; a flute.

زَمِنَ (*a.*) he was worn by time or age; زَمَنٌ and زَمَانٌ (*pl.* أَزْمَانٌ) time, age.

زَمْهَرِيرٌ intense cold, hyperboraean cold.

زَنْجَبِيل ginger; name of a fountain in Paradise.

زَنَى (*i.*) he committed whoredom; زِنَاءٌ fornication, whoredom.

زَهَرَ it shone, glittered; زَهْرٌ (*pl.* أَزْهَارٌ) the flower or blossom of a plant (especially a yellow one).

زَهْوٌ beauty, fairness of countenance; pride.

زَوْجٌ a mate; a fellow; a husband; زَوْجَةٌ a wife; I. زَوَّجَ he united, coupled; he gave in marriage.

زَارَ for زَوَرَ (*u.*) he visited; he made a journey or pilgrimage; مَزَارٌ a place of visiting, a holy shrine.

زَالَ for زَوَلَ (*u.*) he removed, departed; he quitted, left; he ceased; لَمْ تَزَلْ you did not cease; you continued.

زَادَ for زَيَدَ (*i.*) and VII. اِزْدَادَ it was enlarged or increased. زِيَادَةٌ increase, addition.

زَانَ for زَيَنَ (*i.*) he adorned, ornamented; زِينَةٌ ornament, decoration.

س

سَ or سَوْفَ a particle, prefixed to the aorist of a verb; restricting it to a future signification.

سَأَلَ (*a.*) he asked, he inquired; he

begged; مَسْأَلَةٌ a question, querry, demand, request; problem, propositon.

سَبَّ (u.) he cut; سَبَبٌ (pl. أَسْبَابٌ) a cause; an instrument; means; an utensil; سَبٌّ reproach, abuse, cutting reproof; also a man's name.

سَبَحَ (a.) he swam; I. سَبَّحَ he prayed; he praised and glorified God. سُبْحَانٌ praising, glorifying God; سُبْحَانَ اللهِ O God! Merciful God! O Holy God! Good God! Far be it from God!

سَبْعٌ (masc. سَبْعَةٌ) seven; سَبْعُونَ seventy; سَبُعٌ (pl. سِبَاعٌ) fem. سَبُعَةٌ a wild beast, any ferocious beast, a beast of prey; a lion.

سَبَقَ (i. & u.) he went before, preceded, took the lead; he excelled; II. سَابَقُوا, V. تَسَابَقُوا and VII. اِسْتَبَقُوا they strove to excel or get ahead of (each other); they emulated; they preceded; سَابِقٌ preceding, former; aforementioned, foregone.

سَبِيلٌ a road, a way; one's proper course of conduct in life.

سَبَا (i.) he took captive; سَبِيٌّ (pl. سَبَايَا) a captive, prisoner.

سِتٌّ (masc. سِتَّةٌ) for سِدْسٌ six; سِتُّونَ sixty.

سَتَرَ (u.) he covered, he veiled; سِتْرٌ a covering, a veil.

سَجَدَ (u.) he prostrated himself; he adored, سُجُودٌ prostration; adoration, worship; مَسْجِدٌ a place of worship, a mosque.

سَجَنَ (u.) he imprisoned; سِجْنٌ a jail, a prison.

سَحَابَةٌ (pl. سَحَابٌ) a cloud, vapour.

سَخِرَ (a.) he jeered, ridiculed, held in derision; I. سَخَّرَ he subdued, brought under subjection; he compelled to work for nothing; مَسْخَرَةٌ a jest, joke; a laughing-stock.

سَخِطَ (a.) he was incensed, enraged.

سَخَا for سَخَوَ (u.) he was liberal or generous; سَخَاوَةٌ liberality, generosity.

سَدَّ (u.) he stopped, blocked up, obstructed, closed; سَدَادٌ rectitude; the right way; prosperity, happiness.

سَادِسٌ See سِتٌّ. سِدْسٌ the sixth.

سَرَّ (u.) he cut the navel-string (of a new-born child); he was cheerful and joyous; III. أَسَرَّ he concealed, secreted; سِرٌّ a secret; a mystery; سُرُورٌ joy, gladness; مَسْرُورٌ joyful; a man's name.

سَرَابٌ a peculiar vapour of the desert, which at a distance appears like a sheet of water; the mirage.

سَرَجَ (u.) he saddled; سَرْجٌ a saddle; سِرَاجٌ (pl. سُرُوجٌ) a lamp. a lanthorn; a torch.

سَرُعَ (u.) and III. أَسْرَعَ he was quick, active; he made haste; سُرْعَةٌ quickness, haste, celerity; سَرِيعٌ quick, prompt, expeditious; سَرِيعًا quickly; أَسْرَعُ quicker, speedier, very quick.

سَرَقَ (i.) and VII. إِسْتَرَقَ he stole; he took by stealth.

سَطَحَ (a.) he spread out; سَطْحٌ (pl. سُطُوحٌ) a flat roof; a terrace, a platform.

سَعَدَ (a.) it was propitious; سَعِدَ (a.) he was happy and fortunate; III. أَسْعَدَ he blessed; he made happy; he aided; سَعِيدٌ happy, prosperous.

سَعَرَ (a.) he kindled, excited (flame or war); سَعِيرٌ a burning fire.

سَعَى (a.) he endeavoured, laboured, strove; سَعْيٌ endeavour, effort, exertion, pains.

سَفَحَ (a.) also سَفَكَ (i.) he poured out, he shed (blood); سَفَّاحٌ a bloodshedder, a cruel tyrant.

سَفَقَ (a.) he flapped or clapped his wings (a bird, etc.)

سَفَكَ (i.) he shed (blood); see سَفَحَ.

سَفَلَ (u.) he was low, base, inferior; سَفِلَةٌ or سِفْلَةٌ the lowest of the people, rabble; أَسْفَلُ inferior; lowest; the bottom.

سَفِينَةٌ (pl. سَفَائِنُ) a ship.

سَقَمٌ disease, sickness; سَقِيمٌ sick.

سَقَى (i.) and III. أَسْقَى he irrigated, watered; he gave to drink; سَقْيٌ watering; giving to drink; سَاقٍ for سَاقِيٌ a water-carrier; a cupbearer.

سَكَتَ (u.) he was silent, he held his peace; سُكُوتٌ silent, tranquil, taciturn, quiet.

سَكِرَ (a.) he was intoxicated; سَكْرَةٌ

سَكَنَ (pl. سَكَرَاتٌ) the agony of death; fainting; سَكْرَانُ (pl. سُكَارى) intoxicated; a drunkard.

سَكَنَ (u.) he was fixed, setteld; he abode, dwelt, inhabited; III. أَسْكَنَ he caused to dwell; gave as a habitation; مَسْكَنٌ or مَسْكِنٌ a place of residence, a habitation, abode; مِسْكِينٌ poor, miserable, wretched.

سُلَحْفَاةٌ (pl. سَلَاحِفُ) a tortoise; a crab.

سَلَخَ (u. & a.) he flayed, skinned; VI. اِنْسَلَخَ he was flayed, skinned; مَسْلَخٌ a place of slaughter, shambles.

سَلْسَبِيلٌ name of fountain in Paradise.

سِلْسِلَةٌ (pl. سَلَاسِلُ) a chain.

سَلِطَ (a.) he was vehement, bold; سُلْطَانٌ a monarch, emperor, king.

سَلِمَ (a.) he was sound and unblemished; he was safe, secure; I. سَلَّمَ he saved, made secure; he delivered, committed, consigned; he saluted; he blessed; he submitted, became

subservient; III. أَسْلَمَ he submitted, obeyed; he yielded submission to the will of God; he became a Muslim; سَلَامٌ peace, safety; a salutation; إِسْلَامٌ submission; مُسْلِمٌ a believer; a Muslim; سُلَيْمَانُ Solomon.

سَمَاوَةٌ name of place between Kūfa and Syria.

سَمِعَ (a.) he heard; I. سَمَّعَ he caused to be heard; IV. تَسَمَّعَ he heard, listened, obeyed; سَمْعٌ hearing; the ear; سَمِيعٌ a hearer; سَمَاعٌ act of hearing, listening; سَمْعَانُ name of an Arab tribe.

سَمَلَ he cleansed; he dug out; he tore out or knocked out (an eye); he gouged.

سَمِنَ (a.) he was fat; سَمِينٌ also سَامِنٌ fat, corpulent.

سَمَوَ (u.) he was high, for سَمَا (pl. سَمَاوَاتٌ) eminent, conspicuous; I. سَمَّى he named; سَمَاءٌ the sky; إِسْمٌ (pl. أَسْمَاءٌ) a name.

سَنَّ (u.) he formed, fashioned; he polished (a sword); he bit with the teeth; III. أَسَنَّ he was aged,

سُنْدُسّ

advanced in years; مُسِنٌّ old, aged, stricken in years.

سُنْدُسٌ a species of rich or costly silk; brocade.

سَنة (*a*.) he was old and full of years; سَنَةٌ (*pl*. سِنُونَ and سَنَوَاتٌ) a year.

سَنَا for سَنَوَ (*u*.) it shone, was splendid; سَنِيٌّ splendid, precious, eminent.

سِنَّوْرٌ (*pl*. سَنَانِيرُ) a cat.

سَهُلَ (*u*.) it was plain, flat, smooth, easy, or simple; سَهْلٌ (*pl*. سُهُولٌ) a plain; level ground.

سَاءَ for سَوَأَ (*u*.) he did evil; he sinned; he was wicked, vicious; III. أَسَاءَ he rendered bad, he vitiated; سِئَةٌ and سَوْءٌ, سَوَاءٌ, سُوءٌ a sin, crime; سَوْءٌ evil, sin, deformity, misery, wretchedness; سَيِّءٌ wicked, bad; wretched; مَسَاءَةٌ (*pl*. مَسَاوِي) vice, evildoing.

سَاحَةٌ a court, quadrangle; an area or open space surrounded by buildings (*rt*. سَاحَ for سَوَحَ).

سَادَ for سَوَدَ (*u*.) he was chief; was black; I. سَوَّدَ he blackened, he made black;

سَارَ

VIII. اِسْوَدَّ he became black; سَيِّدٌ (*pl*. سَادَة) a chief, lord, noble; a descendant from the Prophet Muḥammad. أَسْوَدُ (*fem*. سَوْدَاءُ) black; a Negro, an Ethiop; سَوَادٌ blackness.

سَوَرَ for سَارَ (*u*.) he scaled (a wall); he rushed on, he attacked; سِوَارٌ (*pl*. أَسَاوِرُ) a bracelet; سُورَةٌ a structure; a course (of bricks), a row (of stones) in a wall; a chapter of the Qur'ān (of which there are in all 114).

سَاعَةٌ a space of time; an hour; a moment (*rt*. سَاعَ for سَوَعَ).

سَوْفَ a prefix. See سَ.

سَوَقَ for سَاقَ (*u*.) he drove; سِيقَانٌ (*pl*. سِيقَانٌ) the leg; سُوقٌ a market.

سَوَمَ for سَامَ (*u*.) he asked for, demanded, or solicited.

سَوَى (*a*.) he intended, proposed, designed; I. سَوَّى he made equal or like; he proportioned; he perfected; سَوَاءٌ equal, straight; سِوَى besides, except.

سَيَرَ for سَارَ (*i*.) he went, departed; he travelled; I. سَيَّرَ he sent, despatched; سَائِرٌ remainder, rest (although often employed to signify the whole); مَسِيرٌ departing, going a journey, travelling; a journey; سِيرَةٌ conduct, mode of life.

سَيْفٌ a sword, a scimitar. (The author of the lexicon, entitled Kāmūs, asserts that in Arabic, the words for a sword exceed a thousand).

سَالَ for سَيَلَ (*i.*) it (blood or water) flowed, gushed out.

ش

شَامٌ the left side or quarter; اَلشَّامُ Syria (being situate to the left of the Arabs as they looked north).

شَأْنٌ (*pl.* شِئَانٌ and شُؤُونٌ), an affair thing; habit, character, disposition.

شَبَّ (*i.*) he was young, in the vigour of youth; شَابٌّ a youth; a man between the age of twenty-four and forty; شَبَابٌ the season of youth.

شَبِعَ (*a.*) he was satiated, sated; his appetite was satisfied; III. أَشْبَعَ satisfied, he filled, he satiated.

شِبْهٌ similitude, likeness; IV. تَشَبَّهَ he was like, he resembled.

شَتَّ (*i.*) he was separate, distinct; I. شَتَّتَ and III. أَشَتَّ he separated, he dispersed.

شَتَمَ (*i.*) he reviled, abused, vilified.

شَتَا for شَتَوَ (*u.*) he wintered; شِتَاءٌ winter.

شَجَرَةٌ (*pl.* أَشْجَارٌ) and شَجَرٌ a tree.

شَجُعَ he was brave or valiant; شُجَاعٌ bravery, valour; a species of large serpent; brave, intrepid.

شَحَّ (*u. & i.*) he was avaricious, niggardly; شُحٌّ avarice, greediness.

شَحَنَ (*a.*) he filled; he loaded (a ship with cargo); شَحْنَاءُ enmity, hatred.

شَخَصَ (*a.*) he gazed with fixed eyes, he stared; his sight was immovable; he arose, appeared; he departed; he went from one country to another; III. أَشْخَصَ he conveyed; he sent from place to place; شَخْصٌ (*pl.* أَشْخَاصٌ) a person, individual.

شَدَّ (*u. & i.*) he tied, he bound; he

شَرُفَ (u.) he was high, eminent, noble; III. أَشْرَفَ he looked down upon; he was over against; he impended, overhung; he was near, at the point of; شَرَفٌ eminence, nobility; ذُو شَرَفٍ and شَرِيفٌ noble, eminent.

شَرَقَ (u.) (the sun) rose; مَشْرِقٌ the place of the sun's rising, the east.

شَرِكَ (a.) and VII. اِشْتَرَكَ he became an associate; (pl. and du.) they became partners, entered into partnership or association.

شَرِهَ (a.) he was very greedy; شَرَهٌ avidity, cupidity, greediness.

شَرَي or شَرَا (i.) also VII. اِشْتَرَي he purchased, bought.

شَطَنَ (u.) he was proud, rebellious, disobedient; شَيْطَانٌ (pl. شَيَاطِينُ) Satan, the devil.

شَعَرَ (u.) he knew; he understood; he perceived; he was acquainted with; شِعْرٌ knowledge; poetry, verse; شَعْرٌ (pl. شُعُورٌ) hair; شَاعِرٌ a poet; شَعِيرٌ barley (as being bearded).

شَغَلَ (a.) and III. أَشْغَلَ he kept

—

strengthened; VII. اِشْتَدَّ it waxed strong; it became intense and severe; شِدَّةٌ violence, strength, greatness; intensity, severity; شَدِيدٌ (pl. أَشِدَّاءُ) intense; vehement, violent, strong; أَشَدُّ stronger, more violent.

شِدْقٌ (pl. أَشْدَاقٌ) that part of the face adjoining the mouth; the chaps or corners of the mouth (especially in a hound, or lion, etc.)

شَذْرَةٌ a particle or grain (of gold); a small pearl.

شَرَّ for شَرِرَ (u. & i.) he sinned; he was wicked; شَرٌّ (pl. شُرُورٌ) evil, wickedness, harm; شَرِيرٌ wicked, vicious; أَشَرُّ very wicked; most or more wicked.

شَرِبَ (a.) he drank; شُرْبٌ drinking; شَرَابٌ drink; liquor; wine; شَرْبَةٌ sherbet, negus; any refreshing drink.

شَرَحَ (a.) he explained, elucidated; laid open; شَرْحٌ explanation, comment.

شَرَعَ (a.) he ordained; he legislated; شَرِيعَةٌ the divine law.

occupied, employed, engaged; V. تَشَاغَلُوا they were reciprocally occupied; they engaged with each other; they kept each other employed, and distracted the attention of one another; شُغْلٌ occupation, business, employ.

شَفَقَ (u.) he acted kindly; he commiserated; شَفَقٌ and إِشْفَاقٌ condolence, kindness, compassion.

شَفَةَ (a.) he was idle, unoccupied; شَفَةٌ for شَفَهَةٌ (pl. شِفَاهْ) a lip.

شَقَّ (u.) he split, he clove; VI. اِنْشَقَّ it was split or cleft; شَقٌّ splitting, breaking; شَاقٌّ painful, grievous.

شَقِيَ (a.) he was miserable, wretched; شَقَاوَةٌ and شَقَاءٌ wretchedness, pain, misery; unhappiness; شَقِيٌّ miserable, hapless, wretched.

شَكَّ he doubted; شَكٌّ doubt.

شَكَرَ (u.) he thanked, rendered thanks; شُكْرٌ (pl. شُكُورٌ) thanks, acknowledgement of a favour; مَشْكُورٌ praised, شَكُورٌ grateful; acceptable, rewarded.

شَكَلَ (u.) he fastened; II. شَاكَلَ he resembled, he was like unto; شَكْلٌ figure, form, shape; similitude.

شَكَرَ (u.) he complained; for شَكْوًا he lamented; he stated his grievance.

شَمَّ (a.) he smelt, inhaled, snuffed.

شَمِتَ (a.) he rejoiced or exulted at the misfortunes of another; he reviled.

شَمْسٌ (pl. شُمُوسٌ) the sun.

شَمْعٌ or شَمَعٌ (pl. شِمَاعٌ) wax; a wax-light, a taper, a candle.

شَمَلَ (a.) he comprehended, included, surrounded; شَمَلٌ the whole, totality; شَمَالٌ the left quarter; the north.

شَهِدَ (a.) he witnessed; he gave evidence; III. أَشْهَدَ he called to witness; he solemnly attested; شَهَادَةٌ (pl. شُهُودٌ) شَاهِدٌ a witness; testifying, witnessing; testimony; شُهْدٌ and شَهْدٌ (pl. شِهَادٌ) honey.

شَهِيَ (u.) he longed for, he wished; VII. إِشْتَهَى the same; شَهْوَةٌ desire, lust.

شَارَ for شَوَرَ (u.) he acquired, obtained; III. أَشَارَ he pointed out; he advised, counselled;

he ordered; شَوْرٌ advice, suggestion; مُشَاوَرَةٌ deliberation; مَشْوَرَةٌ counsel, consultation.

شَاكَ for شَوَكَ (u.) it punctured; شَوْكٌ the prickle of a thorn, etc.

شَالَ for شَوَلَ (u.) he raised; he removed, took away; شَوَّالٌ name of the tenth month in the Islamic calendar.

شُوهَةٌ a species of kite or small vulture.

شَاءَ (يَشَاءُ) he wished, he willed; شَيْءٌ (pl. أَشْيَاءُ) a thing; an affair;

شَابَ for شَيَبَ (i.) he became grey; he grew hoary; شَيْبٌ hoariness, greyness of hair.

شَاخَ for شَيَخَ (u.) he was aged; شَيْخٌ (pl. مَشَائِخُ) an old man; an elder; a chief; شَيْخُوخَةٌ and شَيْخِيَّةٌ old age.

شَادَ for شَيَدَ (i.) he plastered; I. he built or raised up; he erected, exalted.

ص

صَبَّ (u.) he poured out.

صُبْحٌ the dawn; صَبَاحٌ the morning; the early part of the dawn.

صَبَرَ (i.) he was patient; he endured; he abstained or kept himself away from; صَبْرٌ patience.

صَبَا for صَبَوَ (u.) he was an infant, or child; صَبِيٌّ a boy, a child; صَبِيَّةٌ a girl.

صَحَّ (i.) he was sound in (body); he was sincere; صِحَّةٌ sincerity; good health.

صَحِبَ (a.) and VII. إِصْطَحَبَ he associated with or was a companion to (another); صَاحِبٌ a companion; a master, or owner; possessed of, endowed with; صُحْبَةٌ society, intimacy, cohabitation.

صَحْفَةٌ (pl. صِحَافٌ) a plate, dish, or platter.

صَحَا for صَحَوَ (u.) it (the sky) was cloudless and serene; صَاحٍ for صَاحِيٌّ one possessed of a serene mind.

صَدَرَ (u.) he proceeded, flowed,

صَدَعَ

emanated; صُدُورٌ (.pl) the breast; the upper seat, or chief place.

صَدَعَ (a.) he split; صُدَاعٌ a headache, megrim.

صَدَقَ (u.) he was sincere and true; he spoke the truth; I. صَدَّقَ he gave credit to; he believed; he verified; II. صَادَقَ he behaved as a friend; he cultivated friendship; IV. تَصَدَّقَ he bestowed alms; he gave in charity; صِدْقٌ truth, veracity; صَدَقَةٌ alms; whatever is dedicated to pious purposes; صَدَاقَةٌ friendship; صَدُوقٌ true, sincere; صَدِيقٌ a friend.

صَرَخَ (a.) he screamed or roared; صُرَاخٌ roaring, bellowing.

صِرَاطٌ (.pl صُرُطٌ) a road, way, path.

صَرَفَ (i.) he changed; he turned; VI. اِنْصَرَفَ he turned himself; he returned; he retired, he departed.

صَعَدَ and III. أَصْعَدَ he ascended, he mounted, he climbed; صُعُودٌ ascending, going up; ascension.

صَغُرَ (u.) he was small, mean; IX. اِسْتَصْغَرَ he deemed little; he

صَلْعَمْ

despised; صِغَارٌ (.pl) صَغِيرٌ small, little; junior, minor.

صِفَةٌ quality, description (rt. وَصَفَ).

صَفَحَ (a.) he forgave, pardoned.

صَفَرٌ (a.) name of the second month in the Islamic calendar.

صَفَقَ (i.) and I. صَفَّقَ he clapped his hands; he flapped his wings; he beat one thing against another.

صَفَا for صَفَوَ (u.) it was pure, clear, bright; IX. اِسْتَصْفَى he took the whole; he exhausted; he confiscated.

صَلَبَ (i.) he crucified; صَلُبَ he was strong, robust, hardy; صُلْبٌ (.pl أَصْلُبٌ and أَصْلَابٌ) the loins.

صَلَحَ (u.) he was good, honest; III. أَصْلَحَ he amended, fitted, bettered; he reconciled, made peace; صَالِحٌ just, sincere, honest; إِصْلَاحٌ amendment, amelioration, emendation, correction.

صَلْعَمْ a contraction of the formula صَلَّى اللَّهُ عَلَيْهِ وَسَلَّمَ may the blessing and peace of God be upon him!

صَلَا for صَلَوَ (*u.*) he thrust into the fire; he roasted; صَلَّى he prayed; he prayed to God; he blessed; he sanctified; صَلَّى اللّٰهُ عَلَيْهِ may God bestow his blessing upon him! صَلَاةٌ and صَلْوةٌ prayer.

ضَمَّ (*u.*) he corked or closed with a stopple.

صَمْتَ (*u.*) he was silent; صَمْتٌ silence.

صَمَدَ (*u.*) he sought; he made for; he strove to attain; صَمَدٌ a master; eternal, everlasting; sublime.

صَنْدُوقٌ a chest, a coffer.

صَنَعَ (*a.*) he made, formed, constructed; he did; VII. he benefited (another); صِنَاعَةٌ (*pl.* صَنَائِعُ) art, invention, work, workmanship.

صَنْفٌ (*pl.* أَصْنَافٌ) a species, sort, kind.

صَنَمٌ (*pl.* أَصْنَامٌ) an idol.

صَابَ for صَوَبَ (*u.*) it went straight or direct; III. أَصَابَ he reached, overtook; he came upon, found, or acquired; it befell; مُصَابٌ hurt, afflicted; affliction, visitation (from God); مُصِيبَةٌ an accident, misfortune, affliction, calamity.

صَاتَ for صَوَتَ (*u. & a.*) he called; he cried out; صَوْتٌ (*pl.* أَصْوَاتٌ) a sound, voice, noise, shout.

صَارَ for صَوَرَ (*u.*) he cut and divided; I. صَوَّرَ he formed, fashioned; he drew; he painted; صُورَةٌ (*pl.* صُوَرٌ) a form, image, figure, species; تَصْوِيرٌ drawing, painting; a picture; مُصَوِّرٌ a painter, a limner.

صَاغَ for صَوَغَ (*u.*) (the metallist) cast, formed, founded.

صَافَ for صَوَفَ (*u.*) it was wooly; صُوفٌ wool, a fleece.

صَانَ for صَوَنَ (*u.*) he guarded, preserved.

صَاحَ for صَيَحَ (*i.*) he screamed, or cried out; he called aloud.

صَادَ for صَيَدَ (*i. & a.*) he hunted or fished; صَيَّادٌ a huntsman; a fisher-man; صَيْدٌ anything caught by hunting or fishing; prey, game.

صَارَ for صَيَرَ (*i.*) he became; he

صَافَ went; he departed; مَصِيرٌ departure.

صَافَ for صَيَفَ (*i.*) he spent the summer; he summered; صَيْفٌ summer (i.e. May and June); صَائِفَةٌ the summer; a summer campaign.

صِينٌ China; صِينِيُّ Chinese.

ض

ضَجَّ (*i.*) he cried out; he groaned.

ضَجِرَ (*a.*) he became tired, wearied.

ضَحِكَ (*a.*) he laughed; he derided.

ضَحَا (*u.*) it appeared; it was clear and conspicuous; ضَحْوَةٌ the morning, forenoon, when the sun has ascended halfway to the meridian.

ضَرَّ (*u.*) he hurt, injured; ضَرُورِيٌّ necessary, indispensable; مَضَرَّةٌ (*pl.* مَضَارٌّ) harm, hurt, injury, detriment, disadvantage.

ضَرَبَ (*i.*) he struck, beat; ضَرْبٌ beating; a blow.

ضَعْضَعَ *quadril.* he humiliated; he diminished.

ضَعُفَ (*u.*) he was weak, infirm, powerless; II. ضَاعَفَ he doubled; IX. اِسْتَضْعَفَ he contracted illness; he was weak, infirm; ضُعْفٌ weakness, infirmity; ضَعِيفٌ weak, feeble, infirm; أَضْعَافٌ double; as much more.

ضَلَّ (*i.*) he wandered, or deviated (from the right way); he erred and strayed; ضَالٌّ erring, straying.

ضَلَعَ (*a.*) he was strong, robust; ضِلْعٌ (*pl.* أَضْلَاعٌ) a side; a rib.

ضَمَّ (*u.*) he gathered up, or tightened (his garments).

ضَاعَ for ضَيَعَ (*i.*) he perished, was lost and undone; ضَيْعَةٌ (*pl.* ضِيَاعٌ) a plain, a field; a farm.

ضَافَ for ضَيَفَ (*i.*) he visited; he was a guest; ضَيْفٌ a guest, visitor.

ط

طَبَّ for طَبِبَ (*i. & u.*) he practised medicine; he was skilful, scientific; طَبِيبٌ (*pl.* أَطِبَّاءُ) a doctor, physician; طِبَابَةٌ the practice of physic, the medical art.

طَبَخَ he cooked; مَطْبَخ place for cooking, kitchen.

طَبَعَ (*a.*) he stamped, marked, impressed; مَطْبُوعٌ impressed (by nature); stamped, printed; طَبْعٌ or طِبَاعٌ and طَبِيعَةٌ impress, character, nature, disposition.

طَبِقَ (*a.*) (the hand) was closed; أَطْبَقَ he covered, overspread.

طَبْلٌ (*pl.* طُبُولٌ) a drum or tabor.

طَحَنَ (*a.*) he ground, crushed; طَحْنٌ grinding, pounding, crushing.

طَرَحَ (*a.*) he cast, threw; he fixed, placed, laid (a foundation).

طَرَدَ (*a.*) he drove pell-mell; he hunted.

طَرَفَ (*i.*) he averted; turned aside; he closed his eyes; he winked; طَرْفٌ the eye; a glance; طَرَفٌ (*pl.* أَطْرَافٌ) a side, quarter; a district.

طَرَقَ (*u.*) he came by night; طَرِيقٌ (*pl.* طُرُقٌ) a road, a way.

طَشْتٌ a basin, a large cup or bowl.

طَعِمَ (*a.*) he ate, he tasted food; III. أَطْعَمَ he fed; he gave to eat; طَعَامٌ food, meat, victuals.

طَغِيَ (*a.*) he transgressed; he rebelled; طَاغٍ for طَاغِيٌّ (*pl.* طُغَاةٌ) a sinner, transgressor; a rebel.

طَفَقَ (*i.*) he began, set about, engaged in.

طَفُلَ (*u.*) it was soft or tender; IV. تَطَفَّلَ he acted like Tufail, i.e., he came where he had not been invited; طِفْلٌ a child, an infant.

طَقْطَقَ *quadril.* he hooted, uttered a tumultuous noise.

طَلَبَ (*u.*) he sought; he inquired; he begged; طَالِبٌ a seeker; also a man's name; طَلَبٌ pursuit, search; مَطْلَبٌ intention; desire, demand, request; means.

طَلَعَ (*a.* & *u.*) it (the sun or a star) ascended, appeared, or rose; طُلُوعٌ ascending, rising; rise, ascent.

طَلَقَتْ (*u.*) she (a wife) was divorced, dismissed; III. أَطْلَقَ he divorced, repudiated, set free; طَلَاقٌ divorce; مُطْلَقًا absolutely, wholly, simply.

طَلَا or طَلَى (*i.*) he anointed, smeared.

طَمَّ (*u.*) he blocked, stopped, or

choked up; he filled.
طَنَبَ (i.) (the horse) was long in the body and back; III. أَطْنَبَ he spoke with sublimity, or hyperbolically.

طَهَرَ and طَهُرَ (u.) he was pure, and undefiled طَهُورٌ that by which any thing is purified or cleansed; طَهَارَةٌ cleanliness, purification.

طَاسَ for طَوَسَ (u.) he flourished, he convalesced; طَاوُوسٌ or طَاوُوسٌ (pl. طَوَاوِيسُ) a peacock.

طَاعَ for طَوَعَ (u. & a.) he obeyed; III. أَطَاعَ he followed, obeyed, submitted; IX. اِسْتَطَاعَ he was able, and capable; he could; طَاعَةٌ obedience, submission; worship.

طَافَ for طَوَفَ (u.) and III. أَطَافَ he surrounded, went round, circumambulated; he approached softly, he stole upon; طَائِفَةٌ (pl. طَوَائِفُ) a people, nation, party, body, class; an itinerant band; طُوفَانٌ surrounding, pervading all things; a flood, the universal deluge.

طَاقَ for طَوَقَ (u.) and III. أَطَاقَ he was able; he endured; he could; طَاقَةٌ power, ability, strength; power of endurance.

طَالَ for طَوَلَ (u.) it was long; it lasted long; it continued; III. أَطْوَلَ he prolonged; طَوِيلٌ long, lengthy; أَطْوَلُ longer, longest; very long; طُولٌ length, extent, duration.

طَابَ for طَيَبَ (i.) it was good, pleasing, or delicious; I. طَيَّبَ he pleased, gratified, delighted; he found good or beautiful; he approved; طَيِّبٌ good, pleasant, grateful, agreeable, sweet, fragrant; طَيِّبَةٌ (fem. of طَيِّبٌ) (pl. طُوبَى) good; a thing good, lawful, and excellent; أَطْيَبُ more or most delicious, or agreeable.

طَارَ for طَيَرَ (i.) he flew, he was borne rapidly along; IX. اِسْتَطَارَ it flew far and wide; it dispersed itself abroad; طَيْرٌ (pl. طُيُورٌ) a bird.

ظ

ظَبْيٌ a wild buck, chevril; ظَبْيَةٌ a roe, a doe.

ظَلَّ (*a.*) he ceased not, he persevered; I. ظَلَّلَ he shaded, he shadowed; IV. تَظَلَّلَ he shaded himself, he sought or he enjoyed the shade; ظِلٌّ (*pl.* ظِلَالٌ) a shade, a shadow.

ظَلَم (*i.*) he was unjust, tyrannical; ظَالِمٌ a tyrant, oppressor; a sinner; ظَلُومٌ extremely tyrannical; ظُلْمٌ and ظُلَامَةٌ injustice, oppression, tyranny, injury.

ظَنَّ (*u.*) he thought; he was of opinion.

ظَهَرَ (*u.* & *i.*) he appeared, was conspicuous and manifest; I. ظَهَّرَ he displayed, manifested; III. أَظْهَرَ he revealed, made known, declared; ظَهْرٌ (*pl.* ظُهُورٌ) the back; ظُهْرٌ noon, mid-day, or a little time after the sun has passed the meridian, when it is most sultry; ظَاهِرٌ exterior, outward, external; clear, conspicuous, ظَاهِراً apparently; outwardly; إِظْهَارٌ a declaring, shewing forth, making manifest, revealing, publishing.

ع

عَبَدَ (*a.*) he adored, worshipped; عَبْدٌ (*pl.* عَبِيدٌ and عِبَادٌ) a servant, a slave; name; عِبَادَةٌ adoration, devotion. (In addition to these two forms of plural, the word عَبْدٌ has thirteen others.)

عَبَرَ (*u.*) he passed over, he crossed; he went up to; عَابِرٌ one who passes over.

عَبَسَ (*i.*) he was harsh and austere in countenance; عَبُوسٌ austere, crabbed; dismal, calamitous.

عَتَدَ (*u.*) he was prepared, ready; III. أَعْتَدَ he prepared, made ready.

عَتِقَ (*i.*) he was freed; III. أَعْتَقَ he freed, set free, manumitted.

عَجِبَ and III. أَعْجَبَ, and IV. تَعَجَّبَ, also VII. إِعْتَجَبَ he wondered, he marvelled, he was astonished; it pleased him.

عَجَزَ (*i.*) he was weak, impotent,

or destitute; عَجُوزٌ weak, frail, feeble; عَجُوزَةٌ a frail old woman.

عَجِلَ (a.) he hastened; عَاجِلٌ hastening, hasty; عَاجِلًا hastily; عَاجِلٌ and عَاجِلَةٌ(opposed to آجِلَةٌ) this transitory, fleeting life; عَجَلَةٌ precipitation, haste, hurry.

عَجَمٌ a term applied generally to such people as are not Arabs, and more especially to the Persians; it is equivalent to what the Greeks termed "Barbarians."

عَجَنَ (i. & u.) he kneaded; عَجْنٌ kneading.

عَدَّ (u.) he numbered, counted, reckoned up; III. أَعَدَّ he prepared, arranged; IX. إِسْتَعَدَّ he prepared, got ready, إِسْتِعْدَادٌ preparation, readiness, aptitude, dexterity, skill, proficiency.

عَدَلَ (i.) he dealt justly; he administered justice; he deviated, turned aside; VII. إِعْتَدَلَ it was temperate; and moderate; it was equal; عَادِلٌ a just man; an epithet of Nūshirivān, who was king of Persia in the time of the Prophet Muḥammad.

عَدِمَ (i.) he was deficient, or wanting; he was without; عَدِيمٌ deficient, wanting (in intellect).

عَدَنَ (i. or u.) he dwelt permanently (in some place); مَعْدِنٌ (pl. مَعَادِنُ) a mine (of gold, etc.)

عَدَا for عَدَوَ (u.) he passed by, or over; he transgressed; he erred; he was unjust and inimical; I. عَدَّى he caused to pass; he turned aside (his face); عَدَا beside, beyond, save, except; عَدُوٌّ (pl. أَعْدَاءُ) an enemy, a foe; عَدَاوَةٌ (pl. عَدَاوَاتٌ) enmity, hatred, hostility, strife, animosity.

عَذَبَ (i.) he prevented, forbade, hindered; عَذَابٌ punishment, torment, torture.

عَرِبَ he was brisk, lively, and joyful; عَرَبٌ an Arab, peculiarly, one inhabiting a city (the term أَعْرَابٌ denoting an Arab of the desert).

عَرْبَدَةٌ brutality, rudeness,

عَشَا / عَرَش

violence, uproar, quarrelsomeness; (in anglo-American phrase) rowdyism.

عَرَشَ (*u. & i.*) he constructed, framed, erected (a booth or an edifice of wood); عَرْشٌ a throne, seat.

عَرَضَ (*u.*) he met, or came against; it occured, happened; it appeared, or presented itself; II. عَارَضَ he opposed, he contended with; عِرْضٌ odour, effluvia (of the body); reputation, honour, character.

عَرَفَ (*i.*) he knew, was acquainted with; he discovered; I. عَرَّفَ he made known, informed, taught; عُرْفٌ known, notorious, acknowledged; the name by which a person or thing is generally called (or known); commonly called; alias; عُرْفًا notoriously, confessedly; مَعْرُوفٌ known.

عِرْقٌ (*pl.* عُرُوقٌ) root (of a tree, etc.)

عَرَكَ (*u.*) he attacked; he rubbed.

عَرِيَ (*u.*) he was naked; عُرْيَانٌ naked.

عَزَّ (*i.*) it was precious, excellent; he was noble, eminent; I. عَزَّزَ he honoured, held in esteem; عَزِيزٌ precious, dear, valuable; mighty, powerful; a king (especially of Egypt).

عَزَمَ (*i.*) he designed, he determined, intended, resolved, purposed; he vowed; عَزِيمَةٌ (*pl.* عَزَائِمُ) an incantation, spell, charm, amulet.

عَزِيَ (*a.*) he received consolation; IV. تَعَزَّى he received consolation, he was consoled, comforted; عَزَاءٌ condolence, lamentation, mourning.

عَسَلٌ honey; also the honeycomb.

عُشْبٌ grass, green crop (as opposed to حَشِيشٌ *q.v.*)

عَشَرَ (*u.*) he decimated; II. عَاشَرَ he associated with; he was intimate with; عَشْرٌ and *masc.* عَشَرَةٌ ten; إِحْدَى عَشْرَةَ *fem.* eleven; عِشْرُونَ twenty; مَعْشَرٌ (*pl.* مَعَاشِرُ) a crowd, an assembly; society, company.

عَشَا for عَشَوَ (*u.*) he came in the evening; عِشَاءٌ the afternoon, evening.

عَصَفَ (*i.*) it (the wind) blew violently; عَصْفٌ and عَصْفَةٌ the force or fury of the wind; عَاصِفٌ a fierce wind.

عُصْفُورٌ (*pl.* عَصَافِيرُ) a sparrow.

عَصَى (*i.*) he disobeyed; he rebelled against; عَصًا a staff, stick, cudgel, bludgeon; a mace.

عَضَّ (*a.*) he crunched or ground with his teeth.

عَضَدَ (*a.*) he aided or assisted; مُعَاضَدَةٌ assistance, mutual aid; عَضُدٌ or عَضَدٌ the arm from the shoulder to the elbow, the upper arm.

عَضَا for عَضَوَ (*u.*) he cut into pieces; he dissected; عِضْوٌ and عُضْوٌ (*pl.* أَعْضَاءٌ) a member, a limb, a joint.

عَطِشَ (*a.*) he was thirsty; عَطْشٌ thirst; عَطْشَانُ thirsty.

عَطَا (*u.*) he received into his hands; he took; III. أَعْطَى he bestowed; he gave.

عِظَةٌ admonition, exhortation (from وَعَظَ *q.v.*)

عَظُمَ (*u.*) it was grave and important; عَظِيمٌ great; grievous; عَظَمَةٌ and عِظَمٌ and greatness, magnificence; مُعْظَمٌ the greater part (of anything).

عَفَّ (*i.*) he abstained (from anything forbidden); she was modest, chaste; عِفَّةٌ abstinence, chastity.

عَفَرَ (*i.*) he cast on the ground; عِفْرِيتٌ a gigantic or horrible monster, a hideous spectre.

عَفَا for عَفَوَ (*u.*) he obliterated; he pardoned, forgave; عَافِيَةٌ safety, health, welfare.

عُقَابٌ (*pl.* عُقْبَانٌ) an eagle.

عَقَدَ (*i.*) he knotted; he tied in a knot; VII. اِعْتَقَدَ he believed firmly; he was confident.

عَقْرَبٌ (*pl.* عَقَارِبُ) a scorpion.

عَقَلَ (*i.*) he was sensible and intelligent; he understood; عَقْلٌ understanding, sense; عِقَالٌ a rope which binds together the feet and neck of a camel to make him obedient when disposed to be untractable; a fetter.

عَكِرَ (*i.*) it was turbid or muddy (water, etc.); I. عَكَّرَ he rendered muddy, he dirtied, polluted, defiled.

عِلَّةٌ (*pl.* عِلَلٌ and أَعْلَالٌ) a disease,

عَلَجَ illness, ailment; a cause, motive.

عَلَجَ he overcame; II. عَالَجَ he managed; he treated (a disease); مُعَالَجَةٌ and عِلاجٌ medicine; treatment of a disease, cure.

عَلَفَ (*a.*) he pastured; he foddered; he fed himself; he was nourished; عُلُوفَةٌ and عَلَفٌ (*pl.* أَعْلَافٌ and عِلَافٌ) hay, fodder, food for cattle; مَعْلَفٌ a stable, crib, boose, stall, manger.

عَلَقَ (*u.*) he depended, or hung from; he adhered, he clung; I. عَلَّقَ he suspended; تَعْلِيقٌ suspension; exhibition.

عَلِمَ (*a.*) he knew; he was learned, or well-informed; I. عَلَّمَ he taught, informed; III. أَعْلَمَ he published, revealed, made known; تَعَلَّمَ he submitted to be taught; he learnt; عِلْمٌ science, knowledge, learning; عَالِمٌ (*pl.* عُلَمَاءُ) learned, wise; a sage; عَالَمٌ the world; all created things; عَلِيمٌ knowing, omniscient.

عَلَنَ (*u.* & *i.*) it was divulged; it was published; III. أَعْلَنَ he discovered, revealed; عَلَانِيَةٌ that which is manifest; outward behaviour, conduct.

عَلَا for عَلَوَ (*u.*) he was high, lofty, sublime; V. تَعَالَى he was elevated, exalted, supreme; أَعْلَى (عَالِيَةٌ *fem.*) high, lofty; عَالٍ the highest; the summit; عَلَى upon, against; عَلِيٌّ noble, eminent.

عَمِرَ (*a.*) he lived long; عُمْرٌ life, age; عَمَرَ (*u.*) he cultivated, built, repaired; عَامِرٌ an inhabited place (opposed to عَامِرٌ); also a man's name; عِمَارَةٌ a building, mansion.

عَمُقَ (*u.*) it was deep (a well, etc.); عَمِيقٌ deep, profound.

عَمِلَ (*a.*) he acted, did; he composed; he laboured; he constructed; IX. اِسْتَعْمَلَ he used, employed; عَمَلٌ (*pl.* أَعْمَالٌ) work, labour; a deed, act, action; عَامِلٌ (*pl.* عُمَّالٌ) an agent; an officer; a governor.

عَمِيَ (*a.*) he was blind; أَعْمَى (*fem.* عَمْيَاءُ) blind; الْأَعْمَى a man's name (or rather his epithet).

عَنْ off, from, from off;

عَاشَ for عَيْشَ (*i*.) he lived; he enjoyed life; مَعِيشَةٌ (*pl*. مَعَايِشُ)

back; he returned according to habit; عَائِدًا by way of visiting; عَادَةٌ custom, habit, usage.

عَوْرَةٌ (*pl*. عَوْرَاتٌ) the nudities (rt. عَارَ).

عَوْسَجٌ the bramble-tree or bush.

عَوَضَ (*u*.) for عَاضَ he exchanged, he substituted; عِوَضٌ a compensation, recompense, exchange, substitute.

عَوَّلَ (*u*.) for عَالَ and I. he confided in, trusted.

عَامَ (*u*.) he swam, floated.

عَوَنَ (*u*.) for عَانَ he helped; II. عَاوَنَ and III. أَعَانَ he aided and assisted; IX. اِسْتَعَانَ he implored aid, he sought assistance, he demanded or prayed for help; عَوْنٌ (*pl*. أَعْوَانٌ) assistance, aid, help.

عَيِيَ he hesitated; he was incapable; II. عَايَى he was tired; III. أَعْيَى he baffled.

عَابَ for عَيَبَ (*i*.) it was defective, faulty, bad; عَيْبٌ a fault, defect, blemish; a vice.

عِيْسَى Jesus.

---

concerning, about, of, touching.

عِنْدَ with, near, at, among, according to.

عَنْزٌ (*pl*. عُنُوزٌ) also عَنْزَةٌ a she-goat; a fawn, or doe.

عُنُقٌ the neck; the throat.

عَنِيَ originally عَنَوَ, (*u*.) he was wearied, tired; عَنَاءٌ care, labour, distress.

يَعْنِي (*i*.) it signified, it meant; it means, that is to say, to wit; مَعْنًا or مَعْنًى meaning, moral (of a tale, etc.); III. أَعْنَى it concerned or referred to.

عَهِدَ (*a*.) he stipulated; II. عَاهَدَ he engaged; he entered into a compact (with any one); he pledged himself; عَهْدٌ a promise; a compact; a will or testament; commission, appointment to office; time, reign.

عَوِجَ (*a*.) it was bent, distorted; I. عَوَّجَ he curved; VIII. اِعْوَجَّ it was bent; اِعْوِجَاجٌ crookedness, deformity.

عَادَ for عَوَدَ (*u*.) he visited (the sick); he returned; he repeated; II. عَاوَدَ he came also مَعَاشٌ living, life; livelihood.

عَيَّطَ he vociferated, cried out, shouted.

عَانَ for عَيَنَ (the water or the tears) flowed; عَيْنٌ (pl. عُيُونٌ) an eye; a fountain; II. عَايَنَ he saw clearly.

غ

غَامِرٌ (the reverse of عَامِرٌ) an uninhabited region; a place that has been laid waste by a flood.

غَايَةٌ end, extremity, termination, final point, goal, terminus; extreme, utmost.

غَبَنَ (a.) he deceived, he defrauded; تَغَابُنٌ mutually deceiving or defrauding; the inflicting of loss upon one another.

غدا (u.) he came in the morning; غَدًا tomorrow; in the morning.

غَذَا (u.) he ate; he fed, etc.

غَرَّ (u.) he deceived, beguiled; غُرُورٌ deception; VII. اِغْتَرَّ he was deceived, beguiled, cozened, cheated.

غَرَبَ (u.) he was absent, distant; (the sun) set; غُرَابٌ a crow, a raven; غَرِيبٌ an alien, a stranger; مَغْرِبٌ the west; sunset.

غَرْبَلَ quadril. he sifted; غِرْبَالٌ a sieve, a searce; مُغَرْبَلٌ sifted, cleansed.

غَرَسَ (i.) he planted; غَرْسٌ planting.

غَرِضَ (a.) he desired; he sought earnestly; غَرَضٌ aim, end, object, purpose, design, interest, business.

غَرِقَ he was plunged, immersed, or submerged; غَرْقٌ submersion.

غَرِمَ (a.) he was involved in debt; III. أَغْرَمَ he made addicted, or devoted (to anything); مُغْرَمٌ desirous, wishful; addicted, given up to.

غَزَلَ (i.) he spun; غَزْلٌ spinning; غَزَالٌ (pl. غِزْلَانٌ) a gazelle, a fawn, a young deer.

غَزَا for غَزَوَ (u.) he attacked; he invaded; he warred, he waged war.

غَسَلَ (i.) he washed.

غَشَّ (u.) he deceived; غِشٌّ deceit;

مَغْشُوشٌ adulterated, counterfeited, falsified; deceitful.

غَشِيَ (a.) he veiled or covered.

غَصَبَ (i.) and VII. اِغْتَصَبَ he carried off by force or fraud.

غُصْنٌ (pl. أَغْصَانٌ) a branch, a bough.

غَضِبَ (a.) he was angry, incensed; I. غَضَّبَ and III. أَغْضَبَ he made angry; he incensed; غَضَبٌ anger, ire, rage, wrath.

غَفَرَ (i.) he covered; he pardoned, he forgave; IX. اِسْتَغْفَرَ he asked pardon, he besought to forgive and absolve; غَفُورٌ merciful, forgiving, pardoning.

غَفِلَ (a.) he was negligent, heedless, idle; مُغَفَّلٌ destitute of genius, attention or presence of mind; careless, thoughtless, heedless, incurious, ignorant, dull, stupid.

غَلَّ (u.) he inserted (one thing into another); غُلٌّ (pl. أَغْلَالٌ) a collar, or any thing put round the neck (whether of iron, wood, or a skin with the hair on); a yoke.

غَلَبَ (i.) he overcame, conquered, was superior; VI. اِنْغَلَبَ he was conquered, etc.; أَغْلَبُ (fem. غَلْبَاءُ) superior; more or most powerful, stronger, strongest; فِي الْأَغْلَبِ for the most part.

غَلَقَ (i.) and III. أَغْلَقَ he shut up; he locked or fastened (a door).

غَلِمَ (a.) he burned with lust; he desired; غُلَامٌ (pl. غِلْمَانٌ) a boy, lad, youth; a servant; adolescent, pubescent.

غَمَّ (u.) he afflicted, distressed; VII. اِغْتَمَّ he suffered affliction; he was glum and sad; he grieved; غَمٌّ grief, sadness, distress.

غَمَى (u.) he covered; he roofed; in the passive غُمِيَ عَلَيْهِ and III. أُغْمِيَ عَلَيْهِ he swooned, fainted (synonymous with غُشِيَ عَلَيْهِ).

غَنِيَ (a.) he enjoyed; he was contented, satisfied; IX. اِسْتَغْنَى he was contented; he wanted nothing; he was independent, or able to do without, and to dispense with; غَنِيٌّ wealthy, rich; غِنَاءٌ a song; music; غِنًى contentedness of mind; wealth.

مَغَارَةٌ and مَغَارٌ also (pl. غِيرَانٌ), غَارٌ (pl. مَغَائِرُ) a cave, a cavern; a den.

غَاصَ (u.) he dived; غَوَّاصٌ for a diver; also name of a bird.

غَوْغَاءٌ a mob; tumult, uproar, confusion.

غَالَ for غَوَلَ (u.) he surprised; he attacked insidiously and destroyed; غِيلَةٌ a treacherous or unexpected attack.

غَوَى (i.) he erred; he was deceived; غَيٌّ error, sin; غَايَةٌ the extremity; the extreme limit.

غَابَ for غَيَبَ (i.) he was absent, invisible; he disappeared; غَيْبٌ whatever is hidden from us and invisible; mystery; futurity; I. غِيبَةٌ slandering of the absent, backbiting.

غَارَ for غَيَرَ (i.) he was jealous; I. غَيَّرَ he changed; IV. تَغَيَّرَ it was changed, altered (generally for the worse); غَيْرٌ alteration; different, other, except; بِغَيْرِ without, besides.

غَاظَ for غَيَظَ (i.) he was inflamed with anger; he was incensed; غَيْظٌ anger, indignation, rage.

ف

ف an inseparable particle, signifying then, therefore; so that, in order that.

فَأْرٌ (fem. فَأْرَةٌ) a mouse.

فَتَحَ (a.) he opened, unclosed; فَاتِحَةٌ an opening or beginning; the first chapter of the Qur'ān; مِفْتَاحٌ a key.

فَتَنَ (i.) he tried, he proved or tested; فِتْنَةٌ a trial, temptation; trouble, strife, sedition, tumult, insurrection, cabal; evil, pest.

فَجَرَ (u.) he poured forth; he was false, vicious, or dissolute; I. فَجَّرَ he caused to burst forth, he set a flowing; he allowed (water) to run and diffuse (itself); تَفْجِيرٌ a diffusing, a causing to flow; فُجُورٌ dissipation; debauchery; فَاجِرٌ and فَجُورٌ dissipated.

فَخَرَ (a.) he gloried over; VII. اِفْتَخَرَ he boasted; he took credit to himself; فَاخِرٌ precious, excellent; fine, gorgeous, or

sumptuous (apparel),
splendid, showy (dress).
فَدَّانٌ a yoke of oxen; a plough.
فَدَا (i.) he ransomed; he devoted
himself for another.
فَرَّ (i.) he fled away; فَرَارٌ flight,
running away.
فَرِحَ (a.) he was joyful, cheerful; I.
فَرَّحَ he exhilarated, delighted;
فَرِحٌ joy, gladness, delight,
glee; فَرْحَانٌ joyful, joyous,
happy, pleased.
فَرَدَ (u.) and VI. اِنْفَرَدَ he was
separated, withdrew, retired,
was alone.
فَرَسَ (i.) and VII. اِفْتَرَسَ he (the
lion, etc.) grasped by the
neck; he tore with his teeth;
فَرَسٌ a horse; a mare; اَلْفُرْسُ the
Persian, Persia.
فَرَشَ (u.) he spread (a carpet); he
paved, he laid down
(flag-stones); فَرْشٌ a bed; a
couch; any thing spread out,
on which one reclines.
فَرَصَ (a.) he cut, he cleaved, he
split, he tore; فُرْصَةٌ
opportunity, occasion, fit
time, convenience; leisure;
suspension of public business

for a season; freedom, ease,
relief; rest; a time, turn.
فَرَعَ (a.) and IV. تَفَرَّعَ he excelled,
overtopped; فَرْعٌ the summit or
apex; the branch of a tree
(especially the top); anything
arising or produced from
another; effect, result; أَصْلٌ
وَفَرْعٌ root and branch; cause
and effect, principal and
accessory.
فِرْعَونٌ Pharaoh; any cruel tyrant;
imperious, haughty,
overbearing.
فَرَغَ (a.) he finished, brought to a
close, concluded, terminated;
he ceased; فِرَاغٌ leisure,
disengagement; cessation
from labour; freedom from
care, ease.
فَرَقَ (u.) he separated; he parted;
II. فَارَقَ he quitted; he departed
from; VII. اِفْتَرَقَ he was
separated; اِفْتِرَاقٌ removal,
absence, distance, separation.
فَزَّ (i.) he retired, he departed; he
sprung up; he was roused; IX.
اِسْتَفَزَّ he alarmed; he roused.
فَسَدَ (u.) it was corrupt, vicious;
III. أَفْسَدَ he corrupted, vitiated,

destroyed, spoilt; he practised evil; فَسَادٌ corruption, depravity, evil, vice, iniquity; mutiny, rebellion; a deseased state, distemper, unsoundness (of mind or body).

فَسَقَ (*i.* & *u.*) he committed sin (especially fornication); فَاسِقٌ a dissolute, worthless, impudent fellow; impious, abandoned, profligate.

فَشَا (*u.*) it was divulged; it extended; it became public; III. أَفْشَى he divulged, revealed, or spread abroad.

فَصَحَ (*u.*) he was eloquent; فَصَاحَةٌ eloquence, perspicuity, clearness.

فَصَلَ (*i.*) he separated; he dissected; فَصْلٌ a section; a division; chapter (of a book).

فِضَّةٌ silver (rt. فَضَّ *u.*)

فَضَحَ (*a.*) he exposed to infamy; فُضُوحٌ disgrace, ignominy.

فَضَلَ (*u.*) it was redundant; it exceeded; I. فَضَّلَ he preferred, exalted, distinguished; IV. تَفَضَّلَ he excelled, was eminent; he conferred a favour, he favoured, he obliged; he presumed, was arrogant; فَضْلٌ excellence, superiority, knowledge; فَضْلًا even, in the last, at all; فَضُولٌ busy, meddling, officious; a tomfool; فُضُولٌ a busy, meddling spirit; folly; impertinent interference.

فَطَحَ (*a.*) he widened; أَفْطَحُ broad-headed; hence, الْأَفْطَحُ the bull.

فَعَلَ (*a.*) he did; he acted; فِعْلٌ (*pl.* أَفْعَالٌ) and فَعَالٌ a deed, act, action.

فَقَدَ (*i.*) he sought and found out (what he had lost); he desired; he missed.

فَقُرَ (*u.*) he was poor; III. أَفْقَرَ he impoverished, he reduced to indigence; فَقِيرٌ indigent, poor; فَقْرٌ poverty, destitution.

فَكِهَ he was lively, gay, merry, facetious, jocular; فَاكِهَةٌ (*pl.* فَوَاكِهُ) fruit.

فُلَانٌ such a one; so and so (whose name is known, yet not mentioned).

فَلَحَ (*a.*) he ploughed, he tilled (the ground); أَفْلَحَ he

فَلَقَ prospered; he was blessed; مُفْلِحٌ successful, prosperous, happy.

فَلَقَ (i.) he cleft or split; VI. اِنْفَلَقَ it was split or shivered, it burst.

فَمّ the mouth. In construction, it is declined like أَبٌ as; nom. فَمٌ, gen. فِي acc. فَا (pl. أَفْوَاهٌ) as if from فُوهٌ, of which فَمٌ is said to be a corruption.

فَنّ he drove; I. فَنَّنَ he classed; he distributed into orders; فَنٌّ species, form, kind; art, science, skill, trick, knack.

فَنَى for فَنِي (a.) it was destroyed; it disappeared; III. أَفْنَى he made disappear; he wasted, consumed, annihilated.

فَهِمَ (a.) he comprehended, he understood; فَهْمٌ understanding, sense.

فَاتَ for فَوَتَ (u.) it passed by; it elapsed, escaped, slipped away; it perished; فَوْتٌ failure; death.

فَازَ for فَوَزَ (u.) he obtained possession of; he enjoyed; فَوْزٌ triumph, victory; happiness, enjoyment.

فَاقَ for فَوَقَ (u.) he was superior; he excelled; III. أَفَاقَ he recovered (from sickness, swoon, intoxication, etc.) فَوْقَ above, over, more than; فَاقَةٌ poverty, destitution; starving, extreme hunger.

فُولٌ a species of bean.

فِي prep. in, into, among, concerning, on.

فَادَ for فَيَدَ (i.) he derived emolument; he was benefited; III. أَفَادَ he benefited; he enriched; he instructed; فَائِدَةٌ advantage, benefit, profit, gain, emolument, use.

فَيْفٌ and فَيْفَاءُ (pl. فَيَافِي) a plain, a desert void of water.

ق

قَبُحَ he was ugly, deformed, base; IX. اِسْتَقْبَحَ he deemed base; he abhorred; قَبِيحٌ deformed, hideous, ugly, abhorrent; قُبْحَةٌ ugliness, deformity.

قَبَضَ (i.) he took; he seized; he grasped, clutched; قَبْضٌ taking, seizing; capture,

قَبِلَ seizure, distraint; possession. قَبِلَ (*a*.) he approached; he admitted, accepted, adopted; III. أَقْبَلَ he approached; he advanced towards; he began; قَبْلَ before; قَبْلَ أَنْ before that; مِنْ قَبْلِ formerly, before; قِبَلَ at, near, with; مِنْ قِبَلِ in respect of, through, from; قَبِيلَةٌ (*pl*. قَبَائِلُ) a tribe, family, race.

قَتَلَ (*u*.) he slew; he killed; II. قَاتَلَ and V. تَقَاتَلَ he sought to slay; he fought or contended with; III. أَقْتَلَ he put to death; he exposed (to danger or destruction); he gave up to be killed; VII. اِقْتَتَلَ he fought, combated; قِتَالٌ war, battle, conflict.

قَدْ *an affirmative particle*, signifying truly, indeed, verily.

قَدَحٌ a cup, a glass, drinking vessel.

قَدِرَ (*i*.) he was able; he was powerful; I. قَدَّرَ he measured; he fixed he decreed; قَدِيرٌ powerful, able, omnipotent تَقْدِيرٌ measurement, proportioning; decreeing; supposition, hypothesis; قُدْرَةٌ power; قِدْرٌ (*pl*. قُدُورٌ) a kettle, pot, or cauldron.

قَدُسَ (*u*.) he was pure, holy; I. قَدَّسَ he sanctified; he consecrated; he glorified; قُدْسٌ purity, sanctity.

قَدَمَ (*u*.) he preceded, went before, was prior to; I. قَدَّمَ he brought forward; preferred, promoted; he offered, presented; he served up, set (food) before; IV. تَقَدَّمَ he stepped forward, he advanced; قَدَمٌ (*pl*. أَقْدَامٌ) the foot; a step; قُدَّامَ before, in front of; قَدِيمٌ old, ancient, olden, former.

قَدَا for قَدَوَ (*u*.) he moved on rapidly; VII. he imitated; he took for his model or exemplar (قَدْوَةٌ).

قَذَرَ (*u*.) it was impure or unclean; قَاذُورَةٌ impurity; a dunghill, mixen.

قَرَّ (*i*. & *a*.) he rested; he remained firm and still; it was cold; III. أَقَرَّ he fixed, established, appointed; he confirmed, ratified; he averred, he affirmed; IX. اِسْتَقَرَّ he was

قَرَأَ

fixed; he abode, sojourned, dwelt, settled; مَقَرٌّ a place of residence; قَارُورَةٌ (pl. قَوَارِيرُ) a vase, flask, glass bottle, decanter; a glass urinal, in which the urine of sick person is shewn to the physician.

قَرَأَ (a. & u.) he read; he intoned; قُرْآنٌ reading; the Qur'ān.

قَرُبَ (a.) he approached; he drew near; I. قَرَّبَ he brought forward; he advanced; he placed near; V. تَقَارَبُوا they were near to, or adjoining (each other); they approached (each other); قَرِيبٌ (pl. أَقْرِبَاءُ) near, nearly related; a relation.

قَرَضَ (i.) he recompensed; he repaid; III. أَقْرَضَ he lent; قَرْضٌ a loan; a debt.

قَرَنَ (i.) he joined; he united; قَرْنٌ (pl. قُرُونٌ) a horn; an age, period, cycle.

قَسَا for قَسَوَ (u.) (the heart) was hard, obdurate; II. قَاسَى he endured, he suffered; he became callous.

قَصَبَ (i.) he cut in pieces or joints; قَصَّابٌ a butcher.

قِصَّةٌ (pl. قِصَصٌ) a tale, narrative,

قَطَفَ

history.

قَصَدَ (i.) he pursued, made for, aimed at, went towards; قَصْدٌ aim, tendency.

قَصَرَ (u.) he was deficient, fell short; he was unequal to; I. قَصَّرَ he failed; he did less than he ought, he was deficient; قَصْرٌ (pl. قُصُورٌ) a palace; قَصَّارٌ a fuller, bleacher; a washerman.

قَصَفَ he diverted himself; he danced uproariously.

قَضَّ and VI. اِنْقَضَّ he rushed on (the enemy); he pounced on (the prey).

قَضَى (i.) he decreed, determined; he concluded; VI. اِنْقَضَى it was concluded, determined, finished; اِنْقِضَاءٌ completion, termination, expiration; قَاضٍ a judge; اَلْقَاضِي the Qādi, or judge.

قِطٌّ (pl. قِطَاطٌ) a male or female cat.

قَطَعَ (a.) he cut; he separated; VI. اِنْقَطَعَ it was cut, broken, interrupted; it ceased, stopped, failed.

قَطَفَ (i.) he picked; he gathered (grapes); قِطْفٌ (pl. قُطُوفٌ) grapes, a bunch of grapes

قَطَنَ

قَطِيفَةٌ (pl. قَطَائِفُ) velvet; a kind of cake made of flour, honey, and oil.

قَطَنَ (u.) he inhabited; قَاطِنٌ an inhabitant, a settled resident.

قَعَدَ (u.) he sat down.

قَفَرَ he tracked; he followed; قَفْرٌ (pl. قُفُورٌ) a desert destitute of water and herbage.

قَفِعَ (a.) he was shrunk.

قَفَلَ (i. & u.) he returned from his journey; قَافِلَةٌ a caravan, a company of travellers, a coffle.

قَفَا for قَفَوَ (u.) he followed; قَفَا the hind-head; back part, or nape of the neck, the nuke; عَلَى قَفَاهِ after him, behind him.

قَلَّ it was small, little, few, deficient; قَلِيلٌ small, little, wanting, few; أَقَلُّ less, least; more or most deficient; fewer, fewest; قِلَّةٌ smallness, scantiness, paucity, fewness.

قَلَبَ (i.) he turned; he inverted; VI. اِنْقَلَبَ it was inverted, turned transposed; مُنْقَلَبٌ returning, futurity; قَلْبٌ (pl. قُلُوبٌ) the heart; the mind.

قَمَرٌ (pl. أَقْمَارٌ) the moon (especially from the third day to the end); III. أَقْمَرَ it was bright moonlight; he had the full moon shining on him.

قَمْطَرِيرٌ a dismal; calamitous day.

قَنِعَ (a.) he was contented; قَنِعٌ content, satisfied, contented.

قَهَرَ (a.) he vanquished, he overcame; قَاهِرٌ a conqueror; اَلْقَاهِرَةٌ victrix; the city of Cairo in Egypt.

قَادَ for قَوَدَ (u.) he led; he governed; he retaliated; VI. اِنْقَادَ he was led; he obeyed, he was submissive; IX. اِسْتَقَادَ he took retaliation; he indemnified himself; قَائِدٌ (pl. قُوَّادٌ) a leader, ruler, commander, chief, قَوَدٌ retaliation; lex talionis.

قَالَ for قَوَلَ (u.) he said, he spoke; قَوْلٌ (pl. أَقْوَالٌ) speech; a word, saying; مَقَالٌ and مَقَالَةٌ speaking, saying; a speech, discourse.

قَامَ for قَوَمَ (u.) he stood; he arose; III. أَقَامَ he caused to stand, he set on foot; he raised; he erected; he stayed, rested, abode; he was earnest and

قَوِيَ

persevering in prayer and supplication; مَقَامٌ a place; a station; اِسْتِقَامَةٌ erectness; rectitude; constancy, stability; مُسْتَقِيمٌ erect, upright, straight; قَائِمَةٌ (pl. قَوَائِمُ) the fore or hind foot of a quadruped; إِقَامَةٌ قَوْمٌ staying, standing still; (pl. أَقْوَامٌ) a crowd, tribe, multitude.

قَوِيَ (a.) he was strong, powerful; قُوَّةٌ (pl. قُوًى) force, strength, exertion; قَوِيٌّ strong, powerful, robust.

قَيْسٌ strength, power; a man's name.

قَيْصَرٌ the ruler of the Byzantine Empire.

قَانَ for قَيَنَ (i.) he hammered (the iron), he forged; قَيْنَةٌ (pl. قِيَانٌ) a girl; a female slave, singer, or musician.

ك

كَ *particle of similitude*, like, as; كَ *masc*. and كِ *fem. affixed pron. 2nd pers.* thee, thine; كَأَنَّ as if, like.

كَثُرَ

كَأْسٌ a drinking-cup; a wine-glass.

كَبُرَ (u.) he was large, corpulent; I. كَبَّرَ he magnified; he highly estimated; he expressed surprise, etc., by exclaiming اَللَّهُ أَكْبَرُ God is Great! IV. تَكَبَّرَ he was haughty, presumptuous; تَكَبُّرٌ haughtiness; كِبَرٌ greatness, pride; كَبَرٌ grandeur; كَبِيرٌ (pl. كِبَارٌ) great, large; adult; كُبَارًا and كَبِيرًا greatly, very much; أَكْبَرُ greater, greatest, elder, eldest.

كَبْشٌ (pl. كِبَاشٌ) a male lamb, a ram.

كَتَبَ (u.) he wrote; كِتَابٌ (pl. كُتُبٌ) a writing; a letter, book; law; اَلْكِتَابُ the book, the sacred volume.

كَتِفٌ (pl. كِتَفَةٌ and أَكْتَافٌ) the shoulder or shoulder-blade.

كَثُرَ (u.) it was abundant; I. and III. أَكْثَرَ he multiplied; he increased; he used a plentiful supply; كَثِيرٌ numerous, many, much; كَثِيرًا exceedingly, in a high degree; كِثْرَةٌ much, abundance; أَكْثَرُ more, most.

كَدَّ (u.) he laboured; كَدّ labour, work, diligence; fatigue.

كَذَا like that, so, such.

كَذَبَ (i.) he lied; I. كَذَّبَ he accused of falsehood, called a liar, gave the lie, declared false; كَذِبٌ and كِذْبٌ falsehood; كَاذِبٌ and كَذُوبٌ a liar.

كَرُمَ (u.) he was generous, munificent, liberal; I. كَرَّمَ he honoured, he revered; III. أَكْرَمَ he honoured, respected, venerated; he treated with attention and ceremony; كَرِيمٌ (pl.; كِرَامٌ) generous, bountiful, benign, beneficent, gracious (one of the epithets of God).

كَرِهَ (a.) he abhorred, detested; he was averse from.

كَرَا for كَرَوَ (u.) he placed; VII. اِكْتَرَى he hired, he rented.

كَسَبَ (i.) he gained, he acquired; III. أَكْسَبَ he gained for another; he caused to gain; he conferred.

كَسَرَ (i.) he broke to pieces.

كِسْرَى and كَسْرَى the name of several Persian kings, more especially of Nūshīrwān (the Chosroes of the Greeks).

كَسَفَ (i.) he cut; it underwent an eclipse; he was in evil plight.

كَسِلَ (a.) he was lazy; كَسَلٌ laziness, idleness.

كِسْوَةٌ an upper garment; a large veil; raiment, clothing.

كَشَفَ (i.) he exposed, he laid open; VI. اِنْكَشَفَ it was open, bare, exposed.

كَظَمَ (i.) he restrained (his wrath), he compressed (his anger).

كَفٌّ (pl. كُفُوفٌ) the hand, or palm of the hand; the fist.

كَفَأَ (a.) he turned back; he inverted; كَفُوٌ like, similar, equal.

كَفَرَ (u.) he believed not (in God); he was unbelieving, impious, and ungrateful; I. كَفَّرَ he expiated a crime, or the breach of an oath (by doing penance or paying a mulct as an atonement); كُفْرٌ impiety, infidelity, blasphemy; كَافِرٌ and كَفُورٌ an unbeliever, an infidel; كُفُورٌ infidelity.

كَفَنَ (u.) he wrapped (a dead body) in a winding sheet.

كَفَى (i.) it was enough; it sufficed; II. كَافَى he compensated, he remunerated; VII. اِكْتَفَى he was satisfied, he was content.

كَلَّ he was fatigued; (the vision) was dim, (the sword) was blunt; كَلِيلٌ blunt (sword); dim (vision); كُلُّ the whole, all, entire, universal, total, every, each; كُلَّمَا as often as, whensoever.

كَلَّا by no means, not in the least.

كَلَاءٌ pasturage, green crop, grass.

كَلْبٌ (pl. كِلَابٌ) a dog, a hound.

كَلِفَ (a.) he engaged earnestly (in any undertaking); he was engrossed (by any thing); I. كَلَّفَ he imposed labour or trouble; he compelled and obliged (another) to undertake (something) difficult or above (his) strength; and also without making (him) any remuneration for it.

كَلَمَ (u.) he wounded; I. كَلَّمَ he addressed, he spoke to; كَلَامٌ a word, speech, discourse; logic; rhetoric; metaphysics; كَلِمَةٌ a saying, a word.

كَلِيلَةُ وَ دِمْنَةُ the Arabian name or title for the work known as the "Fables of Pilpay."

كَمْ how much? how many?

كُمْ (oblique كِمْ) affixed pron. 2nd pers. pl. masc. you, yours.

كَمَّ (u.) he covered; he concealed; كُمٌّ the sleeve (of a garment).

كَمَا as, like as, such as.

كَمَلَ (u.) it was perfect, complete, entire; كَامِلٌ perfect, accomplished, full; adroit, expert; كَمَالٌ perfection, excellence, accomplishment.

كَنَزَ (i.) he hid (underground); كَنْزٌ a treasure, more especially gold or silver hidden underground.

كَنَافَةٌ a species of sweetmeat.

كَهْفٌ (pl. كُهُوفٌ) a cave, cavern, grot.

كَهَنَ (a. & u.) he predicted, he prophesied; كَاهِنٌ (pl. كَهَنَةٌ) a soothsayer, augur, astrologer, sorcerer; a priest, a prophet.

كُوبٌ (pl. أَكْوَابٌ) a cup, a bowl, a

كَادَ vessel without handles.

كَادَ for كَوَدَ (*u.*) he was just on the point, he was little short of, he did all but.

كُوفَةٌ name of a celebrated city in Irāq.

كَانَ for كَوَنَ (*u.*) he was; he became; كَوْنٌ being, nature, essence; لِكَوْنِهِ on account of his being, because he was.

كَادَ for كَيَدَ (*i.*) he deceived; كَيْدٌ deception, deceit, fraud, treachery.

كَيْفَ how, in what manner.

ل

لَ *an inseparable particle* (generally used in the middle of a sentence), indeed, truly; *also for* لِ to, for; *as* لَهُ to him; لَكَ to you; لِ *an inseparable particle,* to, for, towards; on account of; (prefixed to the aorist it gives it the force of an imperative), as لِيَنْصُرْ let him assist.

لَا no, not; there is not.

لِأَنَّ because, since, in order to.

لُبٌّ the heart, mind; a kernel.

لَبِثَ (*a.*) he delayed, he tarried.

لَبِسَ (*a.*) he put on (a garment, dress clothes, robe, vesture, raiment, habit, garb, appare, attire.)

لَبَطَ (*i.*) (a camel) struck or pawed the ground with his forefeet; لَبْطٌ a striking or pawing of the ground.

لَبَنٌ (*pl.* أَلْبَانٌ) milk; the sap of a tree.

لَبْوَةٌ (*pl.* لَبْآتٌ and لَبَوَاتٌ) a lioness.

لَجَأَ (*a.*) he fled for refuge; III. أَلْجَأَ he drove away; he compelled, he forced.

لِجَامٌ a bridle, reins.

لَحِسَ (*a.*) he licked with his tongue.

لَحَظَ (*a.*) and II. لَاحَظَ he viewed, beheld, looked or glanced at.

لَحِقَ (*a.*) he overtook, he reached; III. أَلْحَقَ he caused to meet; he joined; he affixed, he suffixed; he conveyed.

لَحَمَ (*a.*) he fed with flesh; لَحْمٌ (*pl.* لُحُومٌ) flesh, meat, animal food.

لَحْنٌ (*pl.* أَلْحَانٌ) a sound, tone, note; melody, modulation.

لَذَّ it was delicious; IV. تَلَذَّذَ he

took pleasure; he enjoyed himself; لَذِيذٌ delicious, agreeable, pleasant; أَلَذُّ sweeter, more or most delicious.

لِسَانٌ (pl. اَلْسِنَةٌ) the tongue; language; بِلِسَانِ الْحَالِ with the tongue of the condition (not with that organ itself; but, for example, with ragged clothes or a haggard countenance, etc.).

لَطَمَ (i.) he slapped; he smote on the cheek; لَطْمَةٌ a blow, slap, box.

لَعِبَ (a.) he played, he sported.

لَعِقَ (a.) he licked (his finger, etc.); لَعْقَةٌ one single lick (of the finger).

لَعَلَّ perhaps; لَعَلَّكَ perhaps you.

لَعَنَ (a.) he cursed; لَعْنٌ a curse, imprecation; لَعِينٌ accursed; execrable, abominable.

لَغَا for لَغَوَ (u.) he talked triflingly and nonsensically; لُغَةٌ language, speech, dialect, idiom; لَغْوٌ vain, frivolous or nonsensical talk.

لَفَّ (u.) and VII. اِلْتَفَّ he wrapped himself up, he folded up; لَفَّةٌ a turban.

لَفَتَ (i.) he turned; he twisted; VII. اِلْتَفَتَ he turned towards one, he regarded; he paid attention.

لَقَبٌ (pl. اَلْقَابٌ) a surname, title; a nickname, byname; I. لَقَّبَ he gave a surname, style, title, or nickname; he surnamed; he dubbed.

لَقَدْ verily, truly.

لُقْمَانُ name of celebrated sage.

لَقِيَ (a.) he met; he opposed; he saw; III. اَلْقَى he threw down; he imparted, communicated; he injected, he infused; he inspired; لِقَاءٌ seeing, meeting, encountering; aspect; face, countenance.

لٰكِنَّ also لٰكِنْ but, yet, still.

لَمْ not (when prefixed to the aorist it usually gives it a past signification).

لِمَا for what, why, wherefore. لِمَاذَا for what reason, why so.

لَمَّا when; after that; not yet.

لَمَسَ (u.) he touched or felt with his hand; VII اِلْتَمَسَ he sought for, searched, desired; he besought.

لِهٰذَا on this account, therefore.

لَهِمَ (a.) he swallowed quickly; he gulped down; III. أَلْهَمَ he inspired; he revealed.

لَهَا for لَهَوَ (u.) he played, sported, diverted himself; لَهْوٌ amusement, diversion, play, sport, fun.

لَوْ; if; but, had but; لَوْلَا if not, unless.

لَاذَ for لَوَذَ (u.) he fled to; he took refuge with; he was under the protection of another.

لَوْزٌ an almond; لَوْزِينَج a confection of almonds; a sweetmeat prepared with almonds (Pers. لَوْزِينَه).

لُوْلُوٌ a pearl; a precious gem.

لَامَ for لَوَمَ (u.) and I. he blamed, he reproached, he chided; لَوْمٌ blame, censure, reproach, reproof.

لَوْنٌ (pl. أَلْوَانٌ) colour; species, sort.

لَيْسَ he (or it) is not; لَسْتُ I am not; لَسْتَ you are not, etc. (through each person of the preterite).

لَيْلٌ and لَيْلَةٌ (pl. لَيَالٍ) night; لَيْلًا by night; اَللَّيْلَةَ tonight.

م

مَا that which, what, whatsoever; not, nothing; what? how! what! مَا أَطْيَبَ how delicious!

مَاءٌ (pl. مِيَاهٌ and أَمْوَاهٌ) for مَوَهٌ water; liquor; juice, sap.

مَأَي (i.) he extended, stretched; مِائَةٌ a hundred.

مِبْرَدٌ (pl. مَبَارِدُ) a file, rasp.

مَتَعَ (a.) he enjoyed; IX. اِسْتَمْتَعَ he took enjoyment; he reaped fruit.

مَتَى when, if at any time.

مِثْقَالٌ name of a weight of nearly one drachm and a half; also the name of a gold coin (rt. ثَقَلَ).

مَثَلَ (u.) he was like, he resembled; مِثْلٌ likeness; similar, resembling; مَثَلٌ (pl. أَمْثَالٌ) like, equal to; a proverb, an adage; مِثَالٌ similitude; a representation, description; a form, figure.

مَجَدَ (u.) he excelled; مَجْدٌ glory, splendour, excellence.

مَحَنَ (a.) and VII. اِمْتَحَنَ he tried,

مِخْلَبٌ

he proved, he put to the test; he struck; مُمْتَحَنٌ experienced, skilled; مِحْنَةٌ experience; labour, toil, moil; calamity (by which men are tested); اِمْتِحَانٌ test, trial, examination.

مِخْلَبٌ (pl. مَخَالِبُ) a claw or talon.

مَدَّ (u.) he extended, he stretched out; مُدَّةٌ space of time, period; season; length of time, interval.

مَدَنَ he stayed, he sojourned; مَدِينَةٌ a city, a town.

مَرَّ (u.) he passed by; he departed; he went on; مَرٌّ a passing by; مَمَرٌّ a place of passage; مَرَّةٌ once upon a time; formerly.

مَرَأَ (a.) (Food) did (one) good, digested well; مَرِيءٌ easy of digestion; nutritious. See هَنَّا; اِمْرَأَةٌ a man; اِمْرَأَةٌ a woman.

مُرَاءَاةٌ hypocritically, deceptively (rt. رَأَى).

مَرِحَ (a.) he was cheerful, lively, joyous; مَرَحٌ mirth, merriment.

مَرَخَ (a.) and I. مَرَّخَ he anointed (with oil); تَمْرِيخٌ an anointing.

مَرَدَ (u.) and IV. تَمَرَّدَ he was insolent, stubborn, disobedient, or rebellious.

مَسَحَ

a (مِرْزَبَاتٌ .pl) مِرْزَبَةٌ a sledge-hammer.

تَمَارَضَ .V ;he fell sick (.i) مَرِضَ he feigned sickness; مَرَضٌ disease, illness, sickness; hypocrisy; unbelief.

مَرُوَ (u.) he was manly, for مَرُأَ virtuous; مُرُوَّةٌ manliness, valour, virtue.

مَرْوَانُ a man's name; the fourth Caliph of the Umayyad dynasty.

مَرَى (i.) he inflicted blows; II. مَارَى he disputed, contended; مِرَاءٌ contention, disputation.

مَرْيَمُ Mary, the mother of the Prophet 'Īsā.

مَزَجَ (a.) he mixed; he tempered; VII. اِمْتَزَجَ it was congenial; it agreed with one; he was disposed or inclined; مِزَاجٌ temperament, constitution; a mixture; whatever is mixed with wine.

مَزَحَ (a.) he jested; he sported; II. مَازَحَ he sported or jested (with another); مَزَاحٌ jesting; a joke, jest, fun, frolic.

مَسَحَ (a.) he drew his hand over his head; he wiped (his head); he anointed; مَسِيحٌ anointed;

ٱلْمَسِيحُ the anointed; the Messiah.

مَسَكَ (*i.*) and III. أَمْسَكَ he seized, grasped, held, laid hold of.

مَسَا for مَسَوَ and مَسَى (*u.*) he came in the evening; مَسَاءٌ the evening.

مَشَجَ he mixed; he confounded; مَشِيجٌ (*pl.* أَمْشَاجٌ) mixed; a mixture, a miscellany.

مَشَى (*i.*) he walked; he went; مَشْيٌ and مِشْيَةٌ walking, marching, proceeding; مَاشِيَةٌ (*pl.* مَوَاشِي) a quadruped; cattle.

مَضَغَ (*a.* & *u.*) he chewed; he masticated; مَضْغٌ the act of chewing.

مَضَى (*i.*) he passed by; he went, he departed.

مَطَرَ (*u.*) it rained; مَطَرٌ (*pl.* أَمْطَارٌ) rain; a shower.

مَطَا for مَطَوَ (*u.*) he drew; he extended; IV. تَمَطَّى he stretched himself; he yawned.

مَعَ or مَعْ with, together with.

مَغَارَةٌ (*pl.* مَغَائِرُ) a cave, cavern.

مَكَّةُ the city of Makkah.

مَكَرَ (*u.*) he plotted, he devised; he deceived, he cheated; مَكْرٌ fraud, deceit, contrivance, machination, art, stratagem; مَكَّارٌ a deceiver, knave, cheat.

مَكُنَ (*u.*) he was powerful; I. and III. أَمْكَنَ he gave power, he enabled, he rendered capable; IV. تَمَكَّنَ he was able; he had in his power, he possessed authority, he was powerful; he settled, he took up his abode; مَكَانٌ (*pl.* أَمْكِنَةٌ and أَمَاكِنُ) a place, spot, station.

مَلَّ (*a.*) he became disgusted, he felt tired.

مَلَأَ (*a.*) he filled; VII. اِمْتَلَأَ he was filled; مَلَأٌ a concourse of people, a host, assembly; مَلْآنٌ and مَمْلُوءٌ full, filled.

مِلَّةٌ religion, faith; a sect; a nation, people.

مَلَحَ (*a.*) he salted; he seasoned with salt; مِلْحٌ salt.

مَلِقَ he flattered, soothed; تَمَلُّقٌ flattery, fawning, blandishment, coaxing.

مَلَكَ (*i.*) he possessed; he had dominion and power; he reigned; I. مَلَّكَ he caused to possess; he constituted king; مُلْكٌ and مَمْلَكَةٌ a kingdom,

مَلَا

مَلِكٌ (pl. مُلُوكٌ) a king; مَلَكٌ (pl. مَلَائِكَةٌ) an angel; مَالِكٌ a king; a lord; a posssessor; مَلِكَةٌ a queen; مَلَكُوتٌ kingdom, dominion, empire, sovereignty.

مَلَا for مَلَوَ (u.) he went rapidly; مَلِيٌّ lasting long; a long time.

مِمَّا for مِنْ مَا from, that, which.

مَنْ pronoun of common gender, singular and plural, he who, they who, whosoever.

مِنْ from, from out of, of, for, than (after the comparative degree); مِنْ غَيْرِ without; مِنْ أَنْ besides, notwithstanding.

مَنَّ (u.) he was kind or liberal (towards another); مَنٌّ a gift; manna.

مَنْدَلٌ (pl. مَنَادِيلُ) an enchanter's circle described on the ground; a magic circle.

مَنَعَ (a.) he prevented, he hindered; IV. تَمَنَّعَ he was inaccessible; he kept himself aloof; he drew back, he abstained.

مَهَرَ (a.) he was quick in understanding; مَاهِرٌ skilful, expert, clever, acute,

مَالَ

excellent; مَهَارَةٌ skill, excellence, expertness, proficiency.

مَهَلَ (a.) he did anything slowly and by degrees; III. أَمْهَلَ he deferred, prolonged, granted a delay; VII. اِمْتَهَلَ he evinced patience, shewed forbearance; مَهْلٌ delay; مَهْلًا or مَهْلًا gently, softly, slowly.

مَوْتٌ for مَوَتَ (u.) he died; (مَوْتَى and أَمْوَاتٌ pl. مَيِّتٌ) death; dead; extinct; dying, moribund.

مَالَ for مَوَلَ (u.) he was wealthy; مَالٌ (pl. أَمْوَالٌ) wealth; riches.

مَادَ for مَيَدَ (i.) he served up food; مَائِدَةٌ (pl. مَوَائِدُ) a tray or table covered with victuals.

مَازَ for مَيَزَ (i.) and I. مَيَّزَ he discriminated, reflected, considered.

مَالَ for مَيَلَ (i.) he inclined, he leaned; III. أَمَالَ he caused to lean, bend or incline, he gave a bias.

ن

نَاسٌ for أُنَاسٌ men, mankind; the human race (as opposed to irrational animals). See under أَنِسَ .rt.

نَامُوسٌ and نَامُوسَةٌ a gnat, midge, mosquito.

نَبَأَ (*a.*) he went from one country to another; he announced; he proclaimed; نُبُوٌّ announcing, declaring; نَبِيٌّ a prophet; نُبُوَّةٌ prophecy; the prophetical office or gift.

نَبَتَ (*u.*) (vegetation) sprung up, was produced, grew; نَبْتٌ and نَبَاتٌ vegetation, herbage; grass, vegetables.

نَبَرَ (*i.*) he raised up, he exalted; مِنْبَرٌ (*i.*) a pulpit, a reading-desk.

نَتَجَتْ (*i.*) and III. أَنْتَجَتْ (the camel or mare) foaled; (the sheep) yeaned.

نَتَنَ (*u.*) and III. أَنْتَنَ it smelt badly, it stunk; مُنْتِنٌ stinking, fetid.

نَثَرَ (*u. & i.*) he scattered; he dispersed; V. تَنَاثَرَ it was dispersed; (the hair flowed loose and was dishevelled.)

نَجِسَ (*a.*) he was dirty, nasty, filthy, unclean; نَجَاسَةٌ impurity, filth, dirt.

نَجَا for نَجَوَ (*u.*) he escaped; I. نَجَّى and III. أَنْجَى he liberated; he saved; مُنْجِي for مُنْجِ a liberator.

نَحْلٌ and نَحْلَةٌ the honey-bee.

نَحْنُ *pers. pron, of the comm. gender, dual and plural,* we two, or we.

نَحَا for نَحَوَ (*a. & u.*) he went towards; he aimed at; نَحْوَ as, about, to, towards; نَاحِيَةٌ (*pl.* نَوَاحِي) a district, quarter, tract, extent of country.

نَخْلٌ, نَجِيلٌ and نَخْلَةٌ a palm-tree.

نَدَرَ (*u.*) he remained alone; نَادِرٌ singular, unique; rare, uncommon, unusual; فِي النَّادِرِ rarely, seldom, occasionally.

نَدِمَ (*a.*) he repented; he regretted; نَدْمٌ and نَدَامَةٌ penitence, regret, sorrow; نَدِيمٌ a boon companion, an intimate friend.

نَذَرَ (*i. & u.*) he vowed; he dedicated to God; نَذْرٌ a vow; a promise; a present or offering

نَزَعَ from an inferior to a superior, holy man or prince.

نَزَعَ (*i*.) he removed; he stripped; he tore out; V. تَنَازَعُوا they disputed together, altercated, wrangled, litigated; تَنَازُعٌ altercation, disputing, litigation.

نَزَغَ (*i*.) he sowed dissension; he slandered, reviled; نَزْغٌ suggesting of evil; exciting to what is bad; temptation.

نَزَلَ (*i*.) he descended, he alighted; I. نَزَّلَ he made to descend, he sent down; he revealed (from heaven); III. أَنْزَلَ he caused to descend; he brought down; he invited (a guest) to alight, he entertained, he received hospitably; مُنْزِلٌ causing to alight; receiving and entertaining hospitably; تَنْزِيلٌ sending down, revealing; مَنْزِلٌ an inn, caravansery, or place for travellers to alight; hotel, stage, station; مَنْزِلَةٌ a house of accommodation for travellers; a step, post of honour; rank, dignity, authority; نُزُولٌ

descent.

نَسَبَ (*u*. & *i*.) he referred; he derived; he attributed.

نَسَجَ (*u*. & *i*.) he wove; نَسْجٌ weaving.

نَسْرٌ (*pl*. نُسُورٌ) the eagle or vulture.

نَسِيمٌ a gentle breeze, a zephyr.

نَسِيَ (*a*.) he forgot; he neglected; نِسْوَةٌ and نِسَاءٌ (for the singular of which إِمْرَءَةٌ is used), women, the female sex.

نَشَأَ (*a*.) he grew up; he was brought up, he was educated.

نَشَرَ (*u*.) he spread out, extended; he scattered, diffused; he promulgated, propagated.

نَصَبَ (*u*.) he placed, set up, planted, erected.

نَصَحَ (*a*.) he admonished, he counselled, he advised; he was sincere; نُصْحٌ also نَصْحٌ advising, admonishing; نَاصِحٌ a monitor, a faithful adviser; a sincere friend; نَصُوحٌ sincere, genuine; نَصِيحَةٌ admonition, advice, counsel.

نَصَرَ (*u*.) he assisted, he aided; نَاصِرٌ (*pl*. أَنْصَارٌ) an assistant; a

نَصَفَ (u.) he halved; نِصْفٌ a half, a moiety; the middle.

نَضَرَ (u.) or نَضِرَ (a.) it was bright, brilliant, blooming, and beautiful; نَضْرَةٌ splendour, brightness, bloom, freshness (of complexion); opulence, affluence.

نَطَحَ (a.) he butted with his horns, he gored; نَطِيحٌ butted, gored to death.

نِطْعٌ a sheet of leather, dressed and prepared, which serves for a table or table-cloth.

نَطَفَ (i. & u.) (water) flowed; نُطْفَةٌ pure water; clear water, lymph; sperma genitale.

نَطَقَ (i. & u.) he spoke, he articulated distinctly; نُطْقٌ speech, eloquence, pronunciation; مَنْطِقٌ a discourse, oration; مِنْطَقَةٌ a belt, zone, girdle.

نَظَرَ (u.) he looked, gazed, beheld, observed, regarded; نَظَرٌ sight; regard, consideration; مَنْظَرٌ aspect, appearance.

نَظُفَ (u.) he was clean; نَظِيفٌ clean, pure.

نَعِمَ (a. u. & i.) it was convenient, soft, easy, agreeable; III. أَنْعَمَ he bestowed abundance, he conferred favours and benefits; نِعْمَ excellent! good! well done! نَعَمْ *a particle of affirmation*, good, well, be it so, yes; نَاعِمٌ convenient, agreeable, delicious; نَعِيمٌ affluence, pleasure, enjoyment, delicate living, luxury; نِعْمَةٌ (*pl.* نِعَمٌ) wealth, riches, opulence, abundance; favour, a benefit.

نَغَمَ (u. & i.) he read or sang with a low soft voice; نَغْمَةٌ a sweet and musical voice, melody, song, modulation, soft intonation.

نَفَثَ (i. & u.) he (the necromancer) blew (when making incantations or playing tricks); مُنَافَثَةٌ conversation, talking together in private.

نَفَخَ (a.) he blew, he puffed; he

inspired or breathed into; VII.
اِنْتَفَخَ he was inflated or puffed
out; he was swollen.

نَفَذَ (the arrow) penetrated,
pierced through and through,
coming out on the other side;
he pervaded, passed by or
through; III. أَنْفَذَ he caused to
pass, penetrate, or pervade; he
transmitted; he despatched (a
letter or messenger).

نَفَرَ (*u. & i.*) he shunned; he fled
in terror; I. نَفَّرَ he terrified; he
scared; he put to hight, he
drove away; V. تَنَافَرُوا they fled
from each other, they shunned
one another (through panic,
etc.); نَفَرٌ a number of persons,
from three to ten; a person,
individual; one of the
common people; a private
soldier.

نَفْسٌ (*pl.* أَنْفُسٌ and نُفُوسٌ) the soul,
spirit; self; فِي نَفْسِهِ to himself;
within himself.

نَفَشَ (*u.*) he plucked or teased
(wool or cotton) with his
fingers; نَفَشٌ wool (plucked or
picked, not shorn).

نَفَضَ (*u.*) he shook (the tree); VII.

اِنْتَفَضَ it was shaken; he
trembled; he shivered.

نَفَعَ (*a.*) it was useful, profitable,
serviceable; it availed; نَفْعٌ
also مَنْفَعَةٌ (*pl.* مَنَافِعُ) advantage,
profit, use, benefit.

نَفَقَ (*u.*) it perished, failed, was
lost, or spent; III. أَنْفَقَ he
expended, disbursed; he laid
out in the cause of God; he
bestowed (his goods) for the
support of others.

نَقَدَ (*u.*) he paid ready money; VII.
اِنْتَقَدَ he separated (good coin)
from bad; نَقْدٌ cash, ready
money, prompt payment.

نَقَشَ (*a.*) he painted, printed, or
stained (of two or more
colours); he drew; he
designed; نَقْشٌ painting,
printing; carving, engraving;
نَقَّاشٌ a painter; a draughtsman;
a sculptor.

نَقَصَ (*a.*) and VII. اِنْتَقَصَ it was
defective or deficient; it was
diminished; it suffered loss;
was damaged; نُقْصَانٌ and نَقْصٌ
loss, detriment, damage,
diminution.

نَقْضٌ violation (of an agreement),

نَقَلَ (u.) he transported, transplanted; he carried from one place to another; VII. اِنْتَقَلَ he was transported, transplanted, translated; he was carried; he emigrated.

نَقَمَ (i.) he was angry; he chided, reproved; VII. اِنْتَقَمَ he punished, chastised; he took vengeance; he retaliated; اِنْتِقَامٌ revenge, vengeance, retaliation.

نَقِيَ (a.) it was clean or pure; I. نَقَّى he cleansed; he sifted; he trimmed, weeded (the flowers, etc.)

نَكَثَ (u.) he violated (an agreement), he rebelled; نَكْثٌ perfidy, rebellion, violation of agreement.

نَكِرَ (a.) and III. أَنْكَرَ he denied, he ignored, he disowned, he disavowed; he rejected, repudiated; مُنْكِرٌ one who denies or is ignorant of; مَنْكَرٌ disallowed, unlawful, evil (the opposite of مَعْرُوفٌ); أَنْكَرُ more or most offensive, displeasing, grating to the ear, unpleasant.

نَكَسَ (u.) I. نَكَّسَ and III. أَنْكَسَ he turned down, he inverted, he placed topsy-turvy; مُنَكِّسٌ one who casts down.

نَكِلَ (i.) he took example; he received chastisement; I. نَكَّلَ he made an example of; he punished in an exemplary manner.

نَمَّ (u.) he calumniated, he slandered; نَمَّامٌ a slanderer, calumniator, whisperer.

نِمْسٌ (pl. نُمُوسٌ) a kind of large weasel or rat; the ichneumon.

نَهَرَ (a.) he dug a canal; he checked, chided, cried out (to cattle); نَهْرٌ (pl. أَنْهَارٌ) a stream, river, canal, water-course, rivulet, rill, brook; abusive language addressed (to horses or beasts of burden); نَهَارٌ the day (in opposition to لَيْلٌ the night).

نَهَشَ (a.) (the serpent) bit; he punctured; V. تَنَاهَشُوا they bit or stung (each other).

نَهَضَ (a.) he raised himself up; he arose.

نَهِكَ (i.) he committed excess; he afflicted; he tortured,

tormented; he punished severely; VII. اِنْتَهَكَ he harassed, vexed; he enfeebled, he emaciated; he violated (honour, virtue, or respect). نَهَى (*a.*) he forbade, he prohibited; إِنَّهُ forbid you; VII. اِنْتَهَى it came to an end, it concluded; he abstained, desisted, refrained; نَهْيٌ prohibition, interdict; نِهَايَةٌ extremity, end, termination; term, goal, boundary, limit, utmost point; excess; نَاهٍ (from نَاهِيٌّ) a forbidder; مَنْهِيٌّ forbidden.

نَابَ for نَوَبَ (*u.*) he supplied (another's place); نَابٌ (*pl.* أَنْيَابٌ) a dog's tooth; a canine tooth; نَائِبَةٌ (*pl.* نَوَائِبُ) an accident, misfortune, disaster, calamity.

نَاحَ for نَوَحَ (*u.*) he lamented, complained; he mourned and sorrowed (for a deceased relative).

نَارَ for نَوَرَ (*u.*) it shone; it was brilliant; نُورٌ (*pl.* أَنْوَارٌ) fire; نَارٌ light, splendour, refulgence, brightness; مَنَارَةٌ a candlestick; a lighthouse; a minaret or tower from which the muezzin or crier proclaims the hour of prayer; مُنِيرٌ shining, illuminating, enlightening, splendid, illustrious.

نَوْرُوزٌ (incorrectly نَيْرُوزٌ) the Persian New Year's day; a grand festival held on that day.

نَوْعٌ (*pl.* أَنْوَاعٌ) species, kind, sort; manner, mode.

نَالَ for نَوَلَ (*a. & u.*) he bestowed, he gave; he presented, was liberal; he took; he got, he obtained; V. تَنَاوَلَ he took (meat or drink); he received (gifts); نَوَالٌ a gift, present.

نَامَ for نَوَمَ (*u.*) he slept; نَائِمٌ (*pl.* نِيَّامٌ) sleeping, asleep; a sleeper; نَوْمٌ sleep, dreaming.

نَالَ for نَيَلَ (*a. or i.*) he acquired, he obtained.

ه

هُ (and هِ when preceded by *kasra*); affixed pronoun, 3d pers. *masc.* him, his, it; هَا *fem.* her, hers.

هَا behold! here! well! she; it.

هَاتِ give.

هَاهُنَا here, in this place.

هَبَّ (*u.*) (the wind) blew; (*i.*) he began; هُبُوبٌ a fresh blowing of the wind, stiff breeze, smart gale.

هَجَرَ (*u.*) he left, abandoned, deserted, forsook; he spoke deliriously, he raved, he talked at random.

هَجَمَ (*i.*) he attacked, invaded, charged, rushed upon; he came upon unawares, he surprised; he undertook; هَجْمَةٌ and هُجُومٌ a sudden assault, a violent rush.

هَدَأَ (*a.*) he rested, he remained quiet.

هُدْهُدْ the hoopoe, the lapwing.

هَدَى (*i.*) he directed, guided; he led into the right way; هُدًى direction, guidance (into the path of salvation).

هٰذَا *masc.* and هٰذِهِ *fem.* this.

هَرَّ (*u. & i.*) he abhorred; هِرٌّ a male cat, a tom-cat; هِرَّةٌ a female cat.

هَرَبَ (*u.*) he fled, he ran away, he absconded, he vanished; هَارِبٌ a fugitive, a runaway.

هَرَسَ he pounded, he bruised;

هَرِيسَةٌ a kind of thick pottage made of bruised wheat, meat, and spices.

هَرَمٌ old age, decrepitude.

هَرَا for هَرَوَ and IV. تَهَرَّى he beat with a stick, he cudgelled.

هَزَأَ (*a.*) he mocked, derided, ridiculed, laughed at, made game of; هُزْءٌ derision, mockery, ridicule, irony.

هَزَمَ (*i.*) he put to flight, he routed; VI. اِنْهَزَمَ he was routed, he was put to flight and discomfited; اِنْهِزَامٌ act of running away; rout, flight; مُنْهَزِمٌ routed, put to flight.

هٰكَذَا in this manner.

هَلْ an interrogative particle; whether or not.

هَلَكَ (*i. & a.*) and هَلِكَ (*a.*) he perished, he died; III. أَهْلَكَ he caused to perish; he involved in ruin, led to perdition; he killed, destroyed; هَلَكٌ destruction; مُهْلِكٌ ruinous, destructive.

هَمَّ (*u.*) he revolved in his mind; he anxiously considered; he cared for or tended; he resolved; VII. اِهْتَمَّ he

هَنَأ

concerned himself; هَمٌّ (pl. هُمُومٌ) anxiety, care, serious concern, solicitude.

هَنَأَ (a.) (his food) was light and easy of digestion; I. هَنَأَ (a.) he caused (food) to digest and to nourish; he congratulated; he wished health, saying "may it do you good;" IV. تَهَنَّأَ he throve; he was refreshed with food; he digested easily; هَنِىٌّ (food) light of digestion, nutritious; هَنِيئًا وَمَرِيئًا a form of salutation; a good digestion to you; much good may it to you; هَنَاءٌ being joyful, glad, merry; pleasure, enjoyment.

هُنَاكَ there (at a distance).

هُوَ pron. 3rd pers. he. it; هِيَ she, it.

هَادَ for هَوَدَ (u.) he repented; he returned to his duty; he became a Jew; يَهُودٌ Jews.

هُوذَا lo! behold! هُوذَا أَنَا behold me! here am I.

هَانَ for هَوَنَ (u.) it was light and easy; it was insignificant, vile, or contemptible; I. هَوَّنَ he made light of; he reviled; he facilitated; III. أَهَانَ he despised, condemned; أَهْوَنُ

وَأَد

more or most easy, or tolerable; هَوَانٌ contempt, scorn; misery, distress; إِهَانَةٌ contempt, indignity, insult, scorn, slight, affront; مُهِينٌ ignominious, degrading (punishment); مُهَانٌ despised.

هَؤُلَاءِ (pron.) they, those.

هَوَى (i.) he soared; he fell from a height; هَوَاءٌ air, atmosphere, sky; هَوَى desire, wish.

هَاءَ for هَيَأَ (i.) it was prepared, made ready; IV. تَهَيَّأَ he prepared himself; he got ready; هِيئَةٌ external form, aspect, appearance, bearing, manner.

هَيْتَ لَكَ come here! apporach.

و

و and; too, also (in swearing) by; as وَاللهِ by God. !وَ interj. oh! alas!

وَأَدَ (يَئِدُ) he dug a grave, and buried a daughter alive (a custom with the Pagan Arabs); he was heavy; he moved slowly; IV. تَوَأَدَ he proceeded

وَحَشَ

وَجَدَ (يَجِدُ) he found, he discovered; it was found, it existed; مَوْجُودٌ found; extant, existing.

وَجَعَ (يَجَعُ) he was in pain; III. he hurt, he pained; he beat; وَجَعٌ pain, ache, suffering, disease; مُوجِعٌ painful, grievous (blow).

وَجُهَ (u.) he was in honour; VII. اِتَّجَهَ it pertained, it belonged; وَجْهٌ (pl. وُجُوهٌ) the face, visage, aspect, countenance; a mode, manner, reason, cause; a leader, chief person, chieftain; a noble; I. وَجَّهَ he turned towards; he despatched or sent; IV. تَوَجَّهَ he turned to, he set his face towards.

وَحِدَ (يَجِدُ) he was sole, alone, separate; وَاحِدٌ one; وَحْدَةٌ unity; solitariness, solitude.

وَحَشَ (يَحِشُ) he threw away (cloak, arms, or spear) in flight; IX. اِسْتَوْحَشَ he was gloomy, melancholy, sad; he shunned (society), he avoided (company); وَحْشٌ (pl. وُحُوشٌ) a wild beast; a fierce, shy, untamed, or untameable animal.

وَادٍ

gently and slowly; تَوَدُّدٌ precaution, deliberation.

وَادٍ (from وَادِيٌّ) a valley; a river.

وَبَقَ he perished; III. أَوْبَقَ he destroyed, he killed.

وَبَلَ (يَبِلُ) he struck with a stick; he inflicted punishment by blows; وَبَالٌ a crime, sin; punishment; harshness, severity.

وَثَبَ (يَثِبُ) he sprung upon, he assaulted, leaped; وَثْبَةٌ and وَثْبٌ a leap, bound, or spring (as of a lion).

وَثَقَ (يَثِقُ) he trusted or relied upon ثِقَةٌ confiding, trusting; confidence, trustworthy; a trusty friend, one to be relied on; وُثْقَى (fem. أَوْثَقُ) firmer, firmest, very firm; عُرْوَةٌ وُثْقَى a very strong handle; مَوْثِقٌ a compact, agreement, treaty, or solemn promise.

وَجَبَ (يَجِبُ) it was necessary, it behoved; IX. اِسْتَوْجَبَ he deemed necessary; he deserved; was worth, merited; وَاجِبٌ necessary, needful, proper, incumbent; وَاجِبًا necessarily, properly.

وَحَى and III. أَوْحَى he suggested, he revealed, he inspired.

وَخَطَ (يَخِطُ) (hoariness) sprinkled a few white hairs over (his head).

وَدَّ (u.) he loved; he liked; he esteemed; IV. تَوَدَّدَ he showed love; he gained the affections.

وَدَعَ (يَدَعُ) he placed; he deposited; he left at liberty; he permitted; he abandoned, he quitted; I. وَدَّعَ he bade farewell; he took leave; IX. اِسْتَوْدَعَ he requested (another) to keep a deposit; he committed; he commended; he entrusted; he deposited; دَعْ imper. leave, let alone, permit, grant; وِدَاعٌ adieu, farewell, leave-taking; مُسْتَوْدَعٌ a person with whom, or a place where any thing is deposited; a depository; a receptacle, depot.

وَدَى (يَدِي) he paid the mulct or compensation for homicide; دِيَةٌ the fine paid to expiate murder; the price of blood; وَادِي a valley; a river.

وَذَرَ (يَذِرُ) he left, he quitted.

وَرَاءَ behind, beyond, after; besides.

وَرِثَ (يَرِثُ) he became heir; he succeeded by inheritance; I. وَرَّثَ and III. أَوْرَثَ he made heir; he bequeathed as an inheritance.

وَرَدَ (يَرِدُ) he approached; he arrived; he was present; وَارِدٌ one who comes to draw water; one who goes on before to draw water for a caravan.

وَرَقٌ (pl. أَوْرَاقٌ) a leaf (of a tree or of paper).

وَزٌّ and وَزَّةٌ a goose.

وَزَرَ (يَزِرُ) he bore (a burden); he sustained; IX. اِسْتَوْزَرَ he appointed vizier; وَزِيرٌ (pl. وُزَرَاءُ) a vizier, a minister of state, premier.

وَزَنَ (يَزِنُ) he weighed; he paid or weighed out money; وَزْنٌ weight; measure.

وَسَطٌ the middle, the centre.

وَسِعَ (يَسَعُ) it was made capacious, wide, spacious; وَاسِعٌ or وَسِيعٌ extensive, ample, spacious, roomy.

وَسَمَ (يَسِمُ) he excelled in beauty; وَسِيمٌ handsome, beautiful,

وَصَفَ

comely; distinguished by or sealed with a wen or large wart on the body (characteristic of a prophet and heavenly messenger). وَصَفَ (يَصِفُ) he described; صِفَةٌ (pl. أَوْصَافٌ and صِفَاتٌ) description; quality; property (physical or moral). وَصَلَ (يَصِلُ) he joined; he united; he reached, attained, or arrived at; III. أَوْصَلَ he conveyed, caused to arrive; VII. اِتَّصَلَ he adjoined or was contiguous to; وُصُولٌ arrival. وَصَى (يَصِي) he joined, he connected together; I. وَصَّى and III. أَوْصَى he enjoined, commanded, charged, recommended; he made a will or testament; he bequeathed; وَصِيٌّ a testator, a guardian; an executor, administrator; a trustee; وَصِيَّةٌ a precept, command, mandate; a last will or testament; instruction. وَضَعَ (يَضَعُ) he placed; he deposited; VII. اِتَّضَعَ he was humiliated, abased; وَضْعٌ position, situation; مَوْضَعٌ (pl.

وَفِقَ

مَوَاضِعُ) a place; مَوْضُوعٌ placed; an object; subject (of a speech), text.
وَطَنَ (يَطِنُ) he abode, he resided (in a place); وَطَنٌ a country, residence, dwelling, home.
وَعَدَ (يَعِدُ) he promised; he threatened; he foretold; he prognosticated; وَعْدٌ a promise. وِعَاءٌ a vessel, case, sheath, a sack.
وَعَظَ (يَعِظُ) he preached; he admonished, exhorted; VII. اِتَّعَظَ he was admonished; he received admonition; وَعْظٌ admonition; a sermon, homily; وَاعِظٌ a monitor, a preacher; مَوْعِظَةٌ (pl. مَوَاعِظُ and مَوَاعِيظُ) admonition, good counsel.
وَفَرَ (يَفِرُ) it was full, copious, abundant; وَافِرٌ abundant, plentiful, exuberant, copious; rich, opulent.
وَفِقَ (يَفِقُ) it was suitable, apt, convenient; it succeeded, it prospered; I. وَفَّقَ he directed, assisted, prospered; II. وَافَقَ he assented, he agreed to; VII. اِتَّفَقَ it happened, it occured; he agreed, he consented; اِتِّفَاقٌ

وَفَى | وَكَلَ

consent, concurrence, agreement; اِتِّفَاقًا by chance, accidentally; أَوْفَقُ more or most suitable, or advantageous, better; تَوْفِيقٌ the favour or guardian grace of God.

وَفَى (يَفِي) and III. أَوْفَى he performed his promise, he fulfilled his engagement; he paid; he satisfied; he gave full (measure); IV. تَوَفَّى (God) took (the believer) to himself; he made to die; *passively,* he paid the debt of nature, he died; IX. اِسْتَوْفَى he demanded, received or paid the whole of what was due; he satisfied completely; اِسْتِيفَاءٌ a final settlement; وَفَاءٌ performance of a promise, observance of good faith, fidelity, sincerity; وَفَاةٌ decease, demise, death.

وَقْتٌ (*pl.* أَوْقَاتٌ) time, season; and hour; فِي الْوَقْتِ immediately, at this moment.

وَقَرَ (يَقِرُ) he was venerable, dignified, modest; وَقْرٌ deafness, heaviness of hearing; وَقَارٌ dignity, gravity,

modesty, sedateness, seriousness.

وَقَعَ (يَقَعُ) he fell; it fell out, befell, or happened; he fell upon or attacked; III. أَوْقَعَ he surprised; he attacked; وُقُوعٌ a fall; an occurence; وَاقِعَةٌ an event, incident, occurence; news, history, story.

وَقَفَ (يَقِفُ) he stood; he stopped, halted, paused; he was stationary; وَاقِفٌ standing.

وَقَى (يَقِي) he took care of, he preserved; VII. اِتَّقَى he was devout; he feared God.

وَكَّا he leaned upon; III. أَوْكَأَ he caused to recline; VII. اِتَّكَأَ he leaned against, he reclined upon.

وَكَدَ (يَكِدُ) and I. وَكَّدَ he established, confirmed, strengthened; he was instant and urgent.

وَكَلَ (يَكِلُ) he entrusted, he committed (his affairs to another); IV. تَوَكَّلَ he trusted, he confided (in God); he was resigned; وَكِيلٌ an advocate, attorney, pleader; a governor, protector; a witness; مُتَوَكِّلٌ

وَلَجَ (يَلِجُ) he entered (his hiding-place); I. وَلَّج and III. أَوْلَجَ (God) caused the day to enter into the night, and vice versa (according as the days and nights lengthen and shorten).

وَلَدَتْ (تَلِدُ) she brought forth, bore, produced; V. تَوَالَدُوا they generated again and again; they begot and brought forth in great numbers; they increased and multiplied; وَلَدٌ (pl. أَوْلَادٌ) a son, a child; وَلِيدٌ (pl. وِلْدَانٌ) a son, a boy, lad, servant; وَالِدٌ a father, a parent; وَالِدَانِ parents, father and mother; مَوْلُودٌ born; offspring, a son.

وَلِيَ (يَلِي) he presided over, he governed; I. وَلَّى he appointed to a government, he set over; he turned the back, he fled; IV. تَوَلَّى he was appointed, he received an appointment; he assumed; he undertook or took in hand; he withdrew, he ran away, he turned tail; he shunned; he fled, he turned his back; IX. اِسْتَوْلَى he had complete power and authority; he mastered; he obtained possession of; وَلِيٌّ a helper, protector; trustee; وَلِيُّ الْعَهْدِ an heir apparent, a destined or acknowledged successor; مَوْلًى a lord, master; a freed-man; manumitted slave; مَوْلَايَ my lord; وِلَايَةُ الْعَهْدِ the rank of heir apparent (to a throne), nomination to the succession.

وَنَى (يَنِي) he became faint or tired; V. تَوَانَى he lingered or delayed; تَوَانٍ (from تَوَانِي) or تَوَانِيٌّ) fatigue; delay.

وَهَبَ (يَهَبُ) he gave, he bestowed; هَبْ imper. give, grant.

وَهَمَ (يَهِمُ) he conceived, he thought, he imagined; I. وَهَّمَ he made to believe; he persuaded; he caused to doubt.

وَهْنٌ weakness, feebleness, faintness.

وَهِيَ (يَهِي) it was broken or torn; وَاهٍ (from وَاهِيٌ) weak, broken (heart).

وَيْلٌ woe, misery, misfortune;

وَيْلَكَ woe to thee! fie upon thee! الوَيْلُ alas; woe (unto me, etc.).

ي

ي *affixed pron.* me, mine.
يَا *interj.* O! tell me!
يَئِسَ he despaired; VII. إِيتَأَسَ he was sad and grieved, and full of complaints.
يَابِسٌ dry, shrunk, withered.
يَاقُوتٌ a ruby.
يَتَمَ (يَيْتَمُ) he was deprived of his father; يَتِيمٌ fatherless, an orphan.
يُجَاوِرُ he takes under his protection; aorist of II. جَارَ (*u*.).
يَدٌ (*pl.* أَيْدٍ) for أَيْدِيٌ the hand; the paw or forefoot (of a quadruped).
يَسَرَ (يَيْسِرُ) he was easy, gentle; he played at dice; IV. تَيَسَّرَ it was prepared, made easy; it became easy and handy; يَسَارٌ the left hand; the left side; يَسِيرٌ easy, trifling; أَيْسَرُ more or most easy, easier; يَسْرَةٌ the left hand or side.

يَقِظَ (*a.*) he was vigilant; he watched; I. يَقَّظَ he awakened or roused up; IX. إِسْتَيْقَظَ he was roused up, he became awake; إِسْتِيقَاظٌ awakening; يَقْظَانُ vigilant; أَبُو يَقْظَانَ father watchful (an epithet of the cock, or of the ass).
يَقِنَ (*a.*) III. أَيْقَنَ and IV. تَيَقَّنَ he was certain, he firmly believed, he knew for sure and certain; he felt fully assured; يَقِينٌ sure, certain; certainty, truth; the true faith; أَيْقَنُ surer, surest, more or most certain.
يَمَنَ (*a.*) he approached on the right side; يَمِينٌ (*pl.* أَيْمَانٌ) an oath (as pledged with the right hand); the right hand; يَمْنَةٌ the right hand; the right hand side.
يَهُودٌ the Jews. See هاد.
يُوسُفُ Joseph.
يَوْمٌ (*pl.* أَيَّامٌ) a day; يَوْمُ الأَحَدِ the first day, Sunday; يَوْمُ الإِثْنَيْنِ the second day, Monday, etc. اَلْيَوْمُ today; يَوْمًا on one day.

☆ ☆ ☆

SUPPLEMENT

آبَاءٌ (pl. أَبٌ) fathers; أَبَوَانِ du. parents, father and mother; both fathers, i.e. father and grandfather; يَا أَبَتِ O father! O my father!

إِبْرَاهِيمُ Abraham.

إِبْرِيقٌ a water-jug, ewer.

أَبْنَاءٌ (pl. of إِبْنٌ for بَنَوٌ) sons.

آتَى (III. of أَتَى he came) he caused to come, he brought; he gave.

أَثَرَ (u.) he preferred.

إِذَا behold! if, in case; إِذًا then, in that case.

إِذْ ذَاكَ then, at that time.

أَذَّنَ (I. of أَذَنَ) he cried; مُؤَذِّنٌ a crier.

اِسْتَبْرَقٌ a kind of thick satin; satin embroidered with gold.

أَسَفٌ grief, sorrow.

آلَى (III. of أَلَا) he swore.

أُمَّةٌ time, an interval of time.

آمِرٌ commanding; a commander.

إِمْرَةٌ dominion, authority; أَمَّارٌ imperious, obstinate, headstrong.

آمِنٌ safe, secure.

أُمُورٌ (pl. of أَمْرٌ) affairs, matters of business.

آمِينٌ amen! so be it.

أَمِينٌ faithful, trusty; a confidential agent, a commissioner, superintendent.

أَنْ lest, that, in case that.

أَهْلٌ a family; a wife.

أَوَّلَ (I. of آلَ for أَوَلَ) he interpreted; تَأْوِيلٌ interpretation.

أَوَى (i.) he repaired, he resorted to for shelter or protection; III. آوَى he received hospitably.

أَيَّدَ (I. of آدَ for أَيَدَ) he strengthened.

إِيمَانٌ faith, religious belief.

ب

بَارٌّ just, righteous, holy.

بَأْسٌ severity, vengeance; اِبْتَأَسَ (VII. of بَئِسَ) he was afflicted;

بِئْسَ الْمَصِيرُ out upon! fie upon! بِئْسَ miserable is the abode whither they will return!

بَالٌ heart, mind, thought.

بَثَّ he dispersed abroad, he diffused, disseminated; بَثٌّ grief, sorrow.

بَخْسٌ small, scanty, deficient; trifling.

بَدَأَ (a.) he began.

اِبْتَدَرَ (VII. of بَدَرَ) he ran hastily (to attack); he prepared for; مُبْدِرٌ full (moon).

بَدَا for بَدَوَ he (or it) appeared; (the idea) entered the mind; III. أَبْدَى he made or he allowed to appear, produced, shewed; بَدْوٌ a desert.

بَرَأَ (I. of بَرَأَ) he absolved, acquitted, he justified; he healed.

بَرِحَ (a.) he quitted.

بُرْهَانٌ a clear judgement or decision; demonstration, proof; conviction.

بَشَرَ (u.) he announced good tidings; بَشِيرٌ or مُبَشِّرٌ a bringer of good tidings, messenger of good news; بُشْرَى good tidings.

بَصِيرَةٌ an evident and convincing proof; demonstration.

بِضْعٌ a small number; بِضَاعَةٌ a capital or stock in trade, a share in a mercantile adventure; purchase-money; money or money's worth for purchasing (corn).

بَاطِلٌ vain, false, frivolous.

بَاطِنٌ inward, inner; the heart.

بَعْثٌ a raising of the dead.

أَبْعَدَ (III. of بَعُدَ) he put to a distance; he alienated.

بَعِيرٌ a full-grown male camel.

بَغْتَةً suddenly, unexpectedly.

بَقَرَاتٌ (pl. of بَقَرَةٌ) oxen, beeves, cows.

بَقْلٌ pot-herbs.

أَبْلَغُ more or most eloquent.

بَاءَ for بَوَأَ (u.) he returned; IV. تَبَوَّأَ he settled, he obtained a settlement; he provided himself a dwelling; he obtained (a wife).

بَاحَ for بَوَحَ (u.) he divulged, he disclosed, he revealed.

بَيَّضَ (بَيَضَ for بَاضَ I. of) he whitened; تَبْيِيضٌ the act of whitening; VIII. اِبْيَضَّ he became white; بَيْضَاءُ blank paper.

بَايَعَ (بَيَعَ for بَاعَ II. of he sold) he struck hands in making a bargain; hence, he saluted and acknowledged one invested with authority; بُويعَ *pass.* he was inaugurated; بَيْعَةٌ inauguration.

habitation; أَكْرَمَ مَثْوَاهُ he received him hospitably; أَحْسَنَ مَثْوَايَ he hath received me hospitably.

ت

تَ used in swearing; as, تَرَبِّ الْكَعْبَةِ by the Lord of the Ka'bah!
تَثْرِيبٌ reproach.
أَتْعَبَ (III. of تَعِبَ) he fatigued, he wearied.
تَكَّاً (a.) and VII. اِتَّكَاً he leaned against; مُتَّكَأً a day-bed, a cushion, couch, sofa, or anything against which people recline; hence, a banquet.
تَلَا for تَلَوَ (u.) he read; he rehearsed.
أَتَمَّ (III. of تَمَّ) he completed, he perfected; he fully accomplished; مُتِمٌّ completing; a perfecter.
تَوْبَةٌ repentance; تَائِبٌ penitent.
تَوْرَاةٌ the Pentateuch.

ث

أَثْمَرَ (III. of ثَمَرَ) it bore fruit.
ثَمَنٌ price, or value.
مَثْوًى a dwelling-place, a

ج

جَامْ (*Pers.*) a cup, a goblet.
جَبَا he collected (tribute). VII. اِجْتَبَى he chose, selected, elected.
جَحَدَ he denied, he disowned.
جَادَلَ (II. of جَدَلَ) he contended with, he disputed with.
جَرَبَ he scraped; تَجْرِبَةٌ (*pl.* تَجَارِبُ) experiment, experience; trial, probation; temptation.
جَرَمَ (*i.*) he cut off; مُجْرِمٌ criminal; a sinner, malefactor.
جَرَى (*i.*) he ran; hasted in his course.
جَزَى (*i.*) he gave an equivalent; he satisfied, made satisfaction; he furnished a substitute; he rewarded, requited; جَازٍ from جَازِيٌ who or what suffices, or makes satisfaction.
جَسَدٌ the body.

جَعَلَ (a.) he began; جَاعِلٌ placing, about to appoint or constitute.

جَالَسَ (II. of جَلَسَ) he sat along with.

أَجْمَعَ (III. of جَمَعَ) he agreed, he concerted; he concluded.

جُمْلَةٌ (pl. جُمْلَاتٌ) a sentence, a complete proposition; أَجْمَلُ fairer, fairest.

جَاهَدَ (II. of جَهَدَ) he fought (especially against infidels in defence of the faith); he contended with, he sought to compel, he urged.

جَهَّزَ (I. of جَهَزَ) he equipped, he furnished; he despatched; IV. تَجَهَّزَ he was furnished; he prepared for, he set out; جِهَازٌ travelling equipage; provisions for an expedition.

جَاهِلِيَّةٌ ignorance; paganism, heathen darkness (as prevailing in Arabia before the time of the Prophet Muḥammad).

إِسْتَجَابَ (IX. of جَابَ for جَوَبَ) he listened to, or received a petition, he granted an answer (to prayer).

جَوَّدَ (I. of جَادَ for جَوَدَ) he did well; تَجْوِيدٌ a doing, or executing well.

جَازَ (جَوَزَ for u.) it was lawful, permitted, allowed, or allowable; V. تَجَاوَزَ he passed beyond.

جَوْهَرٌ (Pers. گوهَرْ) matter, substance, essence.

جَائِرٌ (pl. of جِيرَانٌ) neighbours.

جَيْشٌ an army, a host.

ح

حَاجَّ (II. of حَجَّ) he argued; VII. إِحْتَجَّ he pleaded, he argued, he urged as a plea or argument; حَاجٌّ a pilgrim (or a company of pilgrims) to Makkah.

حَاجَةٌ a wish, want, desire.

أَحَبُّ dearer, more or better beloved.

حَبَّةٌ a grain, a seed.

حَجَّامٌ a barber; a cupper, a bleeder.

حَتَّى in order that.

حَدٌّ a distinctive character; عَلَى حَدِّ according to rule, on the principle of analogy.

أَحْدَثَ (III. of حَدَثَ) he produced, originated, brought into existence; أُحْدُوثَةٌ (pl. أَحَادِيثُ) a story, a tale; a parable or dark saying.

حَارَبَ (II. of حَرَبَ) he waged war.
حَرَصَ he greatly desired.
حَرَضٌ at the point of death.
حَرَّمَ (I. of حَرَمَ) he prohibited, interdicted, made or declared unlawful; حُرْمَةٌ honour, reputation, character.
حَازِمٌ wise, prudent, cautious, discreet.
مَحْزُونٌ grieved, sad, afflicted.
تَحَسَّسَ (IV. of حَسَّ) he made enquiry, he explored, examined.
حُسْنٌ goodness, excellence; مُحْسِنٌ beneficent; a benefactor; مَحَاسِنُ (irreg. pl. of حُسْنٌ) beauties, charms; excellences.
حَضْحَصَ quadril. (the truth) appeared, became manifest, came out.
حَصَادٌ reaping, harvest.
أَحْصَنَ (III. of حَصُنَ) he kept safe.
حَفِظَ (a.) he guarded; حِفْظٌ guarding, protecting, taking care of, preserving; custody; حَافِظٌ or حَفِيظٌ keeper, guardian, preserver, protector.
حَاكِمٌ a judge, chief magistrate, ruler.
حُلْمٌ (pl. أَحْلَامٌ) a dream; مَا أَحْلَمَ how meek!

حِلْيَةٌ an ornament (of a sword, especially on the hilt and sheath); تَحَلَّى (IV. of حَلَّى) he was adorned; he plumed himself.
حَامِلٌ حِمْلٌ a load, burden; pregnant (female), with young, in foal.
حَمِيَّةٌ pride, haughtiness.
حَوَارِيٌّ (pl. حَوَارِيُّونَ) a disciple or an apostle of Jesus Christ.
حَاشَ لِلّٰهِ God forbid!
حَاطَ for حَوَطَ (u.) he encompassed.
حَاقَ for حَوَقَ (u.) it surrounded; (an affliction, or a snare) lighted upon, and overtook.
حَاوَلَ (II. of حَالَ for حَوَلَ) he wished, desired, sought; فِي الْحَالِ immediately; حَالَةٌ state, condition, posture of affairs.
حَبْلٌ craft, wile, sagacity.
أَحْيَاءٌ (pl. of حَيٌّ) the living; alive.

خ

خَتَّارٌ a gross deceiver, arrant knave.
خَدٌّ the cheek.
خَادَعَ (II. of خَدَعَ) he deceived, circumvented; he sought to deceive.

خَاذِلٌ routed, put of flight.

خَرَجَ (III. of) أَخْرَجَ he brought out, produced, shewed; خَارِجٌ outside; إِسْتَخْرَجَ (IX. of خَرَجَ) he drew out.

خَرْدَلٌ mustard.

خَرْقٌ a rent, fissure, hole.

خَزَائِنُ (pl. of خِزَانَةٌ) magazines, granaries, storehouses.

خَاسِرٌ one who loses.

خَصْمٌ an opponent, antagonist.

خُضْرٌ (pl. of أَخْضَرُ and خَضْرَاءُ) green; اِخْضَرَّ IX. it was green; مُخْضَرٌّ green, verdant.

خَاطِئٌ a sinner, transgressor; أَخْطَأ (III. of خَطِيءَ) he erred, sinned, trespassed, transgressed.

خَطْبٌ a thing, affair, matter, cause; مَا خَطْبُكَ what is thy business (or thy design)?

خَاطِرٌ heart, mind, soul.

اِخْتَفَى (VII. of خَفَى) he hid himself.

اِسْتَخْلَصَ (IX. of خَلَصَ) he appropriated (to himself); مُخْلِصٌ pure; demonstrative of sincerity; مُخْلَصٌ sincere, candid, pure, unsullied.

أَخْلَفَ (III. of خَلَفَ) he broke his promise, he disappointed.

خَلْقٌ creation; mankind.

خَلَا for خَلَوَ (u.) (it) was clear.

خُمُولٌ obscurity; خَامِلٌ obscure.

خَوَّرَ (I. of خَارَ for خَوَرَ) he bellowed, he lowed.

خَاضَ for خَوَضَ (u.) he entered, waded, forded, plunged into (a river).

خَانَ for خَوَنَ (u.) he acted perfidiously, he broke a promise, betrayed a turst; خَائِنٌ faithless, perfidious, fraudulent, deceitful.

مُخْتَالٌ self-important, vain, haughty, proud (rt. خَالَ for خَيَلَ).

د

دَأْبٌ custom, habit; دَأْبًا as usual.

دَارَابِنَةٌ (less correct than دَرَابِنَةٌ).

دُبُرٌ the hinder part; مِنْ دُبُرٍ from behind, at the back.

دَاخَلَ (II. of دَخَلَ) he was intimate with; دَاخِلٌ inside.

دَرَجَةٌ (pl. دَرَجَاتٌ) a step, a stair.

دَفَعَ he paid, he handed over.

دَاوَمَ (II. of دَامَ for دَوَمَ) he was

دِين

assiduous and unremitting; مُدَاوَمَةٌ assiduity, continuance. دِينٌ law; judgement; يَوْمُ الدِّين the day of judgement.

ذ

ذَاتُ الصُّدُور whatever revolves in the breast.
ذَرُوا leave you (rt. وَذَرَ).
اِذَّكَرَ (VII. of ذَكَرَ) he recollected himself.
ذَهَابٌ departure, loss; ذَاهِبٌ going away, making off; أَذْهَبَ (III. of ذَهَبَ) he gilded; مُذْهَبٌ gilt.
ذَوُو (pl. of ذُو in compos.) endued with, possessing, possessed of.

ر

أَرَى for أَرْأَي (III. of رَأَى) he shewed; لِيُرِيَكُمْ that he may make you see; رُؤْيَا a vision.
أَرْبَابٌ (pl. of رَبٌّ) lords.
رَتَعَ (a.) he roamed or strolled about.
مَرْجِعٌ a return (to God) (rt. رَجَعَ).
رَحْلٌ (pl. رِحَالٌ) a small camel's saddle.
رَاحِمٌ or رَحِمٌ the womb; رِحْمٌ

مَرْؤُوس

أَرْحَمُ compassionate, merciful; more or most merciful, or compassionate.
أَرَدَّ (III. of رَدَّ) he brought back, he restored; اِرْتِدَادُ الطَّرْفِ the twinkling of any eye.
اِسْتَرْسَلَ (IX. of رَسَلَ) (the stiffened joint) relaxed or hung down.
رَاسِيَةٌ (pl. رَوَاسِي) firm, solid (mountain).
رَشَّ he strewed (litter); مَرْشُوشٌ littered; strewed.
مَرْصُوصٌ held together by cramps (of iron); soldered (rt. رَصَّ).
رِضَا content, satisfaction, good pleasure; رَاضٍ (from رَاضِي) content, satisfied, gratified, acquiescent, complying, consenting, agreeing.
مَرْعُوبٌ terrified (rt. رَعَبَ).
مَرْفُوعٌ removed; redressed (rt. رَفَعَ).
رُكَّابٌ (pl. of رَاكِبٌ) passengers on board a ship.
أَرَاحَ (IV. of رَاحَ) for رُوحٌ mercy; مُسْتَرِيحٌ he caused to rest; رَوَحَ reposing, resting.
رَاوَدَ (II. of رَادَ) for رَوَدَ he begged, solicited, wooed.
مَرْؤُوسٌ headed, commanded (rt. رَأَسَ).

ز

زَعِيمٌ a sponsor, a surety; a leader.
أَزِمَّةٌ (pl. of زِمَامٌ) reins, bridles.
زَاهِدٌ on who esteems lightly; indifferent, unconcerned.
أَزْوَاجٌ (pl. of زَوْجٌ) wives, spouses.
زَالَ for زَوَلَ (a.) he ceased, he desisted; زَائِلٌ transitory, fleeting, evanescent.
تَزَايَدَ (V. of زَادَ for زَيَدَ) it increased, it grew.
زَاغَ for زَيَغَ (i.) he deviated, he declined (from the right way); III. أَزَاغَ he caused to decline; he made to swerve.

س

سَائِلٌ an enquirer; سُؤَالٌ a question, an interrogation; سَلْ (imp.) ask.
أَسْبَغَ (III. of سَبَغَ) he completed; he conferred (favours) in abundance.
سَاجِدٌ (pl. سُجَّدٌ) worshipping; a worshipper; one who does obeisance.
سِحْرٌ magic, enchantment, sorcery.
إِسْحَاقٌ Isaac.
مَسْخَرَةٌ a buffoon, wag, facetious joker.

سَاخِطٌ angry, indignant, incensed, hostile, spiteful.
أَسْخَنَ (III. of سَخَنَ) he boiled (water), he heated.
سَارَعَ (II. of سَرُعَ) he made haste, he hurried; مُسَارَعَةٌ a making haste, hurrying; مُسْرِعٌ expeditious.
سَارِقٌ a thief, a robber.
مِنْ سَاعَتِهِ in the same hour.
سِقَايَةٌ a cup, a drinking vessel.
سُكَّانٌ (pl. of سَاكِنٌ) inhabitants; مَسَاكِنُ (pl. of مَسْكَنٌ) a knife; سِكِّينٌ abodes, dwellings, habitations.
سِمَانٌ (pl. of سَمِينٌ) fat.
سَمَوَاتٌ (pl.) heavens; مُسَمَّى named, called, styled.
سُنْبُلٌ or سُنْبُلَةٌ (pl. سُنْبُلَاتٌ) an ear of corn.
سَوْآتٌ (pl. سَوْأَةٌ) secret parts, privities.
سَوَّلَ (I. of سَالَ for سَوَلَ) he suggested (evil); he devised or contrived.
سَاوَى (II. of سَوَى) it was worth.
سَيِّدٌ a lord or master.
سَاقٌ a stem, a stalk.
سَيَّارَةٌ a body of travellers, a caravan.

ش

تَشَاجَرُوا (V. of شَجَرَ) they contended, disputed, wrangled together.

شِدَادٌ (pl. of شَدِيدٌ) sore, severe; scarce; أَشُدَّ strength and powers (applied chiefly to a young man between 18 and 30).

شَرَعَ he began.

أَشْرَافٌ (pl. of شَرِيفٌ) nobles.

أَشْرَقَ (III. of شَرَقَ) (the sun) arose, shined forth, became radiant and refulgent.

أَشْرَكَ (III. of شَرَكَ) he gave partners or associates; شِرْكٌ polytheism; مُشْرِكٌ a polytheist, an idolater.

شَغَفَ (i.) he wounded in the pericardium or in the heart's core.

شَكَا for شَكَوَ (u.) he complained, he stated the case of his maladies.

شَمَّ the sense of smell; مَشْمُومٌ perfumed; smelled; odoriferous, fragrant (as pastilles, etc.).

فَرَّقَ اللهُ شَمْلَهُم شَمْلٌ a collection; may God break up their confederacy!

مَشِيئَةٌ will, good pleasure (rt. شَاءَ).

ص

أَصْبَحَ (III. of صَبَحَ) he rose betimes; he became, he came or did (a thing) early in the morning; he entered on the morning; he became.

صَبَّارٌ very patient; أَصْبَرُ more or most patient.

صَبَا for صَبَوَ (u.) he acted like a boy; he felt a juvenile affection for.

صَحَّ (i.) it was right, straightforward.

صَاحَبَ (II. of صَحَبَ) he cultivated sociableness with, he bore company; أَصْحَابٌ (pl. of صَاحِبٌ) friends, companions, associates.

صَخْرَةٌ a rock (noun of unity).

صَادِقٌ a speaker of the truth, veracious; صِدِّيقٌ a faithful witness of the truth; مُصَدِّقٌ confirming; a confirmer; تَصَدَّقَ (IV. of صَدَقَ) he bestowed alms; مُتَصَدِّقٌ an almsgiver.

صَعَّرَ (I. of صَعَرَ) he made a wry face

صَاغِرٌ in contempt.

صَاغِرٌ contemptible; one who submits tamely to indignant treatment.

صَفٌّ a row, rank, file (of soldiers).

صُلْبٌ the backbone, the loins; (metaphorically) capital, principal.

أَصْلَحَ (III. of صَلَحَ) he cooked, prepared (food).

أَصَمَّ (III. of صَمَّ) he rendered deaf.

صَنْعَةٌ workmanship; اِصْطِنَاعٌ performance; rendering a service, doing a kindness.

صُنُوفٌ (pl. of صُنْفٌ or صِنْفٌ) different sorts or forms.

صُوَاعٌ a drinking-vessel.

تَصَيَّدَ (IV. of صَادَ for صَيَّدَ) he went a hunting, he looked about for game.

ض

تَضَحَّكَ (IV. of ضَحِكَ) he laughed heartily.

ضُرٌّ damage, loss; famine; اِضْطَرَّ (VII. of ضَرَّ) he compelled, he forced.

اِضْطَرَبَ (VII. of ضَرَبَ) he knocked himself about, was agitated, disturbed, restless, and fidgety.

أَضْعَفُ weaker, weakest.

أَضْغَاثُ الْأَحْلَامِ confused dreams which cannot be interpreted.

أَضَلَّ (III. of ضَلَّ) he made to err, he led astray, he seduced; ضَلَالٌ error.

اِسْتَضَاءَ (IX. of ضَاءَ for ضَوَءَ) he afforded light.

ضَيَّعَ for ضَاعَ III. of أَضَاعَ I. and ضَيَّعَ he suffered to be lost, he allowed to perish.

ط

أَطْفَأَ (III. of طَفِئَ) he extinguished (a fire), he put out (a light).

أَطْلَقَ (III. of طَلَقَ) he loosened, he gave the reins.

تَطَاوَلَ (V. of طَالَ for طَوَلَ) he was long; he exalted himself; he unjustly usurped another's right.

طَيْرٌ (pl. of طَائِرٌ) birds.

ظ

ظُلَّةٌ (pl. ظُلَلٌ) a covering; a shady thing; أَظَلَّ (III. of ظَلَّ) he (or it) shaded.

عَاقِلٌ (I. of عَرَضَ) عَرَّضَ he opposed, objected, gave trouble; مُعْرِضٌ averse.

عِرْفٌ knowledge; أَعْرَفُ more knowing, better acquainted; مَعْرِفَةٌ knowledge, science, learning; مَعْرُوفٌ known; just, acceptable; kindness, courtesy, favour, benefit.

عُرْوَةٌ a handle; a loop.

عِزٌّ glory, dignity, grandeur; عَزِيزٌ a king (of Egypt), a prince; a lord.

عَزَلَ (a.) he removed from office, he deposed.

عَزْمُ الأُمُورِ the divine purpose concerning human affairs.

عَسَى it may be, perhaps.

عُصْبَةٌ a body (of men), from 10 to 40.

عَصَرَ (i.) he squeezed, pressed (grapes).

(IX. of عَصَمَ) اِسْتَعْصَمَ he preserved himself from sin, he abstained from what is unlawful.

عَطَبٌ perishing; destruction.

(IV. of عَقَبَ) تَعَقَّبَ end, issue; عَاقِبَةٌ he followed, he came at the heels; (عَقِبٌ); يَعْقُوبُ Jacob.

عَاقِلٌ intelligent, sensible, wise,

ظُلَامَةٌ أَظْلَمُ redress of grievances; more or most unjust, or iniquitous; مَظْلَمَةٌ (pl. of مَظَالِمُ) oppression, wrong, injustice; requisition of justice, redress of wrongs; مَظْلُومٌ oppressed, injured.

ظَاهِرٌ triumphant, victorious; اَلظَّاهِرُ apparently, evidently; أَظْهَرَ (III. of ظَهَرَ) he exalted, rendered superior, made to triumph.

ع

عَبَرَ he interpreted (a dream); عِبْرَةٌ an instructive example, warning.

عَاجِزٌ weak, puny, feeble.

أَعْجَفُ (pl. عِجَافٌ) lean, emaciated.

عَجَّلَ (I. of عَجِلَ) he made haste; تَعْجِيلٌ making a haste, hastening.

مَعْدُودٌ numbered, counted; few, limited in number (rt. عَدَّ).

عَدْلٌ justice, equity; مُعْتَدِلٌ temperate, middling, moderate.

عَدْنٌ a permanent dwelling; Eden.

عَرَبِيٌّ Arabic, Arabian.

عَرْشٌ a seat of state; a throne.

prudent; an intelligent man.

اِعْتَلَفَ (VII. of عَلَفَ) he ate provender.

عُمُدٌ (pl. of عَمُودٌ) columns, pillars.

عَمَرَ (u.) he built up; III. أَعْمَرَ he cultivated, he rendered habitable; أَعْمَارٌ (pl. of عُمْرٌ) lives.

عَنْ on the authority.

عَائِدًا as a visitor; أَعَادَ (III. of عَادَ for عَوَدَ) he performed a second time, repeated, said, did over again.

مَعَاذَ اللّٰهِ God forbid!

عَامٌ a year; عَامَانِ two years.

مُعَاوَنَةٌ assistance; مُسْتَعَانٌ one whose aid is implored; hence, God.

عَيَاءٌ difficult, incurable (disease); أَعْيَى (III. of عَيَّ) he was wearied (with travelling).

عِيرٌ a caravan.

غ

غَرُورٌ a deceiver; Satan, the devil.

مَغْشِيًّا عَلَيْهِ غَاشِيَةٌ overwhelming; fainted away, unconscious.

غَضَّ he cast down (the eyes); he lowered (the voice).

مَغْضُوبٌ عَلَيْهِ vengeance; غَضَبٌ odious; one against whom anger is felt.

غَافِلٌ remiss, neglectful, negligent, careless, senseless, imprudent, off one's guard; تَغَافَلَ (V. of غَفَلَ) he was intentionally negligent, listless, and indifferent.

غَالِبٌ overcoming, prevailing, victorious; capable of effecting.

غَلِيظٌ coarse, gross, rugged, rough.

غَامِرٌ uninhabited, uncultivated, waste. abondoned (the opposite of عَامِرٌ).

غَنِيمَةٌ plunder, booty, prize-money; اِغْتَنَمَ (VII. of غَنَمَ) he obtained spoil (as booty or a prize); he seized an opportunity.

أَغْنَى (III. of غَنِيَ) he supplied the place (of another); he sufficed; it availed; أَغْنِيَاءُ (pl. of غَنِيٌّ) rich; أَغْنَى richer, richest.

غَيَابَةٌ the bottom (of a well or valley).

غَاثَ for غَيَّثَ (God) gave rain, made it to fall; غَيْثٌ rain widely spread.

ف

مَا تَفْتَأُ (a.) he ceased, left off; تَذْكُرُهُ thou dost not cease to remember him (used also without مَا).

فَتْحٌ victory.

فَتَّشَ (I. of فَتَشَ) he searched diligently.

أَفْتَى (III. of فَتِيَ) he resolved a question of law, or a case of conscience; he expounded; he interpreted; he instructed; IX. اِسْتَفْتَى he consulted a lawyer (*mufti*), he took an opinion, he asked for a *fatwa*; فَتًى du. فَتَيَانِ pl. فِتْيَةٌ a young man, a man servant; فَتَاهُ his servant.

فَحْشَاءُ whoredom, adultery.

فَخُورٌ boastful, vainglorious; a boaster.

فَارِسٌ Persia; the Persians.

فِرَاشٌ a bed, a couch.

فَرَّطَ (I. of فَرَطَ) he acted carelessly in the performance of duty; he behaved perfidiously.

مُتَفَرِّقٌ dispersed, scattered; miscellaneous, various (*rt.* فَرَقَ).

اِفْتَرَى (VII. of فَرَى) he invented (a lie).

فِصَالٌ فَصَلَ he departed, set off; تَفْصِيلٌ a weaning, ablactation; a distinct explanation.

فَضْلٌ grace, favour; فَاضِلٌ excellent, virtuous, pious; learned; أَفْضَلُ more or most excellent, better.

فَطَرَ he created; فَاطِرٌ creator.

فَقَدَ (i.) he missed; فَقْدٌ loss, miss, deprivation.

أَفْلَسَ (III. of فَلَسَ) he became insolvent, he was reduced to bankruptcy.

فُلْكٌ a ship; ships.

فُلَانِيٌّ of, or belonging to so-and-so; of such a place.

فَنَّدَ (I. of فَنَدَ) he regarded as a dotard, he suspected of dotage (from indisposition or from age).

فِي (see فَمٌ); فِيمَا whilst; فِيمَا بَيْنَ between, betwixt; فِيمَا عَدَا over and above.

ق

مِنْ قُبُلٍ from the fore part; قُبَلٌ before, in front; قَبَّلَ (I. of قَبَلَ) he kissed.

قَدَّ (u.) he tore (a garment) length wise.

مِقْدَارٌ quantity, sum, amount; power, strength (*rt.* قَدَرَ).

تَقَدَّسَ (IV. of قَدَسَ) he was sanctified.

قَدَّمَ (I. of قَدَمَ) he sent before; he laid up as a future provision; he provided beforehand; تَقَدَّمَ (IV.) he preceded, he went before.

قَارَبَ (II. of قَرَبَ) he approaches.

أَهْلُ الْقُرَى (*pl.* of قَرْيَةٌ) towns; قُرًى inhabitants of cities, towns people.

قَسَمَ (*i.*) he divided, he apportioned, allotted.

قَسْوَةٌ hardness of heart; قَاسٍ (from قَاسِي) hard, cruel.

قَصَّ (*u.*) he told, related, narrated; قِصَّةٌ (*pl.* قِصَصٌ) a story, fable, tale; an affair; a case.

قَصَدَ he kept or steered in the straight and middle path; he was moderate; he acted uprightly; مُقْتَصِدٌ one who keeps the middle path, or one who halts between two parties.

قَضَى (*i.*) he performed; he paid.

قَطَعَ (I. of قَطَعَ) he hacked, he cut in several pieces or in sundry places; III. أَقْطَعَ he assigned lands on feudal or copyhold tenure (as a prince to a subject); مُتَقَاطِعٌ cut, parted from each other, separated.

قَلَّدَ (I. of قَلَدَ) he put a wreath or chain around; he entrusted (the reins of government).

قَلَمٌ (*pl.* أَقْلَامٌ) a pen.

مُقْمِرٌ bright, moon-shine (night).

قَمِيصٌ a shirt, an inner garment.

قَهَّارٌ powerful; اَلْقَهَّارُ the omnipotent, or avenging (God).

قُوتٌ (*pl.* أَقْوَاتٌ) victuals, food.

قَائِلٌ saying, speaking; a speaker.

قَوْمٌ people; قَيِّمٌ true, right; قَائِمٌ upright, standing, erect; established (market); إِقَامَةٌ a setting up, fixing, establishing, putting in execution.

ك

كَافُورٌ camphor.

كَأَيِّنْ how many.

أَكَبَّ (III. of كَبَّ) he fell prostrate.

كَبُرَ (*u.*) it was great; كَبُرَ عَلَى it was grievous, painful, annoying, disagreeable; III. أَكْبَرَ he

كِتْمَانٌ — مَدَنِيٌّ

viewed as great, he honoured; he praised; IX. اِسْتَكْبَرَ he was proud; كَبِيرٌ very aged; مُسْتَكْبِرٌ disdainful.

كِتْمَانٌ a concealing.

كَذِبٌ false, deceitful.

كُرْسِيٌّ a chair; a seat of state, a throne.

أَكْرَهَ (III. of كَرِهَ) he forced against the will, he compelled; إِكْرَاهٌ compulsion.

كَظِيمٌ oppressed with grief.

كِفَاةٌ (كِفَايَةٌ) a sufficiency, a supply equal to wants.

تَكَلَّمَ (IV. of كَلَمَ) he spoke.

كُلِّيٌّ entire, full, complete.

كَنَسَ he swept; كَنْسٌ sweeping.

كَهْفٌ a cave; أَصْحَابُ الْكَهْفِ companions of the cave, the seven sleepers.

كَوْكَبٌ a star.

كَادَ for كَيَدَ (i.) he laid snares, he devised a plot; كَيْدٌ a plot.

كَالَ for كَيَلَ he measured (grain); VII. اِكْتَالَ he measured (corn); he measured for another; he received by measure; كَيْلٌ measure.

ل

أَلْبَابٌ (pl. of لُبٌّ) hearts.

لَبِثَ he remained, he continued.

أَلْحَقَ (III. of لَحِقَ) he joined, he added, he followed (it) up.

لَدَى or لَدَا to, at, nigh; لَدَيْنَا with us.

لَطِيفٌ subtile; clear-sighted; gracious.

اِلْتَقَطَ (VII. of لَقَطَ) he picked up.

لَقَّى (II. of لَقِيَ) he cast, or shed upon; III. أَلْقَى he met, encountered.

لِمَ wherefore. لَمَّا surely not.

لَنْ verily not, assuredly not.

م

مَتَّعَ (I. of مَتَعَ) he permitted freely to enjoy; he bestowed, conferred upon, granted; مَتَاعٌ merchandize, goods, wares, effects, baggage, clothes, chattels; provisions.

مَدَحَ (a.) he praised, lauded, extolled.

مَدَنِيٌّ of Madinah; (revealed) at Madinah.

مُرْ (imper. of أَمَرَ) command thou; مُرُوا do you bid.

مُرٌّ bitter; bitterness.

مَرَحًا jauntingly, insolently.

مُزْجَى (fem. مُزْجَاة) small, trifling.

مَسَّ he touched; it pressed.

اِسْتَمْسَكَ (IX. of مَسَكَ) he laid hold upon, he held firmly.

مَطْلٌ a deferring, putting off, procrastination.

مَقْتٌ odium, hate.

مَكَانٌ state, condition; مَكِينٌ a dweller; settled, established, firmly fixed; أَمْكَنَ (III. of مَكُنَ) it was possible.

مَكِّيٌّ of Makkah; (revealed) at Makkah.

مَنَّ (u.) he was gracious; مَنٌّ a reproaching, twitting, or casting in the teeth of benefits conferred.

مَنَادِلُ (more correct than مَنَادِيلُ).

مَنَعَ (a.) he forbade, prohibited.

مَوْجٌ a wave, a billow.

مَادَ for مَيَدَ (i.) it quivered, undulated, played, rocked to and fro.

مَارَ for مَيَرَ (i.) he purveyed food for; he brought corn from a distance.

مَائِلٌ inclined (rt. مَالَ for مَيَلَ).

ن

نَبَأَ (a.) he declared; I. نَبَّأَ he prophesied; he announced, informed, made acquainted; نَبَأٌ (pl. أَنْبَاءُ) news, advice; أَنْبِيَاءُ (pl. of نَبِيٌّ) prophets.

أَنْبَتَ (III. of نَبَتَ) he made (corn or grass) to spring up and grow.

نَجِيٌّ the communication of a secret; a private conference, carried on in a whisper; نَاجٍ from نَاجِي one who escapes; escaped, saved.

نَزَغَ he sowed discord.

مُنْزِلٌ a receiver of guests; (pl. مَنَازِلُ) a mansion.

أَنْسَى (III. of نَسِيَ) he made to forget.

نُصْحٌ advice, good counsel.

نَصْرٌ aid, help, assistance.

نَفِدَ it vanished, it became empty, and dried up.

اِنْتَفَضَ (VII. of نَفَضَ) he shook himself.

SECTION I

Miscellaneous Sentences

جُمَلاتٌ مُخْتَلِفَةٌ

◆ اَلدُّنْيَا دَارُ مَمَرٍّ لَا دَارُ مَقَرٍّ. سُلْطَانٌ بِلَا عَدْلٍ كَنَهْرٍ بِلَا مَاءٍ. عَالِمٌ بِلَا عَمَلٍ كَسَحَابٍ بِلَا مَطَرٍ. غَنِيٌّ بِلَا سَخَاوَةٍ كَشَجَرٍ بِلَا ثَمَرٍ. إِمْرَأَةٌ بِلَا حَيَاءٍ كَطَعَامٍ بِلَا مِلْحٍ. لَا تَسْتَصْغِرْ عَدُوّاً وَإِنْ ضَعُفَ. قِلَّةُ الْأَكْلِ يَمْنَعُ كَثِيراً مِنْ أَعْلَالِ الْجِسْمِ. بِالْعَمَلِ يُحَصَّلُ الثَّوَابُ لَا بِالْكَسَلِ.

◆ مَنْ رَضِيَ عَنْ نَفْسِهِ كَثُرَ السَّاخِطُ عَلَيْهِ. إِذَا كُنْتَ كَذُوباً فَكُنْ ذَكُوراً. رَأْسُ الدِّينِ الْمَعْرِفَةُ. اَلسَّعِيدُ مَنْ وُعِظَ بِغَيْرِهِ. اَلصَّبْرُ مِفْتَاحُ الْفَرَحِ. اَلصِّنَاعَةُ فِي الْكَفِّ أَمَانٌ مِنَ الْفَقْرِ. مَنْ تَسَمَّعَ سَمِعَ مَا يَكْرَهُ. قَلْبُ الْأَحْمَقِ فِي فِيهِ وَلِسَانُ

جُمْلَاتٌ مُخْتَلِفَةٌ

الْعَاقِلِ فِي قَلْبِهِ. كُنْ قَنِعاً تَكُنْ غَنِيّاً. كُنْ مُتَوَكِّلاً تَكُنْ قَوِيّاً. حُبُّ الدُّنْيَا يُفْسِدُ الْعَقْلَ وَيُصِمُّ الْقَلْبَ عَنْ سَمَاعِ الْحِكْمَةِ.

◆ شَرُّ النَّوَالِ مَا تَقَدَّمَهُ الْمَطْلُ وَتَعَقَّبَهُ الْمَنُّ. شَرُّ النَّاسِ مَنْ يُعِينُ عَلَى الْمَظْلُومِ وَيَنْصُرُ الظَّلُومَ. شَيْئَانِ لَا يُعْرَفُ فَضْلُهُمَا إِلَّا مِنْ فَقْدِهِمَا الشَّبَابُ وَالْعَافِيَةُ. اَلْكَسَلُ وَكَثْرَةُ النَّوْمِ يُبْعِدَانِ مِنَ اللَّهِ وَيُورِثَانِ الْفَقْرَ. لَيْسَ مِنْ عَادَةِ الْكِرَامِ تَأْخِيرُ الْإِنْعَامِ ـ لَيْسَ مِنْ عَادَةِ الْأَشْرَافِ تَعْجِيلُ الْإِنْتِقَامِ. الصَّدِيقُ الصَّدُوقُ مَنْ نَصَحَكَ فِي عَيْنِكَ وَأَثَرَكَ عَلَى نَفْسِهِ. الْأَمَلُ كَالسَّرَابِ ـ يَغُرُّ مَنْ رَآهُ وَيُخْلِفُ مَنْ رَجَاهُ.

◆ ثَلَاثَةٌ يُمْتَحَنُ بِهِنَّ عَقْلُ الرِّجَالِ ـ اَلْمَالُ وَالوِلَايَةُ وَالْمُصِيبَةُ. إِيَّاكَ وَحُبَّ الدُّنْيَا ـ فَإِنَّهَا رَأْسُ كُلِّ خَطِيَّةٍ وَمَعْدِنُ كُلِّ بَلِيَّةٍ. اَلْحَسَدُ دَاءٌ عَيَاءٌ ـ لَا يَزُولُ إِلَّا بِهَلْكِ الْحَاسِدِ أَوْ مَوْتِ الْمَحْسُودِ. زِدْ فِي اصْطِنَاعِ الْمَعْرُوفِ وَأَكْثِرْ مِنْ أَشِدَّاءِ الْإِحْسَانِ ـ فَإِنَّهُ أَيْقَنُ ذُخْرٍ وَأَجْمَلُ ذُكْرٍ. سَلْ عَنِ الرَّفِيقِ قَبْلَ الطَّرِيقِ ـ سَلْ عَنِ الْجَارِ قَبْلَ الدَّارِ. جَالِسْ أَهْلَ الْعِلْمِ وَالْحِكْمَةِ وَأَكْثِرْ مُنَافَتَتَهُمْ فَإِنَّكَ إِنْ كُنْتَ جَاهِلاً

عَلَّمُوكَ وَإِنْ كُنْتَ عَالِماً ازْدَدْتَ عِلْماً إِلَى عِلْمٍ.

◆ ذُو الشَّرَفِ لَا تُبْطِرُهُ مَنْزِلَةٌ نَالَهَا وَإِنْ عَظُمَتْ كَالْجَبَلِ الَّذِي لَا تُزَعْزِعُهُ الرِّيَاحُ، وَالدَّنِيُّ تُبْطِرُهُ أَدْنَى مَنْزِلَةٍ كَالْكَلَاءِ الَّذِي يُحَرِّكُهُ مَرُّ النَّسِيمِ. خَمْسٌ يُسْتَقْبَحُ فِي خَمْسٍ — كَثْرَةُ الفُجُورِ فِي الْعُلَمَاءِ وَالْحِرْصُ فِي الْحُكَمَاءِ وَالْبُخْلُ فِي الْأَغْنِيَاءِ وَالْقُبْحَةُ فِي النِّسَاءِ وَفِي الْمَشَائِخِ الزِّنَاءُ. قَالَ ابْنُ الْمُعْتَزِّ- أَهْلُ الدُّنْيَا كَرُكَّابِ سَفِينَةٍ - يُسَارِبِهِمْ وَهُمْ نِيَامٌ. صُنْ إِيمَانَكَ مِنَ الشَّكِّ فَإِنَّ الشَّكَّ يُفْسِدُ الإِيمَانَ كَمَا يُفْسِدُ الْمِلْحُ الْعَسَلَ.

◆ طُوبَى لِمَنْ كَظَمَ غَيْظَهُ وَلَمْ يُطْلِقْهُ وَعَصَى إِمْرَةَ نَفْسِهِ وَلَمْ تُهْلِكْهُ. قَالَ الْمَسِيحُ بْنُ مَرْيَمَ (عَلَيْهِ السَّلَامُ)- عَالَجْتُ الْأَكْمَهَ وَالْأَبْرَصَ فَأَبْرَأْتُهُمَا - وَأَعْيَانِي عِلَاجُ الْأَحْمَقِ. قَالَ ابْنُ الْمُقَنَّعِ. إِذَا حَاجَجْتَ فَلَا تَغْضَبْ - فَإِنَّ الْغَضَبَ يَقْطَعُ عَنْكَ الْحُجَّةَ وَيُظْهِرُ عَلَيْكَ الْخَصْمَ. مَثَلُ الْأَغْنِيَاءِ الْبُخَلَاءِ كَمَثَلِ الْبِغَالِ وَالْحَمِيرِ تَحْمِلُ الذَّهَبَ وَالْفِضَّةَ وَتَعْتَلِفُ بِالتِّبْنِ وَالشَّعِيرِ. قَالَ أَبُو مُسْلِمٍ الْخُرَاسَانِيُّ -

خَاطَرَ مَنْ رَكِبَ الْبَحْرَ وَأَشَدُّ مِنْهُ مُخَاطَرَةً مَنْ دَاخَلَ الْمُلُوكَ.

◆ مِثْلُ الَّذِي يُعَلِّمُ النَّاسَ الْخَيْرَ وَلَا يَعْمَلُ بِهِ كَمِثْلِ أَعْمَى بِيَدِهِ سِرَاجٌ يَسْتَضِيءُ بِهِ غَيْرُهُ وَهُوَ لَا يَرَاهُ. أَضْعَفُ النَّاسِ مَنْ ضَعُفَ عَنْ كِتْمَانِ سِرِّهِ ـ وَأَقْوَاهُمْ مَنْ قَوِيَ عَلَى غَضَبِهِ ـ وَأَصْبَرُهُمْ مَنْ سَتَرَ فَاقَتَهُ. وَأَغْنَاهُمْ مَنْ قَنِعَ بِمَا تَيَسَّرَ لَهُ. قَالَ أَمِيرُ الْمُؤْمِنِينَ عَلِيُّ بْنُ أَبِي طَالِبٍ (كَرَّمَ اللَّهُ وَجْهَهُ) مَنْ عُرِفَ بِالْحِكْمَةِ لَاحَظَتْهُ الْعُيُونُ بِالْوَقَارِ. قَالَ بَعْضُ الْحُكَمَاءِ ـ تَحْتَاجُ الْقُلُوبُ إِلَى أَقْوَاتِهَا مِنَ الْحِكْمَةِ كَمَا تَحْتَاجُ الْأَجْسَامُ إِلَى أَقْوَاتِهَا مِنَ الطَّعَامِ.

◆ قَالَ افْلَاطُونُ ـ حُبُّكَ لِلشَّيْءِ سِتْرٌ بَيْنَكَ وَبَيْنَ مَسَاوِيهِ ـ وَبُغْضُكَ لَهُ سِتْرٌ بَيْنَكَ وَبَيْنَ مَحَاسِنِهِ. مَنْ مَدَحَكَ بِمَا لَيْسَ فِيكَ مِنَ الْجَمِيلِ وَهُوَ رَاضٍ عَنْكَ ذَمَّكَ بِمَا لَيْسَ فِيكَ مِنَ الْقَبِيحِ وَهُوَ سَاخِطٌ عَلَيْكَ. قَالَ افْلَاطُونُ الْحَكِيمُ لَا تَطْلُبْ سُرْعَةَ الْعَمَلِ وَاطْلُبْ تَجْوِيدَهُ فَإِنَّ النَّاسَ لَا يَسْأَلُونَ فِي كَمْ فَرَغَ وَإِنَّمَا يَنْظُرُونَ إِلَى إِتْقَانِهِ وَجُودَةِ صَنْعَتِهِ.

وُجِدَ عَلَى صَنَمٍ مَكْتُوبٌ حَرَامٌ عَلَى النَّفْسِ الْخَبِيثَةِ أَنْ تَخْرُجَ مِنْ هَذِهِ الدُّنْيَا حَتَّى تُسِيءَ إِلَى مَنْ أَحْسَنَ إِلَيْهَا.

◆ ثَلَاثَةٌ لَا يَنْفَعُونَ مِنْ ثَلَاثَةٍ شَرِيفٌ مِنْ دَنِيٍّ وَبَارٌّ مِنْ فَاجِرٍ وَحَكِيمٌ مِنْ جَاهِلٍ. قَالَ عَامِرُ بْنُ عَبْدِ الْقَيْسِ إِذَا خَرَجَتِ الْكَلِمَةُ مِنَ الْقَلْبِ دَخَلَتْ فِي الْقَلْبِ ــ وَإِذَا خَرَجَتْ مِنَ اللِّسَانِ لَمْ تَتَجَاوَزْ الْآذَانَ. قَالَ حَكِيمٌ لِآخَرَ يَا أَخِي! كَيْفَ أَصْبَحْتَ؟ قَالَ أَصْبَحْتُ ــ وَبِنَا مِنْ نِعَمِ اللّهِ مَا لَا نُحْصِيهِ مَعَ كَثِيرٍ مَا نَعْصِيهِ فَمَا نَدْرِي أَيُّهُمَا نَشْكُرُ جَمِيلًا مَا يَنْشُرُ أَوْ قَبِيحًا مَا يَسْتُرُ. اِجْتَمَعَ حُكَمَاءُ الْعَرَبِ وَالْعَجَمِ عَلَى أَرْبَعِ كَلِمَاتٍ ــ وَهِيَ ــ لَا تُحَمِّلْ نَفْسَكَ مَا لَا تُطِيقُ ــ وَلَا تَعْمَلْ عَمَلًا لَا يَنْفَعُكَ ــ وَلَا تَغْتَرَّ بِامْرَأَةٍ وَ إِنْ عَفَّتْ ــ وَلَا تَثِقْ بِمَالٍ وَإِنْ كَثُرَ.

◆ اَلْعَالِمُ عَرَفَ الْجَاهِلَ لِأَنَّهُ كَانَ جَاهِلًا ــ وَالْجَاهِلُ لَا يَعْرِفُ الْعَالِمَ لِأَنَّهُ مَا كَانَ عَالِمًا. لَا تَحْمِلْ عَلَى يَوْمِكَ هَمَّ سَنَتِكَ ــ كَفَاكَ كُلَّ يَوْمٍ مَا قُدِّرَ لَكَ فِيهِ ــ فَإِنْ تَكُنِ السَّنَةُ مِنْ عُمْرِكَ فَإِنَّ اللّهَ سُبْحَانَهُ سَيَأْتِيكَ فِى كُلِّ غَدٍ جَدِيدٍ بِمَا

قُسِمَ لَكَ ـ فَإِنْ لَمْ تَكُنْ مِنْ عُمْرِكَ فَمَا هَمُّكَ بِمَا لَيْسَ لَكَ. فِي كِتَابِ كَلِيلَهْ وَ دِمْنَهْ ـ إِذَا أَحْدَثَ لَكَ الْعَدُوُّ صَدَاقَةً لِعِلَّةٍ أَلْجَأَتْهُ إِلَيْكَ فَمَعَ ذَهَابِ الْعِلَّةِ رُجُوعُ الْعَدَاوَةِ ـ كَالْمَاءِ تُسْخِنُهُ فَإِذَا أَمْسَكْتَ عَنْهُ نَاراً عَادَ إِلَى أَصْلِهِ بَارِداً وَالشَّجَرَةُ الْمُرَّةُ لَوْ طَلَيْتَهَا بِالْعَسَلِ لَمْ تُثْمِرْ إِلَّا مُرًّا.

◆ يَوْمٌ وَاحِدٌ لِلْعَالِمِ أَخْيَرُ مِنَ الْحَيَاةِ كُلِّهَا لِلْجَاهِلِ. لَا تُخَاطِبِ الْأَحْمَقَ وَلَا تُخَالِطْهُ فَإِنَّهُ مَا يَسْتَحِي. قَالَ أَمِيرُ الْمُؤْمِنِينَ عَلِيٌّ (كَرَّمَ اللَّهُ وَجْهَهُ) الْأَدَبُ حَلْيٌ فِي الْغِنَى ـ كَنْزٌ عِنْدَ الْحَاجَةِ ـ عَوْنٌ عَلَى الْمُرُوَّةِ ـ صَاحِبٌ فِي الْمَجْلِسِ ـ مُؤْنِسٌ فِي الْوَحْدَةِ تُعْمَرُ بِهِ الْقُلُوبُ الْوَاهِيَةُ ـ وَتُحْيَا بِهِ الْأَلْبَابُ الْمَيِّتَةُ ـ وَتَنْفُذُ بِهِ الْأَبْصَارُ الْكَلِيلَةُ ـ وَيُدْرِكُ بِهِ الطَّالِبُونَ مَا حَاوَلُونَ. قَالَ لُقْمَانُ لِابْنِهِ يَا بُنَيَّ! لِيَكُنْ أَوَّلُ شَيْءٍ تَكْسِبُهُ بَعْدَ الْإِيمَانِ خَلِيلًا صَالِحًا ـ فَإِنَّمَا مَثَلُ الْخَلِيلِ الصَّالِحِ كَمَثَلِ النَّخْلَةِ ـ إِنْ قَعَدْتَ فِي ظِلِّهَا أَظَلَّكَ ـ وَإِنِ احْتَطَبْتَ مِنْ حَطَبِهَا نَفَعَكَ ـ وَإِنْ أَكَلْتَ مِنْ ثَمَرِهَا وَجَدْتَهُ طَيِّبًا.

◆ مَنْ تَرَكَ نَفْسَهُ بِمَنْزِلَةِ الْعَاقِلِ تَرَكَهُ اللَّهُ وَالنَّاسُ

جُمْلَاتٌ مُخْتَلِفَةٌ

بِمَنْزِلَةِ الْجَاهِلِ. مَنْ أَحَبَّ أَنْ يَقْوَى عَلَى الْحِكْمَةِ فَلَا تَمْلِكُ نَفْسَهُ النِّسَاءُ. نَقْلُ الشَّرِّ عَنْ شُرُورِهِ أَيْسَرُ مِنْ نَقْلِ الْمَحْزُونِ عَنْ حُزْنِهِ. ثَلَاثَةٌ لَا يُعْرَفُونَ إِلَّا فِي ثَلَاثَةِ مَوَاضِعَ. لَا يُعْرَفُ الشُّجَاعُ إِلَّا عِنْدَ الْحَرْبِ ـ وَلَا يُعْرَفُ الْحَكِيمُ إِلَّا عِنْدَ الْغَضَبِ ـ وَلَا يُعْرَفُ الصَّدِيقُ إِلَّا عِنْدَ الْحَاجَةِ إِلَيْهِ. قَالَ رَسُولُ اللَّهِ (صَلَّى اللَّهُ عَلَيْهِ وَسَلَّمَ) ثَلَاثٌ مُهْلِكَاتٌ وَثَلَاثٌ مُنْجِيَاتٌ ـ فَأَمَّا الْمُهْلِكَاتُ فَشُحٌّ مُطَاعٌ وَهَوًى مُتَّبَعٌ وَإِعْجَابُ الْمَرْءِ بِنَفْسِهِ ـ وَأَمَّا الْمُنْجِيَاتُ فَخَشْيَةُ اللَّهِ فِي السِّرِّ وَالْعَلَانِيَةِ وَالْقَصْدُ فِي الْغِنَى وَالْفَقْرِ وَالْعَدْلُ فِي الرِّضَا وَالْغَضَبِ.

◆ اَلْكَمَالُ فِي ثَلَاثَةِ أَشْيَاءَ ـ اَلْعِفَّةُ فِي الدِّينِ ـ وَالصَّبْرُ عِنْدَ النَّوَائِبِ ـ وَحُسْنُ الْمَعِيشَةِ. اَلظَّالِمُ مَيِّتٌ وَلَوْ كَانَ فِي مَنَازِلِ الْأَحْيَاءِ ـ وَالْمُحْسِنُ حَيٌّ وَلَوْ كَانَ انْتَقَلَ إِلَى مَنَازِلِ الْمَوْتَ. كَمَا الْبَدَنُ إِذَا هُوَ سَقِيمٌ لَا يَنْفَعُهُ الطَّعَامُ ـ كَذَا الْعَقْلُ إِذَا غَلَقَهُ حُبُّ الدُّنْيَا لَا تَنْفَعُهُ الْمَوَاعِظُ. كُنْ عَلَى حِذْرٍ مِنَ الْكَرِيمِ إِذَا هَوَّنْتَهُ ـ وَمِنَ الْأَحْمَقِ إِذَا مَازَحْتَهُ ـ وَمِنَ الْعَاقِلِ اذَا غَضَّبْتَهُ ـ وَمِنَ الْفَاجِرِ إِذَا عَاشَرْتَهُ. بِسِتَّةِ خِصَالٍ يُعْرَفُ الْأَحْمَقُ

ـ بِالْغَضَبِ مِنْ غَيْرِ شَيءٍ ـ وَالْكَلَامِ فِي غَيْرِ نَفْعٍ ـ وَالثِّقَةِ فِي كُلِّ أَحَدٍ ـ وَبَدَلِهِ بِغَيرِ مَوْضِعِ الْبَدَلِ ـ وَسُؤَالِهِ عَنْ مَا لَا يُعْنِيهِ ـ وَبِأَنَّهُ مَا يَعْرِفُ صَدِيقَهُ مِنْ عَدُوِّهِ.

◆ لَا يَنْبَغِي لِلْفَاضِلِ أَنْ يُخَاطِبَ ذَوِى النَّقْضِ ـ كَمَا لَا يَنْبَغِي لِلصَّاحِي أَنْ يُكَلِّمَ السُّكَارَى. لَا يَنْبَغِي لِلْعَاقِلِ أَنْ يَسْكُنَ بَلَداً لَيْسَ فِيهِ خَمْسَةُ أَشْيَاءٍ ـ سُلْطَانٌ حَازِمٌ وَقَاضٍ عَادِلٌ وَطَبِيبٌ عَالِمٌ وَنَهْرٌ جَارٍ وَسُوقٌ قَائِمٌ. قِيلَ لِأَحْنَفِ بْنِ قَيْسٍ مَا أَحْلَمَكَ. قَالَ لَسْتُ بِحَلِيمٍ وَلَكِنِّي أَتَحَالَمُ ـ وَاللَّهِ إِنِّي.

SECTION II

Fables of Luqmān the Sage

أَمْثَالُ لُقْمَانَ الْحَكِيمِ

١ — إِنْسَانٌ وَأَسْوَدُ

إِنْسَانٌ مَرَّةً رَأَى رَجُلًا أَسْوَدَ وَهُوَ وَاقِفٌ فِي الْمَاءِ يَسْتَحِمُّ فَقَالَ لَهُ يَا أَخِي! لَا تُعَكِّرِ النَّهْرَ ـ فَإِنَّكَ لَا تَسْتَطِيعُ الْبَيَاضَ ـ وَلَا تَقْدِرُ عَلَيْهِ أَبَدَ الدَّهْرِ. هٰذَا مَعْنَاهُ ـ أَنَّ الْمَطْبُوعَ لَا يَتَغَيَّرُ طَبْعُهُ.

٢ — إِنْسَانٌ وَحَيَّتَانِ

إِنْسَانٌ مَرَّةً نَظَرَ حَيَّتَيْنِ تَقْتَتِلَانِ وَتَتَنَاهَشَانِ ـ وَإِذْ بِحَيَّةٍ أُخْرَى قَدْ أَتَتْ فَأَصْلَحَتْ بَيْنَهُمَا. فَقَالَ لَهَا الْإِنْسَانُ ـ لَوْ لَا أَنَّكِ أَشَرُّ مِنْهُمَا لَمْ تَدْخُلِي بَيْنَهُمَا. هٰذَا مَعْنَاهُ ـ أَنَّ إِنْسَانَ السَّوْءِ يَصِيرُ إِلَى أَبْنَاءِ جِنْسِهِ.

٣ — ذِئْبٌ

ذِئْبٌ مَرَّةً اِخْتَطَفَ خِنَّوْصاً صَغيراً ـ وَفيما هُوَ ذاهِبٌ بِهِ لَقِيَهُ الأَسَدُ ـ فَأَخَذَهُ مِنْهُ. فَقالَ الذِّئْبُ في نَفْسِهِ ـ عَجَبْتُ أَنَّ شَيْئاً اِغْتَصَبْتُهُ كَيْفَ لَمْ يَثْبُتْ مَعي. هذا مَعْناهُ ـ أَنَّ ما يُكْسَبُ مِنَ الظُّلْمِ لا يُقيمُ مَعَ صاحِبِهِ ـ وَإِنْ هُوَ أَقامَ مَعَهُ فَلا يَتَهَنَّأُ بِهِ.

٤ — قِطٌّ

قِطٌّ مَرَّةً دَخَلَ إِلى دُكّانِ حَدّادٍ ـ فَأَصابَ الْمِبْرَدَ مَرْمِيّاً. فَأَقْبَلَ يَلْحَسُهُ بِلِسانِهِ ـ وَلِسانُهُ يَسيلُ مِنْهُ الدَّمُ ـ وَهُوَ يَبْلَعُهُ وَيَظُنُّ أَنَّهُ مِنَ الْمِبْرَدِ إِلى أَنِ اِنْشَقَّ لِسانُهُ وَماتَ. هذا مَعْناهُ ـ مَنْ يُنْفِقْ مالَهُ في غَيْرِ الْواجِبِ ثُمَّ أَنَّهُ لا يَحْسُبُ حَتّى يُفْلِسَ وَهُوَ لا يَعْلَمُ.

٥ — غَزالٌ

غَزالٌ مَرَّةً مَرِضَ ـ فَكانَ أَصْحابُهُ مِنَ الْوُحوشِ يَأْتُونَ إِلَيْهِ وَيَعودونَهُ ـ وَيَرْعَوْنَ ما حَوْلَهُ مِنَ الْحَشيشِ وَالْعُشْبِ. فَلَمّا أَفاقَ مِنْ مَرَضِهِ اِلْتَمَسَ شَيْئاً لِيَأْكُلَهُ ـ فَلَمْ يَجِدْ فَهَلَكَ جوعاً. هذا مَعْناهُ ـ مَنْ كَثُرَ أَهْلُهُ وَإِخْوانُهُ كَثُرَتْ أَحْزانُهُ.

٦ — كِلَابٌ وَثَعْلَبٌ

كِلَابٌ مَرَّةً أَصَابُوا جِلْدَ سَبْعٍ. فَأَقْبَلُوا عَلَيْهِ يَنْهَشُونَهُ. فَنَظَرَهُمُ الثَّعْلَبُ ـ فَقَالَ لَهُمْ ـ أَمَّا لَوْ أَنَّهُ كَانَ حَيَّاً ـ لَرَأَيْتُمْ مَخَالِيبَهُ أَحَدَّ مِنْ أَنْيَابِكُمْ وَأَطْوَلَ. هذا مَعْنَاهُ ـ اَلَّذِينَ يَشْمَتُونَ بِقَوْمٍ أَجِلَّاءِ الْمِقْدَارِ إِذَا هُمْ تَضَعْضَعَتْ أَحْوَالُهُمْ.

٧ — كَلْبٌ وَأَرْنَبٌ

كَلْبٌ مَرَّةً طَرَدَ أَرْنَباً. فَلَمَّا أَدْرَكَهُ قَبَضَ عَلَيْهِ وَأَقْبَلَ يَعَضُّهُ بِأَنْيَابِهِ. فَإِذَا جَرَى الدَّمُ لَحِسَهُ بِلِسَانِهِ. فَقَالَ لَهُ الْأَرْنَبُ ـ أَرَاكَ تَعَضُّنِي كَأَنِّي عَدُوُّكَ ـ ثُمَّ تَبُوسُنِي كَأَنَّكَ صَدِيقِي. هذا مَعْنَاهُ مَنْ يَكُونُ فِي قَلْبِهِ غَشٌّ وَدَغَلٌ وَيُظْهِرُ إِشْفَاقاً وَمَحَبَّةً.

٨ — غَزَالٌ وَأَسَدٌ

غَزَالٌ مَرَّةً مِنْ خَوْفِهِ مِنَ الصَّيَّادِينَ اِنْهَزَمَ إِلَى مَغَارَةٍ. فَدَخَلَ إِلَيْهِ الْأَسَدُ فَافْتَرَسَهُ. فَقَالَ فِي نَفْسِهِ ـ اَلْوَيْلُ لِي أَنَا الشَّقِيِ! لِأَنِّي هَرَبْتُ مِنَ النَّاسِ ـ فَوَقَعْتُ فِي يَدِ مَنْ هُوَ أَشَدُّ مِنْهُمْ بَأْساً. هذا مَعْنَاهُ ـ مَنْ يَفِرُّ مِنْ خَوْفٍ يَسِيرٍ فَيَقَعُ فِي بَلَاءٍ عَظِيمٍ.

٩ — غَزَالٌ وَثَعْلَبٌ

غَزَالٌ مَرَّةً عَطِشَ ـ فَنَزَلَ إِلَى جُبِّ مَاءٍ ـ فَشَرِبَ مِنْهُ بِشَرَهٍ. ثُمَّ رَامَ الطُّلُوعَ فَلَمْ يَقْدِرْ. فَنَظَرَهُ الثَّعْلَبُ فَقَالَ لَهُ ـ يَا أَخِي ـ قَدْ أَسَأْتَ فِي فِعْلِكَ ـ إِذْ لَمْ تُمَيِّزْ قَبْلَ نُزُولِكَ كَيْفَ تَطْلُعُ وَبَعْدَ ذَلِكَ نَزَلْتَ. هَذَا مَعْنَاهُ ـ مَنْ يَنْفَرِدُ بِرَأْيِ نَفْسِهِ بِغَيْرِ مَشْوَرَةٍ.

١٠ — أَرَانِبُ وَثَعَالِبُ

اَلنُّسُورُ وَالْأَرَانِبُ مَرَّةً وَقَعَ بَيْنَهُمْ حَرْبٌ. فَمَضَى الْأَرَانِبُ إِلَى الثَّعَالِبِ يَسُومُونَ مِنْهُمُ الْحِلْفَ وَالْمُعَاضَدَةَ عَلَى النُّسُورِ. فَقَالُوا لَهُمْ ـ لَوْ لَا عَرَفْنَاكُمْ وَنَعْلَمُ لِمَنْ تُحَارِبُونَ لَفَعَلْنَا ذَلِكَ. هَذَا مَعْنَاهُ ـ أَنَّهُ مَا سَبِيلُ الْإِنْسَانِ أَنْ يُحَارِبَ لِمَنْ هُوَ أَشَدُّ بَأْسًا مِنْهُ.

١١ — أَرْنَبٌ وَلَبُوءَةٌ

أَرْنَبٌ مَرَّةً عَبَرَ عَلَى لَبُوءَةٍ قَائِلَةً لَهَا ـ أَنَا أُنْتِجُ فِي كُلِّ سَنَةٍ أَوْلَادًا كَثِيرَةً ـ وَأَنْتِ إِنَّمَا تَلِدِينَ فِي كُلِّ عُمْرِكِ وَاحِدًا أَوِ اثْنَيْنِ. فَقَالَتْ لَهَا اللَّبُوءَةُ ـ صَدَقْتِ غَيْرَ أَنَّهُ وَإِنْ كَانَ وَاحِدًا

فَهْوَ سَبْعَةٌ. هذا مَعْناهُ ـ أَنَّ وَلَدًا وَاحِدًا مُبَارَكًا خَيْرٌ مِنْ أَوْلَادٍ كَثِيرَةٍ عَاجِزِينَ.

١٢ ـ امْرَأَةٌ وَدَجَاجَةٌ

امْرَأَةٌ كَانَ لَهَا دَجَاجَةٌ ـ تَبِيضُ فِي كُلِّ يَوْمٍ بَيْضَةَ فِضَّةٍ. قَالَتِ الْمَرْأَةُ فِي نَفْسِهَا ـ إِنْ أَنَا كَثَّرْتُ عَلَفَهَا تَبِيضُ فِي كُلِّ يَوْمٍ بَيْضَتَيْنِ. فَلَمَّا كَثَّرَتْ عَلَفَهَا انْشَقَّتْ حَوْصَلَتُهَا فَمَاتَتْ. هذا مَعْناهُ ـ أَنَّ نَاسًا كَثِيرًا بِسَبَبِ رِبْحٍ يَسِيرٍ يُهْلِكُونَ رُؤُوسَ أَمْوَالِهِمْ.

١٣ ـ بُسْتَانِيٌّ

بُسْتَانِيٌّ يَوْمًا كَانَ يَسْقِي الْبَقْلَ. فَقِيلَ لَهُ لِمَاذَا الْبَقْلُ الْبَرِّيُّ بَهِيُّ الْمَنْظَرِ وَهُوَ غَيْرُ مَخْدُومٍ ـ وَهذَا الْجَوِّيُّ سَرِيعُ الذُّبُولِ وَالْعَطَبِ؟ قَالَ الْبُسْتَانِيُّ لِأَنَّ الْبَرِّيَّ تُرَبِّيهِ أُمُّهُ وَهذَا تُرَبِّيهِ امْرَأَةُ أَبِيهِ. هذا مَعْناهُ ـ أَنَّ تَرْبِيَةَ الْأُمِّ لِلْأَوْلَادِ أَفْضَلُ مِنْ تَرْبِيَةِ امْرَأَةِ الْأَبِ.

١٤ ـ إِنْسَانٌ وَصَنَمٌ

إِنْسَانٌ كَانَ لَهُ صَنَمٌ فِي بَيْتِهِ يَعْبُدُهُ ـ وَكَانَ يَذْبَحُ لَهُ فِي

كُلِّ يَوْمٍ ذَبِيحَةً. فَأَفْنَى جَمِيعَ مَا يَمْلِكُهُ عَلَى ذَلِكَ الصَّنَمِ. فَشَخَصَ لَهُ قَائِلًا ـ لَا تُفْنِ مَالَكَ عَلَيَّ ثُمَّ تَلُومُنِي فِي الْآخِرَةِ. هذَا مَعْنَاهُ ـ مَنْ يُنْفِقُ مَالَهُ فِي الْخَطِيئَةِ ثُمَّ يَحْتَجُّ أَنَّ اللَّهَ أَفْقَرَهُ.

١٥ ــ صَبِيٌّ وَعَقْرَبٌ

صَبِيٌّ مَرَّةً كَانَ يَصِيدُ الْجَرَادَ. فَنَظَرَ عَقْرَبًا ـ فَظَنَّ أَنَّهَا جَرَادَةٌ كَبِيرَةٌ. فَمَدَّ يَدَهُ لِيَأْخُذَهَا ـ ثُمَّ تَبَاعَدَ عَنْهَا. فَقَالَتْ لَهُ ـ أَمَّا لَوْ أَنَّكَ قَبَضْتَنِي فِي يَدِكَ لَتَخَلَّيْتَ عَنْ صَيْدِ الْجَرَادِ. هذَا مَعْنَاهُ ـ أَنَّ سَبِيلَ الْإِنْسَانِ أَنْ يُمَيِّزَ الْخَيْرَ مِنَ الشَّرِّ ـ وَيُدَبِّرَ لِكُلِّ شَيْءٍ تَدْبِيرًا عَلَى حَدِّهِ.

١٦ ــ دِيكَانِ

دِيكَانِ مَرَّةً اقْتَتَلَا فِي قَاذُورَةٍ ــ فَفَرَّ أَحَدُهُمَا وَمَضَى وَاخْتَفَى مِنْ وَقْتِهِ فِي بَعْضِ الْأَمَاكِنِ. فَأَمَّا الدِّيكُ الَّذِي غَلَبَ صَعِدَ فَوْقَ سَطْحٍ عَالٍ ـ وَجَعَلَ يُصَفِّقُ بِجَنَاحَيْهِ وَيَصِيحُ وَيَفْتَخِرُ. فَنَظَرَهُ بَعْضُ الْجَوَارِحِ ـ فَانْقَضَّ عَلَيْهِ وَاخْتَطَفَهُ لِوَقْتِهِ. هذَا مَعْنَاهُ ـ أَنْ لَا يَجُوزُ لِلْإِنْسَانِ أَنْ يَفْتَخِرَ بِقُوَّتِهِ وَشِدَّةِ بَأْسِهِ.

١٧ — اَلْوَزُّ وَالْخُطَّافُ

اَلْوَزُّ وَالْخُطَّافُ اِشْتَرَكَا فِي الْمَعِيشَةِ ـ فَكَانَ مَرْعَى الْجَمِيعِ فِي مَكَانٍ وَاحِدٍ. وَلَمَّا كَانَ ذَاتَ يَوْمٍ أَتَاهُمَا الصَّيَّادُونَ. فَأَمَّا الْخُطَّافُ فَلِأَجْلِ خِفَّتِهِ طَارَ جَمِيعُهُ وَسَلِمَ ـ وَأَمَّا الْوَزُّ فَأَدْرَكَهُ الصَّيَّادُونَ فَذَبَحُوهُ. هَذَا مَعْنَاهُ ـ مَنْ يُعَاشِرُ مَنْ لَا يُشَاكِلُهُ وَلَيْسَ هُوَ ابْنُ جِنْسِهِ.

١٨ — اَلنِّمْسُ وَالدَّجَاجُ

بَلَغَ النِّمْسَ أَنَّ الدَّجَاجَ مَرْضَى. فَقَامَ النِّمْسُ فَلَبِسَ جِلْدَ طَاوُسٍ وَأَتَى يَزُورُهُنَّ. فَقَالَ لَهُنَّ ـ السَّلَامُ عَلَيْكُنَّ أَيَّهَا الدَّجَاجُ ـ كَيْفَ أَنْتُنَّ وَكَيْفَ حَالُكُنَّ؟ فَقَالَ لَهُ الدَّجَاجُ ـ مَا نَحْنُ إِلَّا بِخَيْرٍ يَوْمَ لَا نَرَى وَجْهَكَ. هَذَا مَعْنَاهُ ـ مَنْ يُظْهِرُ الْمَحَبَّةَ رِيَاءً وَفِي قَلْبِهِ الدَّغَلُ وَالْبُغْضُ.

١٩ — كَلْبٌ وَذِئْبٌ

كَلْبٌ مَرَّةً كَانَ يَطْرُدُ ذِئْبًا وَيَفْتَخِرُ بِقُوَّتِهِ وَخِفَّةِ جَرْيِهِ وَانْهِزَامِ الذِّئْبِ بَيْنَ يَدَيْهِ. فَالْتَفَتَ إِلَيْهِ الذِّئْبُ قَائِلًا لَهُ ـ لَا تَظُنَّ

أنَّ خَوْفِي مِنْكَ ـ وَإِنَّمَا خَوْفِي مِمَّنْ هُوَ مَعَكَ يَطْرُدُنِي. هذا مَعْنَاهُ ـ أَنَّهُ لَا يَفْتَخِرُ الإِنْسَانُ إِلَّا بِمَا هُوَ لَهُ ـ وَلَا يَكُونُ افْتِخَارُهُ بِمَا لَيْسَ لَهُ.

٢٠ ــ بَعُوضَةٌ وَثَوْرٌ

بَعُوضَةٌ (يَعْنِي نَامُوسَةٌ) وقَفَتْ عَلَى قَرْنِ ثَوْرٍ ـ وَظَنَّتْ أَنَّهَا قَدْ ثَقُلَتْ عَلَيْهِ. فَقَالَتْ لَهُ ـ إِنْ كُنْتُ قَدْ ثَقُلْتُ عَلَيْكَ فَأَعْلِمْنِي حَتَّى أَطِيرَ عَنْكَ. فَقَالَ الثَّوْرُ ـ يَا هذِهِ! مَا حَسِسْتُ بِكِ فِي وَقْتِ نُزُولِكِ ـ ولَا إِذَا أَنْتِ طِرْتِ أَعْلَمُ بِكِ. هذا مَعْنَاهُ ـ مَنْ يَطْلُبُ أَنْ يَجْعَلَ لَهُ ذِكْرًا وَمَجْدًا وَهُوَ ضَعِيفٌ حَقِيرٌ.

٢١ ــ ذِئَابٌ

ذِئَابٌ أَصَابُوا جُلُودَ بَقَرٍ فِي جَوْرَةِ مَاءٍ تُبَلُّ ـ وَلَيْسَ عِنْدَهَا أَحَدٌ. فَاتَّفَقُوا كُلُّهُمْ جَمِيعًا عَلَى أَنَّهُمْ يَشْرَبُونَ الْمَاءَ كُلَّهُ حَتَّى يَصِلُوا لِلْجُلُودِ وَيَأْكُلُوهَا. فَمِنْ كَثْرَةِ مَا شَرِبُوا مِنَ الْمَاءِ انْفَلَقُوا كُلُّهُمْ وَمَاتُوا وَلَمْ يَصِلُوا إِلَى الْجُلُودِ. هذا مَعْنَاهُ ــ مَنْ هُوَ قَلِيلُ الرَّأْيِ وَيَعْمَلُ عَمَلًا كَمَا لَا يَجِبُ عَمَلُهُ.

٢٢ — صَبِيٌّ

صَبِيٌّ مَرَّةً رَمَى نَفْسَهُ فِي نَهْرِ مَاءٍ ـ وَلَمْ يَكُنْ يَعْرِفُ يَسْبَحُ ـ فَأَشْرَفَ عَلَى الْغَرَقِ. فَاسْتَعَانَ بِرَجُلٍ عَابِرٍ فِي الطَّرِيقِ. فَأَقْبَلَ إِلَيْهِ وَجَعَلَ يَلُومُهُ عَلَى نُزُولِهِ إِلَى النَّهْرِ. فَقَالَ لَهُ الصَّبِيُّ ـ يَا هَذَا خَلِّصْنِي أَوَّلًا مِنَ الْمَوْتِ وَبَعْدَ ذَلِكَ لَوِّ مْنِي. هَذَا مَعْنَاهُ ـ أَنَّهُ لَا يَجِبُ أَنْ يُلَامَ الْإِنْسَانُ عِنْدَ وُقُوعِهِ فِي شِدَّةٍ فِي غَيْرِ مَوْضِعِ اللَّوْمِ.

٢٣ — أَسَدٌ وَثَوْرَانِ

أَسَدٌ مَرَّةً خَرَجَ عَلَى ثَوْرَيْنِ ـ فَاجْتَمَعَا جَمِيعًا وَكَانَا يَنْطَحَانِهِ بِقُرُونِهِمَا ـ وَلَا يُمَكِّنَاهُ مِنَ الدُّخُولِ بَيْنَهُمَا. فَانْفَرَدَ بِأَحَدِهِمَا وَخَدَعَهُ وَوَعَدَهُ بِأَنْ لَا يُعَارِضَهُمَا إِنْ تَخَلَّى عَنْ صَاحِبِهِ. فَلَمَّا افْتَرَقَا افْتَرَسَهُمَا جَمِيعًا. هَذَا مَعْنَاهُ ـ أَنَّ مَدِينَتَيْنِ إِذَا اتَّفَقَ رَأْيُ أَهْلِهِمَا فَإِنَّهُ لَا يُمْكِنُ مِنْهُمَا عَدُوٌّ ـ فَإِذَا افْتَرَقَا هَلِكَا جَمِيعًا.

٢٤ — أَسَدٌ وَثَعْلَبٌ

أَسَدٌ مَرَّةً اشْتَدَّ عَلَيْهِ حَرُّ الشَّمْسِ. فَدَخَلَ إِلَى بَعْضِ الْمَغَائِرِ يَتَظَلَّلُ فِيهَا. فَلَمَّا رَبَضَ أَتَى إِلَيْهِ جُرَذٌ يَمْشِي فَوْقَ

ظَهْرِهِ. فَوَثَبَ قَائِمًا فَنَظَرَ يَمِينًا وَيَسَارًا وَهُوَ خَائِفٌ مَرْعُوبٌ. فَنَظَرَهُ الثَّعْلَبُ فَتَضَحَّكَ عَلَيْهِ. فَقَالَ لَهُ الْأَسَدُ ـ لَيْسَ مِنَ الْجُرَذِ خَوْفِي وَإِنَّمَا كَبُرَ عَلَيَّ احْتِقَارُهُ لِي. هذَا مَعْنَاهُ ـ أَنَّ الْهَوَانَ عَلَى الْعَاقِلِ أَشَدُّ مِنَ الْمَوْتِ.

٢٥ ـ حَمَامَةٌ

حَمَامَةٌ مَرَّةً عَطِشَتْ ـ فَأَقْبَلَتْ تَحُومُ فِي طَلَبِ الْمَاءِ. فَنَظَرَتْ عَلَى حَائِطٍ صُورَةَ صَحْفَةٍ مَمْلُوَّةٍ مَاءً. فَطَارَتْ بِسُرْعَةٍ وَضَرَبَتْ نَفْسَهَا إِلَى تِلْكَ الصُّورَةِ ـ فَانْشَقَّتْ حَوْصَلَتُهَا. فَقَالَتِ الْوَيْلُ لِي ـ أَنَا الشَّقِيَّةُ! لِأَنِّي أَسْرَعْتُ فِي طَلَبِ الْمَاءِ وَأَهْلَكْتُ رُوحِي. هذَا مَعْنَاهُ ـ أَنَّ التَّأْخِيرَ وَالتَّأَنِّيَ عَلَى الْأَشْيَاءِ أَخْيَرُ مِنَ الْمُبَادَرَةِ وَالْمُسَارَعَةِ إِلَيْهَا.

٢٦ ـ سُلَحْفَاةٌ وَأَرْنَبٌ

سُلَحْفَاةٌ وَأَرْنَبٌ مَرَّةً تَسَابَقَا ـ وَجَعَلَا الْحَدَّ بَيْنَهُمَا الْجَبَلَ يَسْتَبِقَانِ إِلَيْهِ. أَمَّا الْأَرْنَبُ فَلِإِدْلَالِهِ بِخِفَّتِهِ وَجَرْيِهِ تَوَانَى فِي الطَّرِيقِ وَنَامَ. وَأَمَّا السُّلَحْفَاةُ فَلِعِلْمِهَا بِثِقَلِ طَبِيعَتِهَا لَمْ تَكُنْ تَسْتَقِرُّ وَلَا تَتَوَانَى فِي الْجَرْيِ. فَوَصَلَتْ إِلَى الْجَبَلِ عِنْدَ

اسْتِيقَاظِ الْأَرْنَبِ مِنْ نَوْمِهِ. هذَا مَعْنَاهُ ـ أَنَّ طُولَ الرُّوحِ وَالْمُدَاوَمَةَ خَيْرٌ مِنَ الْخِفَّةِ وَالْعَجَلَةِ.

٢٧ ــ حَدَّادٌ وَكَلْبٌ

حَدَّادٌ مَرَّةً كَانَ لَهُ كَلْبٌ ـ وَكَانَ لَا يَزَالُ نَائِمًا مَا دَامَ الْحَدَّادُ يَعْمَلُ شُغْلًا. فَإِذَ رَفَعَ الْعَمَلَ وَجَلَسَ هُوَ وَأَصْحَابُهُ لِيَأْكُلُوا خُبْزاً اسْتَيْقَظَ الْكَلْبُ فَقَالَ الْحَدَّادُ ـ يَا كَلْبَ السُّوءِ لِأَيِّ سَبَبٍ صَوْتُ الْمِرْزَبَاتِ الَّذِي يُزَعْزِعُ الْأَرْضَ لَا يُيَقِّظُكَ وَصَوْتُ الْمَضْغِ الْخَفِيُّ إِذَا أَنْتَ سَمِعْتَهُ اسْتَيْقَظْتَ؟ هذَا مَعْنَاهُ ـ مَنْ يَسْمَعُ مَا يُصْلِحُ شَأْنَهُ ـ وَيَتَغَافَلُ عَمَّا لَيْسَ فِيهِ مَنْفَعَةٌ.

٢٨ ــ اَلْبَطْنُ وَالرِّجْلَانِ

اَلْبَطْنُ وَالرِّجْلَانِ تَخَاصَمُوا فِيمَا بَيْنَهُمْ أَيُّهُمْ يَحْمِلُ الْجِسْمَ. قَالَتِ الرِّجْلَانِ ـ نَحْنُ بِقُوَّتِنَا نَحْمِلُ الْجِسْمَ جَمِيعًا. قَالَ الْجَوْفُ ــ أَنَا إِنْ لَمْ أَنَلْ مِنَ الطَّعَامِ شَيْئًا. فَلَا كُنْتُمَا تَسْتَطِيعَانِ الْمَشْيَ فَضْلًا تَحْمِلَانِ شَيْئًا. هذَا مَعْنَاهُ ـ مَنْ يَتَوَلَّى أَمْرًا فَإِنْ لَمْ يَعْضُدْهُ الَّذِي هُوَ أَرْفَعُ وَأَشَدُّ مِنْهُ ـ فَمَا لَهُ قُدْرَةٌ عَلَى خِدْمَتِهِ وَلَا مَنْفَعَةَ لِرُوحِهِ أَيْضًا.

٢٩ — إِنْسَانٌ وَالْمَوْتُ

إِنْسَانٌ مَرَّةً حَمَلَ جُرْزَةَ حَطَبٍ فَثَقُلَتْ عَلَيْهِ. فَلَمَّا أَعْيَا وَضَجِرَ مِنْ حَمْلِهَا رَمَى بِهَا عَنْ كَتِفِهِ ـ وَدَعَا عَلَى رُوحِهِ بِالْمَوْتِ. فَشَخَصَ لَهُ الْمَوْتُ قَائِلًا هُوَذَا أَنَا لِمَاذَا دَعَوْتَنِي؟ فَقَالَ لَهُ الْإِنْسَانُ ـ دَعَوْتُكَ لِتَرْفَعَ هَذِهِ جُرْزَةَ الْحَطَبِ عَلَى كَتِفِي. هَذَا مَعْنَاهُ ـ أَنَّ الْعَالَمَ بِأَسْرِهِ يُحِبُّ الْحَيَاةَ فِي هَذِهِ الدُّنْيَا ـ وَمَا يَمَلُّونَ مِنَ الضَّعْفِ وَالشَّقَاءِ.

٣٠ — غَزَالٌ

أَيَّلٌ (يَعْنِي غَزَالٌ) مَرَّةً عَطِشَ. فَأَتَى إِلَى عَيْنِ مَاءٍ يَشْرَبُ. فَنَظَرَ خَيَالَهُ فِي الْمَاءِ ـ فَحَزِنَ لِدِقَّةِ قَوَائِمِهِ ـ وَسَرَّ وَابْتَهَجَ لِعِظَمِ قُرُونِهِ وَكِبَرِهَا. وَفِي الْحَالِ خَرَجَ عَلَيْهِ الصَّيَّادُونَ ـ فَانْهَزَمَ مِنْهُمْ. فَأَمَّا وَهُوَ فِي السَّهْلِ فَلَمْ يُدْرِكُوهُ ـ فَلَمَّا دَخَلَ فِي الْجَبَلِ وَكَثْرَةِ الشَّجَرِ فَلَحِقَهُ الصَّيَّادُونَ وَقَتَلُوهُ. فَقَالَ عِنْدَ مَوْتِهِ. الوَيْلُ لِي أَنَا الْمِسْكِينُ! الَّذِي ازْدَرَيْتُ بِهِ هُوَ خَلَّصَنِي ـ وَالَّذِي رَجَوْتُهُ أَهْلَكَنِي.

٣١ — أَسْوَدُ

أَسْوَدُ فِي يَوْمٍ ثَلْجٍ نَزَعَ ثِيَابَهُ وَأَقْبَلَ يَأْخُذُ الثَّلْجَ وَيَعْرُكُ بِهِ جِسْمَهُ. فَقِيلَ لَهُ ـ لِمَاذَا تَعْرُكُ جِسْمَكَ بِالثَّلْجِ؟ فَقَالَ لَعَلِّي أَبْيَضُّ. فَأَجَابَهُ رَجُلٌ حَكِيمٌ قَائِلًا لَهُ ـ يَا هَذَا! لَا تُتْعِبْ نَفْسَكَ ـ فَقَدْ يُمْكِنُ أَنَّ جِسْمَكَ يُسَوِّدُ الثَّلْجَ وَهُوَ لَا يَزْدَادُ إِلَّا سَوَادًا. هَذَا مَعْنَاهُ ـ أَنَّ أَهْلَ الشَّرِّ لَا يَسْتَطِيعُونَ فِعْلَ الْخَيْرِ. وَمَعْلُومٌ أَنَّ الشِّرِّيرَ يَقْدِرُ أَنْ يُفْسِدَ الْخَيْرَ ـ وَأَمَّا الْخَيْرُ لَا يَقْدِرُ أَحَدٌ عَلَى إِصْلَاحِ الشِّرِّيرِ.

٣٢ — خُنْفَسَةٌ وَنَحْلَةٌ

خُنْفَسَةٌ مَرَّةً قَالَتْ لِنَحْلَةِ الْعَسَلِ ـ لَوْ أَخَذْتِنِي مَعَكِ لَعَمِلْتُ عَسَلًا مِثْلَكِ وَأَكْثَرَ. فَأَجَابَتْهَا النَّحْلَةُ إِلَى ذَلِكَ. فَلَمَّا لَمْ تَقْدِرْ عَلَى مِثْلِ ذَلِكَ ـ ضَرَبَتْهَا النَّحْلَةُ بِحُمَتِهَا. وَفِيمَا هِيَ تَمُوتُ قَالَتْ فِي نَفْسِهَا ـ لَقَدِ اسْتَوْجَبْتُ مَا نَالَنِي مِنَ السُّوءِ ـ فَلَمْ يَكُنْ لِي بَصِيرَةٌ بِعَمَلِ الزِّفْتِ ـ لِمَاذَا الْتَمَسْتُ عَمَلَ الْعَسَلِ؟ هَذَا مَعْنَاهُ ـ مَنْ يَتَحَلَّى بِمَا لَيْسَ لَهُ ـ وَيَدَّعِي عَمَلَ مَا يَتَّجِهُ لَهُ.

٣٣ ــ أَسَدٌ وَإِنْسَانٌ

أَسَدٌ وَإِنْسَانٌ اصْطَحَبَا عَلَى الطَّرِيقِ ـ فَجَعَلَا يَتَشَاجَرَانِ بِالْكَلَامِ عَلَى كَثْرَةِ الْبَأْسِ. فَجَعَلَ الْأَسَدُ يُطْنِبُ فِي شِدَّتِهِ وَبَأْسِهِ فَنَظَرَ الْإِنْسَانُ عَلَى حَائِطٍ صُورَةَ رَجُلٍ ـ وَهْوَ يَخْنُقُ سَبُعاً فَافْتَخَرَ الْإِنْسَانُ فَقَالَ لَهُ الْأَسَدُ ـ لَوْ أَنَّ السِّبَاعَ مُصَوِّرُونَ دُونَ آدَمَ ـ لَمَا قَدَرَ الْإِنْسَانُ يَخْنُقُ سَبُعًا بَلْ كَانَ السَّبْعُ يَخْنُقُ الْإِنْسَانَ. هذَا مَعْنَاهُ ــ أَنْ مَا يُزَكَّى الْإِنْسَانُ بِشَهَادَةِ أَهْلِ جَلْدَتِهِ.

٣٤ ــ إِنْسَانٌ وَفَرَسٌ

إِنْسَانٌ كَانَ يَرْكَبُ فَرَسًا ـ وَكَانَتْ حَامِلًا. وَفِيمَا هُوَ فِي بَعْضِ الطَّرِيقِ أَنْتَجَتْ ابْنًا. فَتَبِعَ أُمَّهُ غَيْرَ بَعِيدٍ ثُمَّ وَقَفَ وَقَالَ لِصَاحِبِهِ ــ يَا سَيِّدِي! تَرَانِي صَغِيرًا وَلَا أَسْتَطِيعُ الْمَشْيَ. وَإِنْ مَضَيْتَ وَتَرَكْتَنِي هَاهُنَا فَهَلَكْتُ. وَإِنْ أَنْتَ أَخَذْتَنِي مَعَكَ وَرَبَّيْتَنِي إِلَى أَنْ أَقْوَى فَحَمَلْتُكَ عَلَى ظَهْرِي ـ وَأَوْصَلْتُكَ سَرِيعًا إِلَى حَيْثُ تَشَاءُ. هذَا مَعْنَاهُ ــ أَنَّهُ يَجِبُ أَنْ يُشَدَّ الْمَعْرُوفُ لِأَهْلِهِ وَمُسْتَحِقِّيهِ وَلَا يَطْرَحُوهُ.

٣٥ — كَلْبٌ وَشُوهَةٌ

كَلْبٌ مَرَّةً خَطَفَ بَضْعَةَ لَحْمٍ مِنَ المَسْلَخِ ـ وَنَزَلَ يَخُوضُ فِي النَّهْرِ. فَنَظَرَ خَيَالَهَا فِي المَاءِ ـ وَإِذَا هِيَ أَكْبَرُ مِنَ الَّتِي مَعَهُ. فَرَمَى بِهَا فَانْحَدَرَتْ شُوهَةً وَأَخَذَتْهَا. وَجَعَلَ الكَلْبُ يَجْرِي فِي طَلَبِ الكَبِيرَةِ فَلَمْ يَجِدْ شَيْئًا. فَرَجَعَ فِى طَلَبِ الَّتِي كَانَتْ مَعَهُ ـ فَلَمْ يُصِبْهَا. فَقَالَ مَا أَعْرَفُ أَقَلَّ رَأْيٍ مِنِّي لِأَنَّنِي ضَيَّعْتُ مَا كَانَ مَعِي وَطَلَبْتُ مَا لَا يَصِحُّ لِي. هَذَا مَعْنَاهُ — مَنْ يَتْرُكُ شَيْئًا قَلِيلًا مَوْجُودًا وَيَطْلُبُ كَثِيرًا مَفْقُودًا.

٣٦ — اَلشَّمْسُ وَالرِّيحُ

اَلشَّمْسُ وَالرِّيحُ تَخَاصَمَا فِيمَا بَيْنَهُمَا مَنْ مِنْهُمَا يَقْدِرُ أَنْ يُجَرِّدَ الإِنْسَانَ الثِّيَابَ فَاشْتَدَّتِ الرِّيحُ بِالْهُبُوبِ وعَصَفَتْ جِدًّا. فَكَانَ الإِنْسَانُ إِذَا اشْتَدَّتْ هُبُوبُ الرِّيحِ ضَمَّ ثِيَابَهُ إِلَيْهِ وَالْتَفَّ بِهَا مِنْ كُلِّ جَانِبٍ. فَلَمْ تَقْدِرِ الرِّيحُ عَلَى خَلْعِ ثِيَابِهِ مِنْ جَسَدِهِ بِشِدَّةِ عَصْفِهِ. فَلَمَّا أَشْرَقَتِ الشَّمْسُ وَارْتَفَعَ النَّهَارُ وَاشْتَدَّ الحَرُّ وَحَمِيَتِ الرَّمْضَاءُ فَخَلَعَ الإِنْسَانُ ثِيَابَهُ وَحَمَلَهَا

عَلَى كَتِفِهِ مِنْ شِدَّةِ الْحَرِّ. هذَا مَعْنَاهُ ـ مَنْ كَانَ مَعَهُ الإِتِّضَاعُ وَحُسْنُ الْخُلْقِ يَنَالُ مِنْ صَاحِبِهِ جَمِيعَ مَا يُرِيدُهُ.

٣٧ ـ أَسَدٌ وَثَوْرٌ

أَسَدٌ مَرَّةً أَرَادَ أَنْ يَفْتَرِسَ ثَوْرًا ـ فَلَمْ يَجْسُرْ عَلَيْهِ لِشِدَّةِ قُوَّتِهِ. فَمَضَى إِلَيْهِ لِيَحْتَالَ عَلَيْهِ قَائِلًا لَهُ ـ اعْلَمْ أَنَّنِي قَدْ ذَبَحْتُ خَرُوفًا سَمِينًا وَأَشْتَهِي أَنْ تَأْكُلَ عِنْدِي فِي هذِهِ اللَّيْلَةِ خُبْزًا. فَأَجَابَهُ إِلَى ذلِكَ. فَلَمَّا وَصَلَ إِلَى الْمَوْضِعِ وَنَظَرَهُ ـ وَإِذَا قَدِ اسْتَعَدَّ الأَسَدُ حَطَبًا كَثِيرًا وَخَلَاقِينَ كِبَارًا. فَوَلَّى الثَّوْرُ هَارِبًا لَمَّا عَايَنَ ذلِكَ. فَقَالَ لَهُ الأَسَدُ ـ لِمَاذَا وَلَّيْتَ بَعْدَ مَجِيئِكَ إِلَى هَاهُنَا؟ فَقَالَ لَهُ الثَّوْرُ لأَنِّي عَلِمْتُ أَنَّ هذَا الإِسْتِعْدَادَ لِمَا هُوَ أَكْبَرُ مِنَ الْخَرُوفِ. هذَا مَعْنَاهُ ـ أَنَّ مَا سَبِيلُ الْعَاقِلِ أَنْ يُصَدِّقَ عَدُوَّهُ وَلَا يَأْنَسَ إِلَيْهِ.

٣٨ ـ كَلْبَانِ

كَلْبٌ مَرَّةً كَانَ فِي دَارِ أَصْحَابِهِ دَعْوَةٌ. فَخَرَجَ إِلَى السُّوقِ فَلَقِيَ كَلْبًا آخَرَ. فَقَالَ لَهُ اعْلَمْ أَنَّ عِنْدَنَا الْيَوْمَ دَعْوَةٌ ـ فَامْضِ بِنَا لِنَقْصِفَ الْيَوْمَ جَمِيعًا. فَمَضَى مَعَهُ فَدَخَلَ بِهِ إِلَى الْمَطْبَخِ.

فَلَمَّا نَظَرَهُ الْخُدَّامُ قَبَضَ أَحَدُهُم عَلَى ذَنَبِهِ وَرَمَى بِهِ مِنَ الْحَائِطِ إِلَى خَارِجِ الدَّارِ. فَوَقَعَ مَغْشِيًّا عَلَيْهِ ـ فَلَمَّا أَفَاقَ وَانْتَفَضَ مِنَ التُّرَابِ فَرَآهُ أَصْحَابُهُ فَقَالُوا لَهُ ــ أَيْنَ كُنْتَ الْيَوْمَ فَكُنْتَ تَقْصِفُ؟ فَإِنَّنَا نَرَاكَ مَا خَرَجْتَ الْيَوْمَ تَدْرِي كَيْفَ الطَّرِيقُ. هذَا مَعْنَاهُ ـ أَنَّ كَثِيرِينَ يَتَطَفَّلُونَ فَيَخْرُجُونَ مَطْرُودِينَ بَعْدَ الاسْتِخْفَافِ بِهِمْ وَالْهَوَانِ.

٣٩ ــ اَلْعَوْسَجُ

اَلْعَوْسَجُ قَالَ لِلْبُسْتَانِيِّ ـ لَوْ أَنَّ لِي مَنْ يَهْتَمُّ بِي وَيَنْصُبُنِي فِي وَسَطِ الْبُسْتَانِ وَيَسْقِينِي وَيَخْدُمُنِي لَكَانَ الْمُلُوكُ يَشْتَهُونَ يَنْظُرُونَ زَهْرِي وَثَمَرِي. فَأَخَذَهُ وَنَصَبَهُ فِي وَسَطِ الْبُسْتَانِ فِي أَجْوَدِ الأَرْضِ ـ وَكَانَ يَسْقِيهِ فِي كُلِّ يَوْمٍ دَفْعَتَيْنِ ـ فَنَشَى وَقَوِيَ شَوْكُهُ وَتَفَرَّعَتْ أَغْصَانُهُ عَلَى جَمِيعِ الشَّجَرِ الَّتِي حَوْلَهُ. فَجَافَتْ وَأَصَلَتْ عُرُوقُهُ فِي الأَرْضِ وَامْتَلَأَ الْبُسْتَانُ مِنْهُ، وَمِنْ كَثْرَةِ شَوْكِهِ لَمْ يَكُنْ أَحَدٌ يَسْتَطِيعُ أَنْ يَتَقَدَّمَ إِلَيْهِ. هذَا مَعْنَاهُ ـ مَنْ يُجَاوِرُ إِنْسَانَ سُوءٍ فَإِنَّهُ كُلَّمَا أَكْرَمَهُ اشْتَدَّ شَرُّهُ وَتَمَرُّدُهُ ـ وَكُلَّمَا أَحْسَنَ إِلَيْهِ أَسَاءَ هُوَ الْفِعْلَ مَعَهُ.

٤٠ ـ أَسَدٌ وَثَعْلَبٌ

أَسَدٌ مَرَّةً شَاخَ وَضَعُفَ وَلَمْ يَقْدِرْ عَلَى كَسْرِ شَيْءٍ مِنَ الوُحُوشِ. فَأَرَادَ أَنْ يَحْتَالَ لِنَفْسِهِ فِي المَعِيشَةِ. فَتَمَارَضَ وَأَلْقَى نَفْسَهُ فِي بَعْضِ المَغَائِرِ. وَكَانَ كُلَّمَا أَتَاهُ شَيْءٌ مِنَ الوُحُوشِ لِيَعُودَهُ اِفْتَرَسَهُ دَاخِلَ المَغَارَةِ وَأَكَلَهُ. فَأَتَى الثَّعْلَبُ عَائِدًا لَهُ ـ فَوَقَفَ عَلَى بَابِ المَغَارَةِ مُسَلِّمًا عَلَيْهِ قَائِلًا لَهُ ـ كَيْفَ حَالُكَ يَا سَيِّدَ الوُحُوشِ؟ فَقَالَ لَهُ الأَسَدُ ـ لِمَاذَا لَا تَدْخُلُ يَا أَبَا الحُصَيْنِ؟ فَقَالَ لَهُ الثَّعْلَبُ ـ يَا سَيِّدِي! قَدْ كُنْتُ عَوَّلْتُ عَلَى ذَلِكَ غَيْرَ أَنَّنِي أَرَى عِنْدَكَ آثَارَ أَقْدَامٍ كَثِيرَةٍ قَدْ دَخَلُوا ـ وَلَا أَرَى أَنْ خَرَجَ مِنْهُمْ وَلَا وَاحِدٌ. هَذَا مَعْنَاهُ ـ أَنَّ مَا سَبِيلُ الإِنْسَانِ أَنْ يَهْجُمَ عَلَى أَمْرٍ إِلَّا حَتَّى يُمَيِّزَهُ.

٤١ ـ إِنْسَانٌ وَخِنْزِيرٌ

إِنْسَانٌ مَرَّةً حَمَلَ عَلَى بَهِيمَةٍ كَبْشًا وَعَنْزًا وَخِنْزِيرًا ـ وَتَوَجَّهَ إِلَى المَدِينَةِ لِيَبِيعَ الجَمِيعَ. فَأَمَّا الكَبْشُ وَالعَنْزُ فَلَمْ يَكُونَا يَضْطَرِبَانِ عَلَى البَهِيمَةِ ـ وَأَمَّا الخِنْزِيرُ فَإِنَّهُ كَانَ يُعَرِّضُ دَائِمًا وَلَا يَهْدَأُ. فَقَالَ لَهُ الإِنْسَانُ ـ يَا أَشَرَّ الوُحُوشِ لِمَاذَا

الْكَبْشُ وَالْعَنْزُ سَكُوتٌ؟ لَا يَضْطَرِبَانِ ـ وَأَنْتَ لَا تَهْدَأُ وَلَا تَسْتَقِرُّ. قَالَ لَهُ الْخِنْزِيرُ كُلُّ وَاحِدٍ يَعْلَمُ دَاءَ نَفْسِهِ ـ فَأَنَا أَعْلَمُ أَنَّ الْكَبْشَ لِصُوفِهِ وَالْعَنْزَ يُطْلَبُ لِلَبَنِهَا ـ وَأَنَا الشَّقِيُّ لَا صُوفَ لِي وَلَا لَبَنَ. وَأَنَا عِنْدَ وُصُولِي إِلَى الْمَدِينَةِ أُرْسَلُ إِلَى الْمَسْلَخِ ـ لَا مَحَالَةَ. هٰذَا مَعْنَاهُ ـ أَنَّ الَّذِينَ يَغْرَقُونَ فِي الْخَطَايَا وَالذُّنُوبِ الَّتِي قَدَّمَتْ أَيْدِيهِمْ يَعْلَمُونَ سُوءَ مُنْقَلَبِهِمْ وَمَاذَا تَكُونُ آخِرَتُهُمْ.

SECTION III

Miscellaneous Anecdotes

حِكَايَاتٌ مُخْتَلِفَةٌ

١ — اَلْحِكَايَة الْأُولَى

قِيلَ أَنَّ بَعْضَ الْعُلَمَاءِ تَخَاصَمَ مَعَ زَوْجَتِهِ ـ فَعَزَمَ عَلَى طَلَاقِهَا. فَقَالَتْ اُذْكُرْ طُولَ الصُّحْبَةِ. فَقَالَ وَاللَّهِ! مَا لَكِ عِنْدِي ذَنْبٌ سِوَى ذَلِكَ.

٢ — اَلْحِكَايَةُ الثَّانِيَةُ

قِيلَ أَنَّ أَعْرَابِيًّا وُلِّيَ الْبَحْرَيْنِ. فَجَمَعَ الْيَهُودَ وَقَالَ ـ مَا صَنَعْتُمْ بِعِيسَىٰ بْنِ مَرْيَمَ (عَلَيْهِ السَّلَامُ)؟ قَالُوا قَتَلْنَاهُ. قَالَ وَاللَّهِ! لَا تَخْرُجُوا مِنَ السِّجْنِ حَتَّى تُؤَدُّوا دِيَتَهُ. فَمَا خَرَجُوا حَتَّى أَخَذَ مِنْهُمُ الدِّيَةَ كَامِلَةً.

٣ — اَلْحِكَايَةُ الثَّالِثَةُ

قِيلَ اِجْتَازَ بَعْضُ الْمُغَفَّلِينَ بِمَنَارَةٍ ـ وَكَانُوا ثَلَاثَةَ نَفَرٍ. فَقَالَ أَحَدُهُمْ ـ مَا أَطْوَلَ الْبَنَّائِينَ فِي الزَّمَنِ الْأَوَّلِ حَتَّى وَصَلُوا إِلَى رَأْسِ هذِهِ الْمَنَارَةِ! فَقَالَ الثَّانِي ـ يَا أَبْلَهُ! كُلُّ يَبْنِيهَا وَلكِنْ يَعْمَلُونَهَا عَلَى وَجْهِ الْأَرْضِ وَيُقِيمُونَهَا. فَقَالَ الثَّالِثُ ـ يَا جُهَّالُ! كَانَتْ هذِهِ بِئْراً فَانْقَلَبَتْ مَنَارَةً.

٤ — اَلْحِكَايَةُ الرَّابِعَةُ

قَالَ بَعْضُ الْحُكَمَاءِ الْفُرْسِ أَخَذْتُ مِنْ كُلِّ شَيْءٍ أَحْسَنَ مَا فِيهِ. فَقِيلَ لَهُ ـ فَمَا أَخَذْتَ مِنَ الْكَلْبِ؟ قَالَ حُبَّهُ لِأَهْلِهِ وَذَبَّهُ عَنْ صَاحِبِهِ. قِيلَ فَمَا أَخَذْتَ مِنَ الْغُرَابِ؟ قَالَ شِدَّةَ حَذَرِهِ. قِيلَ فَمَا أَخَذْتَ مِنَ الْخِنْزِيرِ؟ قَالَ بُكُورَهُ فِي حَوَائِجِهِ. قِيلَ فَمَا أَخَذْتَ مِنَ الْهِرَّةِ؟ قَالَ تَمَلُّقَهَا عِنْدَ الْمَسْئَلَةِ.

٥ — اَلْحِكَايَةُ الْخَامِسَةُ

قِيلَ أَنَّ بَعْضَ الْبُخَلَاءِ اسْتَأْذَنَ عَلَيْهِ ضَيْفٌ وَبَيْنَ يَدَيْهِ خُبْزٌ وَقَدَحٌ فِيهِ عَسَلٌ. فَرَفَعَ الْخُبْزَ وَأَرَادَ أَنْ يَرْفَعَ الْعَسَلَ ـ وَظَنَّ

الْبَخِيلُ أَنَّ ضَيْفَهُ لَا يَأْكُلُ الْعَسَلَ بِلَا خُبْزٍ. فَقَالَ تَرَى أَنْ تَأْكُلَ عَسَلًا بِلَا خُبْزٍ؟ قَالَ نَعَمْ ـ وَجَعَلَ يَلْعَقُ لَعْقَةً بَعْدَ لَعْقَةٍ. فَقَالَ لَهُ الْبَخِيلُ ـ وَاللَّهِ يَا أَخِي! إِنَّهُ يَحْرِقُ الْقَلْبَ. فَقَالَ صَدَقْتَ ـ وَلَكِنَّ قَلْبَكَ.

٦ — اَلْحِكَايَةُ السَّادِسَةُ

قِيلَ أَنَّ بَعْضَ الْأُدَبَاءِ قَالَ حَضَرَ رَسُولُ مَلِكِ الرُّومِ عِنْدَ الْمُتَوَكِّلِ ـ فَاجْتَمَعْتُ بِهِ ـ فَقَالَ لَمَّا أُحْضِرَ الشَّرَابُ ـ مَا لَكُمْ مَعَاشِرَ الْمُسْلِمِينَ قَدْ حُرِّمَ عَلَيْكُمْ فِي كِتَابِكُمُ الْخَمْرُ وَلَحْمُ الْخِنْزِيرِ فَعَمِلْتُمْ بِأَحَدِهِمَا دُونَ الْآخَرِ؟ فَقُلْتُ لَهُ أَمَّا أَنَا فَلَا أَشْرَبُ الْخَمْرَ فَسَلْ مَنْ يَشْرَبُهَا. فَقَالَ إِنْ شِئْتَ أَخْبَرْتُكَ. قُلْتُ لَهُ قُلْ. فَقَالَ لَمَّا حُرِّمَ عَلَيْكُمْ لَحْمُ الْخِنْزِيرِ وَجَدْتُمْ بَدَلَهُ مَا هُوَ خَيْرٌ مِنْهُ لُحُومُ الطُّيُورِ ـ وَأَمَّا الْخَمْرُ فَلَمْ تَجِدُوا مَا يُقَارِبُهُ فَلَمْ تَنْتَهُوا عَنْهُ. قَالَ فَخَجِلْتُ مِنْهُ وَلَمْ أَدْرِ مَا أَقُولُ لَهُ.

٧ — اَلْحِكَايَةُ السَّابِعَةُ

سَأَلَ بَعْضُ الْمُلُوكِ وَزِيرَهُ ـ الْأَدَبُ يَغْلِبُ الطَّبْعَ أَمِ الطَّبْعُ يَغْلِبُ الْأَدَبَ؟ فَقَالَ ـ الطَّبْعُ أَغْلَبُ لِأَنَّهُ أَصْلٌ وَالْأَدَبُ

حِكَايَاتٌ مُخْتَلِفَةٌ

فَرْعٌ ـ وَكُلُّ فَرْعٍ يَرْجِعُ إِلَى أَصْلِهِ. ثُمَّ أَنَّ الْمَلِكَ اسْتَدْعَى بِالشَّرَابِ ـ وَأَحْضَرَ سَنَانِيرَ بِأَيْدِيهَا الشِّمَاعُ فَوَقَفَتْ حَوْلَهُ. فَقَالَ لِلْوَزِيرِ انْظُرْ خَطَاءَكَ فِي قَوْلِكَ ـ الطَّبْعُ أَغْلَبُ. فَقَالَ الْوَزِيرُ أَمْهِلْنِي اللَّيْلَةَ ـ قَالَ قَدْ أَمْهَلْتُكَ. فَلَمَّا كَانَتِ اللَّيْلَةُ الثَّانِيَةُ ـ أَخَذَ الْوَزِيرُ فِي كُمِّهِ فَأْرَةً وَرَبَطَ فِي رِجْلِهِ خَيْطًا وَمَضَى إِلَى الْمَلِكِ. فَلَمَّا قَبَلَتِ السَّنَانِيرُ بِأَيْدِيهَا الشِّمَاعُ أَخْرَجَ الْفَأْرَةَ مِنْ كُمِّهِ. فَلَمَّا رَأَتْهُ السَّنَانِيرُ رَمَتْ بِالشِّمَاعِ وَتَبِعَتِ الْفَأْرَةَ فَكَادَ الْبَيْتُ أَنْ يَحْتَرِقَ. فَقَالَ الْوَزِيرُ انْظُرْ أَيُّهَا الْمَلِكُ! كَيْفَ غَلَبَ الطَّبْعُ الْأَدَبَ وَرَجَعَ الْفَرْعُ إِلَى أَصْلِهِ. قَالَ صَدَقْتَ لِلَّهِ دَرُّكَ.

٨ ـ اَلْحِكَايَةُ الثَّامِنَةُ

قِيلَ لَمَّا تَشَاغَلَ عَبْدُ الْمَلِكِ ابْنُ مَرْوَانَ بِقِتَالِ مُصْعَبِ ابْنِ الزُّبَيْرِ اجْتَمَعَ وُجُوهُ الرُّومِ إِلَى مَلِكِهِمْ وَقَالُوا ـ قَدْ أَمْكَنَتْكَ الْفُرْصَةُ مِنَ الْعَرَبِ ـ فَقَدْ تَشَاغَلَ بَعْضُهُمْ بِبَعْضٍ ـ وَوَقَعَ بَأْسُهُمْ بَيْنَهُمْ ـ وَالرَّأْيُ أَنْ تَغْزُوَهُمْ فِي بِلَادِهِمْ ـ فَإِنَّكَ تُذِلُّهُمْ وَتَنَالُ حَاجَتَكَ مِنْهُمْ. فَنَهَاهُمْ عَنْ ذَلِكَ ـ فَأَبَوْا عَلَيْهِ

إِلَّا أَنْ يَفْعَلَ. فَلَمَّا رَأَى ذَلِكَ دَعَا بِكَلْبَيْنِ ـ فَأَحْرَشَ بَيْنَهُمَا ـ فَاقْتَتَلَا قِتَالًا شَدِيدًا. ثُمَّ دَعَا بِذِئْبٍ ـ فَخَلَّاهُ بَيْنَهُمَا ـ فَلَمَّا رَأَى الْكَلْبَانِ الذِّئْبَ تَرَكَا مَا كَانَ بَيْنَهُمَا وَأَقْبَلَا عَلَى الذِّئْبِ حَتَّى قَتَلَاهُ. فَقَالَ مَلِكُ الرُّومِ ـ هَكَذَا الْعَرَبُ ـ يَقْتَتِلُونَ بَيْنَهُمَا ـ فَإِذَا رَأَوْنَا وَهُمْ مَجْتَمِعُونَ تَرَكُوا ذَلِكَ وَأَقْبَلُوا عَلَيْنَا. فَعَرَفُوا صِدْقَ قَوْلِهِ ـ وَرَجَعُوا عَمَّا كَانُوا عَلَيْهِ.

٩ ــ اَلْحِكَايَةُ التَّاسِعَةُ

قِيلَ أَنَّ بَعْضَ الْمُلُوكِ كَانَ مُغْرَمًا بِحُبِّ النِّسَاءِ. وَكَانَ وَزِيرُهُ يَنْهَاهُ عَنْ ذَلِكَ. فَرَأَتْهُ بَعْضُ قِيَانِهِ مُتَغَيِّرَ الْحَالِ عَلَيْهِنَّ. فَقَالَتْ يَا مَوْلَايَ مَا هَذَا؟ فَقَالَ لَهَا أَنَّ وَزِيرِي فُلَانَ قَدْ نَهَانِي عَنْ مَحَبَّتِكُنَّ. فَقَالَتِ الْجَارِيَةُ ـ هَبْنِي لَهُ أَيُّهَا الْمَلِكُ ـ وَسَتَرَى مَا أَصْنَعُ بِهِ ـ فَوَهَبَهَا لَهُ ـ فَلَمَّا خَلَابِهَا تَمَتَّعَتْ مِنْهُ حَتَّى تَمَكَّنَ حُبُّهَا مِنْ قَلْبِهِ ـ فَقَالَتْ لَا تَقْرَبْنِي حَتَّى أَرْكَبَكَ وَتَمْشِي بِي خَطَوَاتٍ. فَأَجَابَهَا إِلَى ذَلِكَ ـ فَوَضَعَتْ عَلَيْهِ سَرْجًا وَجَعَلَتْ فِي رَأْسِهِ لِجَامًا وَرَكَبَتْهُ. وَكَانَتْ قَدْ أَرْسَلَتْ إِلَى الْمَلِكِ بِهَذَا الْخَبَرِ فَهَجَمَ عَلَيْهِ وَهُوَ عَلَى تِلْكَ الْحَالَةِ ـ

فَقَالَ مَا هَذَا أَيُّهَا الْوَزِيرُ كُنْتَ تَنْهَانِي عَنْ مَحَبَّتِهِنَّ وَهَذِهِ حَالَتُكَ مَعَهُنَّ. فَقَالَ أَيُّهَا الْمَلِكُ ـ مِنْ هَذَا كُنْتُ أَخَافُ عَلَيْكَ. فَاسْتَحْسَنَ مِنْهُ هَذَا الْجَوَابَ.

١٠ ـ اَلْحِكَايَةُ الْعَاشِرَةُ

قِيلَ أَنَّ قَيْصَرَ مَلِكِ الشَّامِ وَالرُّومِ ـ أَرْسَلَ رَسُولًا إِلَى مَلِكِ فَارِسٍ كِسْرَى أَنُوشِرْوَان صَاحِبِ الْإِيْوَانِ. فَلَمَّا وَصَلَ وَرَأَى عَظَمَةَ الْإِيْوَانِ وَعَظَمَةَ مَجْلِسِ كِسْرَى عَلَى كُرْسِيِّهِ وَالْمُلُوكِ فِي خِدْمَتِهِ ـ مَيَّزَ الْإِيْوَانَ ـ فَرَأَى فِي بَعْضِ جَوَانِبِهِ اِعْوِجَاجًا. فَسَأَلَ التَّرْجَمَانَ عَنْ ذَلِكَ ـ فَقِيلَ لَهُ ـ ذَلِكَ بَيْتٌ لِعَجُوزٍ كَرِهَتْ بَيْعَهُ عِنْدَ عِمَارَةِ الْإِيْوَانِ ـ فَلَمْ يَرَ الْمَلِكُ إِكْرَاهَهَا عَلَى الْبَيْعِ ـ فَأَبْقَى بَيْتَهَا فِي جَانِبِ الْإِيْوَانِ فَذَلِكَ مَا رَأَيْتَ وَسَأَلْتَ. فَقَالَ الرُّومِيُّ وَحَقِّ دِينِهِ! إِنَّ هَذَا الِاعْوِجَاجَ أَحْسَنُ مِنَ الِاسْتِقَامَةِ ـ وَحَقِّ دِينِهِ إِنَّ هَذَا الَّذِي فَعَلَهُ مَلِكُ الزَّمَانِ لَمْ يُؤَرَّخْ فِيمَا مَضَى لِمَلِكٍ وَلَا يُؤَرَّخُ فِيمَا بَقِىَ لِمَلِكٍ. فَأَعْجَبَ كِسْرَى كَلَامَهُ فَأَنْعَمَ عَلَيْهِ وَرَدَّهُ مَسْرُورًا مَحْبُورًا.

١١ — اَلْحِكَايَةُ الْحَادِيَةَ عَشَرَ

قِيلَ أَنَّ أَنُوشِيرِوَانَ وَضَعَ الْمَوَائِدَ لِلنَّاسِ فِي الْيَوْمِ نَيْرُوزَ وَجَلَسَ وَدَخَلَ وُجُوهُ مَمْلَكَتِهِ الْإِيوَانَ. فَلَمَّا فَرَغُوا مِنَ الطَّعَامِ جَاءُوا بِالشَّرَابِ وَأُحْضِرَتِ الْفَوَاكِهُ وَالْمَشْمُومُ فِي آنِيَةٍ مِنَ الذَّهَبِ وَالْفِضَّةِ. فَلَمَّا رُفِعَتْ آلَةُ الْمَجْلِسِ ـ أَخَذَ بَعْضُ مَنْ حَضَرَ جَامَ ذَهَبٍ وَزْنُهُ أَلْفُ مِثْقَالٍ فَخَبَّأَهُ تَحْتَ ثِيَابِهِ ـ وَأَنُوشِيرَوَانُ يَرَاهُ. فَلَمَّا فَقَدَهُ السَّاقِي قَالَ بِصَوْتٍ عَالٍ ـ لَا يَخْرُجَنَّ أَحَدٌ حَتَّى يُفَتَّشَ. فَقَالَ كِسْرَى وَلِمَ ـ فَأَخْبَرَهُ بِالْقِصَّةِ. فَقَالَ قَدْ أَخَذَهُ مَنْ لَا يَرُدُّهُ وَرَآهُ مَنْ لَا يَنُمُّ عَلَيْهِ فَلَا يُفَتَّشُ أَحَدٌ. فَأَخَذَهُ الرَّجُلُ وَمَضَى فَكَسَرَهُ وَصَاغَ مِنْهُ مِنْطَقَةً وَحِلْيَةً لِسَيْفِهِ وَجَدَّدَ لَهُ كِسْوَةً فَاخِرَةً. فَلَمَّا كَانَ فِي مِثْلِ جُلُوسِ الْمَلِكِ ـ دَخَلَ ذَلِكَ الرَّجُلُ بِتِلْكَ الْحِلْيَةِ ـ فَدَعَاهُ كِسْرَى وَقَالَ لَهُ ـ هَذَا مِنْ ذَاكَ. فَقَبَّلَ الْأَرْضَ وَقَالَ نَعَمْ ـ أَصْلَحَكَ اللَّهُ تَعَالَى.

١٢ — اَلْحِكَايَةُ الثَّانِيَةَ عَشَرَ

قِيلَ أَنَّ أَبَا دُلَامَةٍ الشَّاعِرَ ـ كَانَ وَاقِفًا بَيْنَ يَدَيِ السَّفَّاحِ

فِي بَعْضِ الْأَيَّامِ ـ فَقَالَ لَهُ سَلْنِي حَاجَتَكَ. فَقَالَ لَهُ أَبُو دُلَامَةٍ ـ أُرِيدُ كَلْبَ صَيْدٍ. فَقَالَ أَعْطُوهُ إِيَّاهُ ـ فَقَالَ وَأُرِيدُ دَابَّةً أَتَصَيَّدُ عَلَيْهَا. قَالَ أَعْطُوهُ إِيَّاهَا. قَالَ وَغُلَامًا يَقُودُ الْكَلْبَ وَيَصِيدُ بِهِ ـ قَالَ أَعْطُوهُ غُلَامًا. قَالَ وَجَارِيَةً تُصْلِحُ الصَّيْدَ وَتُطْعِمُنَا مِنْهُ. قَالَ أَعْطُوهُ جَارِيَةً. قَالَ هَؤُلَاءِ يَا أَمِيرَ الْمُؤْمِنِينَ ـ لَا بُدَّ لَهُمْ مِنْ دَارٍ يَسْكُنُونَهَا. فَقَالَ أَعْطُوهُ دَارًا تَجْمَعُهُمْ. قَالَ وَإِنْ لَمْ تَكُنْ لَهُمْ ضَيْعَةٌ فَمِنْ أَيْنَ يَعِيشُونَ؟ قَالَ قَدْ أَقْطَعْتُكَ عَشْرَ ضِيَاعٍ عَامِرَةٍ وَعَشْرَ ضِيَاعٍ غَامِرَةٍ. قَالَ وَمَا الْغَامِرَةُ يَا أَمِيرَ الْمُؤْمِنِينَ؟ قَالَ مَا لَا نَبَاتَ فِيهَا. قَالَ قَدْ أَقْطَعْتُكَ يَا أَمِيرَ الْمُؤْمِنِينَ ـ مِائَةَ ضَيْعَةٍ غَامِرَةٍ مِنْ فَيَا فِي بَنِي أَسَدٍ. فَضَحِكَ مِنْهُ وَقَالَ اِجْعَلُوهَا كُلَّهَا عَامِرَةً.

١٣ ــ اَلْحِكَايَةُ الثَّالِثَةَ عَشَرَ

قَالَ رَسُولُ اللَّهِ (صَلَّى اللَّهُ عَلَيْهِ وَسَلَّمَ) خَمْسٌ مَنْ كُنَّ فِيهِ كُنَّ عَلَيْهِ. قِيلَ وَمَا هُنَّ يَا رَسُولَ اللَّهِ؟ قَالَ النَّكْثُ وَالْمَكْرُ وَالْبَغْيُ وَالْخِدَاعُ وَالظُّلْمُ. فَأَمَّا النَّكْثُ فَقَالَ اللَّهُ تَعَالَى ـ فَمَنْ نَكَثَ فَإِنَّمَا يَنْكُثُ عَلَى نَفْسِهِ. وَأَمَّا الْمَكْرُ فَقَالَ

اللَّهُ تَعَالَى ـ وَلَا يَحِيقُ الْمَكْرُ السَّيِّئُ إِلَّا بِأَهْلِهِ. وَأَمَّا الْبَغْيُ فَقَالَ اللَّهُ تَعَالَى ـ يَا أَيُّهَا النَّاسُ إِنَّمَا بَغْيُكُمْ عَلَى أَنْفُسِكُمْ. وَأَمَّا الْخِدَاعُ فَقَالَ اللَّهُ تَعَالَى ـ يُخَادِعُونَ اللَّهَ وَالَّذِينَ آمَنُوا وَمَا يُخَادِعُونَ إِلَّا أَنْفُسَهُمْ. وَأَمَّا الظُّلْمُ فَقَالَ اللَّهُ تَعَالَى ـ وَمَا ظَلَمُونَا وَلَكِنَّ كَانُوا أَنْفُسَهُمْ يَظْلِمُونَ. وَقَالَ (عَلَيْهِ السَّلَامُ) ـ خَمْسَةٌ مِنْ خَمْسَةٍ مُحَالٌ ـ الْحُرْمَةُ مِنَ الْفَاسِقِ مُحَالٌ ـ وَالْكِبْرُ مِنَ الْفَقِيرِ مُحَالٌ ـ وَالنَّصِيحَةُ مِنَ الْعَدُوِّ مُحَالٌ ـ وَالْمَحَبَّةُ مِنَ الْحَسُودِ مُحَالٌ ـ وَالْوَفَاءُ مِنَ النِّسَاءِ مُحَالٌ ـ وَقَالَ (عَلَيْهِ السَّلَامُ) ـ اِغْتَنِمْ خَمْسًا قَبْلَ خَمْسٍ شَبَابَكَ قَبْلَ هَرَمِكَ ـ وَصِحَّتَكَ قَبْلَ سَقَمِكَ ـ وَغِنَاكَ قَبْلَ فَقْرِكَ ـ وَفَرَاغَكَ قَبْلَ شُغْلِكَ وَحَيَاتَكَ قَبْلَ مَوْتِكَ.

١٤ ـ اَلْحِكَايَةُ الرَّابِعَةَ عَشَرَ

عَنِ ابْنِ الْخَرِيفِ قَالَ حَدَّثَنِي وَالِدِي ـ قَالَ أَعْطَيْتُ أَحْمَدَ بْنَ السَّبَّ الدَّلَّالَ ثَوْبًا ـ وَقُلْتُ بِعْهُ لِي. وَبَيِّنْ هَذَا الْعَيْبَ الَّذِي فِيهِ لِمَنْ يَشْتَرِيهِ ـ وَأَرَيْتُهُ خَرْقًا فِي الثَّوْبِ. فَمَضَى وَجَاءَ فِي آخِرِ النَّهَارِ ـ فَدَفَعَ إِلَيَّ ثَمَنَهُ ـ وَقَالَ بِعْتُهُ عَلَى رَجُلٍ

أَعْجَمِيّ غَرِيبٌ بِهَذِهِ الدَّنَانِيرِ. فَقُلْتُ لَهُ ـ وَأَرَيْتُهُ الْعَيْبَ وَأَعْلَمْتُهُ بِهِ؟ فَقَالَ لَا وَاللَّهِ نَسِيتُ ذَلِكَ ـ فَقُلْتُ لَا جَزَاكَ اللَّهُ خَيْرًا اِمْضِ مَعِي إِلَيْهِ. وَذَهَبْتُ مَعَهُ وَقَصَدْنَا مَكَانَهُ فَلَمْ نَجِدْهُ. فَسَأَلْنَا عَنْهُ فَقِيلَ إِنَّهُ رَحَلَ إِلَى مَكَّةَ مَعَ قَافِلَةِ الْحَاجّ. فَأَخَذْتُ صِفَةَ الرَّجُلِ مِنَ الدَّلَّالِ وَاكْتَرَيْتُ دَابَّةً وَ لَحِقْتُ الْقَافِلَةَ وَسَأَلْتُ عَنِ الرَّجُلِ فَدُلِلْتُ عَلَيْهِ فَقُلْتُ لَهُ ـ الثَوْبُ الْفُلَانِيُّ الَّذِي شَرَيْتَهُ أَمْسِ مِنْ فُلَانٍ بِكَذَا وَكَذَا فِيهِ عَيْبٌ ـ فَهَاتِهِ وَخُذْ ذَهَبَكَ. فَقَامَ وَأَخْرَجَ الثَّوْبَ وَطَافَ عَلَى الْعَيْبِ حَتَّى وَجَدَهُ. فَلَمَّا رَآهُ قَالَ ـ يَا شَيْخُ أَخْرِجْ ذَهَبِي حَتَّى أَرَاهُ وَكُنْتُ لَمَّا قَبَضْتُهُ لَمْ أُمَيِّزْ وَلَمْ اَنْتَقِدْهُ. فَأَخْرَجْتُهُ ـ فَلَمَّا رَآهُ قَالَ هَذَا ذَهَبِي اِنْتَقِدْهُ يَا شَيْخُ. قَالَ فَنَظَرْتُ فَإِذَا هُوَ مَغْشُوشٌ لَا يُسَاوِي شَيْئًا. فَأَخَذَهُ وَرَمَى بِهِ وَقَالَ لِي ـ قَدِ اشْتَرَيْتُ مِنْكَ هَذَا الثَّوْبَ عَلَى عَيْبِهِ بِهَذَا الذَّهَبِ. وَدَفَعَ إِلَيَّ بِمِقْدَارِ ذَلِكَ الذَّهَبِ الْمَغْشُوشِ ذَهَبًا جَيِّدًا وَعُدْتُ بِهِ.

١٥ ــ اَلْحِكَايَةُ الْخَامِسَةَ عَشَرَ

قِيلَ أَنَّ مَلِكَ الصِّينِ بَلَغَهُ عَنْ نَقَّاشٍ مَاهِرٍ فِي النَّقْشِ

وَالتَّصْوِيرِ فِي بِلَادِ الرُّومِ. فَأَرْسَلَ إِلَيْهِ وَأَشْخَصَهُ وَأَمَرَهُ بِعَمَلِ شَيْءٍ مِمَّا يَقْدِرُ عَلَيْهِ مِنَ النَّقْشِ وَالتَّصْوِيرِ مِثَالًا يُعَلِّقُهُ بِبَابِ الْقَصْرِ عَلَى الْعَادَةِ. فَنَقَشَ لَهُ فِي رُقْعَةٍ صُورَةَ سُنْبُلَةِ حِنْطَةٍ خَضْرَاءَ قَائِمَةً وَعَلَيْهَا عُصْفُورٌ ـ وَأَتْقَنَ نَقْشَهُ وَهَيْئَتَهُ حَتَّى إِذَا نَظَرَهُ أَحَدٌ لَا يَشُكُّ فِي أَنَّهُ عُصْفُورٌ عَلَى سُنْبُلَةٍ خَضْرَاءَ وَلَا يُنْكِرُ شَيْئًا مِنْ ذَلِكَ غَيْرَ النُّطْقِ وَالْحَرَكَةِ. فَأَعْجَبَ الْمَلِكَ ذَلِكَ وَأَمَرَهُ بِتَعْلِيقِهِ وَبَادَرَ بِإِدْرَارِ الرِّزْقِ عَلَيْهِ إِلَى انْقِضَاءِ مُدَّةِ التَّعْلِيقِ. فَمَضَتْ سَنَةٌ إِلَّا بَعْضَ أَيَّامٍ. وَلَمْ يَقْدِرْ أَحَدٌ عَلَى إِظْهَارِ عَيْبٍ أَوْ خَلَلٍ فِيهِ. فَحَضَرَ شَيْخٌ مُسِنٌّ وَنَظَرَ إِلَى الْمِثَالِ وَقَالَ ـ هَذَا فِيهِ عَيْبٌ. فَأُحْضِرَ إِلَى الْمَلِكِ وَأُحْضِرَ النَّقَّاشُ وَالْمِثَالُ ـ وَقَالَ مَا الَّذِي فِيهِ مِنَ الْعَيْبِ فَأَخْرِجْ عَمَّا وَقَعْتَ فِيهِ بِوَجْهٍ ظَاهِرٍ وَدَلِيلٍ وَإِلَّا حَلَّ بِكَ النَّدَمُ وَالتَّنْكِيلُ. فَقَالَ الشَّيْخُ أَسْعَدَ اللَّهُ الْمَلِكَ وَأَلْهَمَهُ السَّدَادَ ـ مِثَالُ أَيِّ شَيْءٍ هَذَا الْمَوْضُوعُ؟ فَقَالَ الْمَلِكُ مِثَالُ سُنْبُلَةٍ مِنْ حِنْطَةٍ قَائِمَةٍ عَلَى سَاقِهَا وَفَوْقَهَا عُصْفُورٌ. فَقَالَ الشَّيْخُ أَصْلَحَ اللَّهُ الْمَلِكَ ـ أَمَّا الْعُصْفُورُ فَلَيْسَ بِهِ خَلَلٌ وَإِنَّمَا الْخَلَلُ فِي وَضْعِ السُّنْبُلَةِ. قَالَ

الْمَلِكُ وَمَا الْخَلَلُ وَقَدِ امْتَزَجَ غَضَبًا عَلَى الشَّيْخِ. فَقَالَ الْخَلَلُ فِي اسْتِقَامَةِ السُّنْبُلَةِ لِأَنَّ فِي الْعُرْفِ أَنَّ الْعُصْفُورَ إِذَا حَطَّ عَلَى سُنْبُلَةٍ أَمَا لَهَا لِثِقْلِ الْعُصْفُورِ وَضُعْفِ سَاقِ السُّنْبُلَةِ وَلَوْ كَانَتِ السُّنْبُلَةُ مُعْوَجَّةً مَائِلَةً لَكَانَ ذَلِكَ نِهَايَةً فِي الْوَضْعِ وَالْحِكْمَةِ. فَوَافَقَ الْمَلِكُ عَلَى ذَلِكَ وَسَلَّمَ .

١٦ — اَلْحِكَايَةُ السَّادِسَةَ عَشَرَ

قِيلَ إِنَّ عَبْدَ الْمَلِكِ بْنَ مَرْوَانَ خَطَبَ يَوْمًا بِالْكُوفَةِ. فَقَامَ إِلَيْهِ رَجُلٌ مِنْ آلِ سَمْعَانَ ـ فَقَالَ مَهْلًا يَا أَمِيرَ الْمُؤْمِنِينَ اقْضِ لِصَاحِبِي هَذَا بِحَقِّهِ ثُمَّ اخْطُبْ ـ فَقَالَ وَمَا ذَاكَ؟ فَقَالَ إِنَّ النَّاسَ قَالُوا لَهُ مَا يُخَلِّصُ ظُلَامَتَكَ مِنْ عَبْدِ الْمَلِكِ إِلَّا فُلَانٌ. فَجِئْتُ بِهِ إِلَيْكَ لِأَنْظُرَ عَدْلَكَ الَّذِي كُنْتَ تَعِدُنَا بِهِ قَبْلَ أَنْ تَتَوَلَّى هَذِهِ الْمَظَالِمَ. فَطَالَ بَيْنَهُ وَبَيْنَهُ الْكَلَامُ ـ فَقَالَ لَهُ الرَّجُلُ يَا أَمِيرَ الْمُؤْمِنِينَ إِنَّكُمْ تَأْمُرُونَ وَلَا تَأْتَمِرُونَ ـ وَتَنْهَوْنَ وَلَا تَنْتَهُونَ ـ وَتَعِظُونَ وَلَا تَتَّعِظُونَ أَفَنَقْتَدِي بِسِيرَتِكُمْ فِي أَنْفُسِكُمْ أَمْ نُطِيعُ أَمْرَكُمْ بِأَلْسِنَتِكُمْ؟ وَإِنْ قُلْتُمْ أَطِيعُوا أَمْرَنَا وَاقْبَلُوا نُصْحَنَا ـ فَكَيْفَ يَنْصَحُ غَيْرَهُ مَنْ غَشَّ نَفْسَهُ؟ وَإِنْ قُلْتُمْ

خُذُوا الْحِكْمَةَ حَيْثُ وَجَدْتُمُوهَا وَاقْبَلُوا الْعِظَةَ مِمَّنْ سَمِعْتُمُوهَا ـ فَعَلَى مَا قَلَّدْنَاكُمْ أَزِمَّةَ أُمُورِنَا وَحَكَّمْنَاكُمْ فِي دِمَائِنَا وَأَمْوَالِنَا أَوَمَا تَعْلَمُونَ أَنَّ مِنَّا مَنْ هُوَ أَعْرَفُ مِنْكُمْ بِصُنُوفِ اللُّغَاتِ وَأَبْلَغُ فِي الْعِظَاتِ؟ فَإِنْ كَانَتِ الْإِمَامَةُ قَدْ عَجَزْتُمْ عَنْ إِقَامَةِ الْعَدْلِ فِيهَا فَخَلُّوا سَبِيلَهَا وَأَطْلِقُوا عِقَالَهَا يَبْتَدِرُهَا أَهْلُهَا الَّذِينَ قَاتَلْتُمُوهُمْ فِي الْبِلَادِ وَشَتَّتُّمْ شَمْلَهُمْ بِكُلِّ وَادٍ أَمَا وَاللَّهِ لَإِنْ بَقِيَتْ فِي يَدِكُمْ إِلَى بُلُوغِ الْغَايَةِ وَاسْتِيفَاءِ الْمُدَّةِ تَضْمَحِلُّ حُقُوقُ اللَّهِ وَحُقُوقُ الْعِبَادِ؟ فَقَالَ لَهُ كَيْفَ ذَلِكَ؟ فَقَالَ لِأَنَّ مَنْ كَلَّمَكُمْ فِي حَقِّهِ زُجِرَ وَمَنْ سَكَتَ قُهِرَ فَلَا قَوْلُهُ مَسْمُوعٌ وَلَا ظُلْمُهُ مَرْفُوعٌ وَلَا مَنْ جَارَ عَلَيْهِ مَرْدُوعٌ. وَبَيْنَكَ وَبَيْنَ رَعِيَّتِكَ مَقَامٌ تَذُوبُ فِيهِ الْجِبَالُ حَيْثُ مُلْكُكَ هُنَاكَ خَامِلٌ وَعِزُّكَ زَائِلٌ وَنَاصِرُكَ خَاذِلٌ وَالْحَاكِمُ عَلَيْكَ عَادِلٌ. فَأَكَبَّ عَبْدُ الْمَلِكِ عَلَى وَجْهِهِ يَبْكِي ـ ثُمَّ قَالَ لَهُ ـ فَمَا حَاجَتُكَ؟ فَقَالَ عَامِلُكَ بِالسَّمَاوَةِ ظَلَمَنِي وَلَيْلُهُ لَهْوٌ وَنَهَارُهُ لَغْوٌ وَنَظَرُهُ زَهْوٌ. فَكَتَبَ إِلَيْهِ بِإِعْطَائِهِ ظُلَامَتَهُ ثُمَّ عَزَلَهُ.

✯✯✯

SECTION IV

Extracts from the Book of a "Thousand Nights and a Night"

وَاقِعَةُ الْأَخِ الْحَجَّامِ السَّادِسِ — وَهِيَ مَأْخُوذَةٌ مِن كِتَابِ أَلْفِ لَيْلَةٍ وَلَيْلَةٍ

أمّا أخي السّادِسُ ـ فكان فقيرًا بعد أن كان غنيًّا. ومِن أخبارِهِ انّه خرج يوما يطلبُ شيئًا يسدُّ بِهِ جوعَهُ. فرأى في بـعـضِ الطُّرُقِ دارًا حسـنـةً ـ لها دهليزٌ واسعٌ وبابٌ مرتفعٌ ـ وعـلـى البابِ خدمٌ وحشمٌ وأمرٌ ونهيٌ. فسـأل بـعـضَ الـحاضرين هُناك عن صاحب الدّارِ. فقال له ـ هو رجلٌ مِن البَرامِكة. فتقدّم أخي إلى الدّارابنة وطلب منهم صدقةً. فقالوا له ـــ الباب قدّامك ـــ ادخلْ فيه ـ فانّك تجدُ ما تحبُّ وتـختارُ. فدخل أخي ومَشى ساعةً ـ فرأى ساحةً وسيعةً ـ في

وسطها بستانٌ ما رأى مَثَلَه ـ فبقى متحيّرًا فيما رأى. ثمّ انّه مشى نحو مجلسٍ من المجالس. فلمّا دخله وجد فى صدرِه اِنسانًا حسَنَ الوجهِ جالسًا على بساطٍ مُذْهَبٍ ـ فقصده. فلمّا رآه الرّجلُ صاحب المجلسِ رحّب به وسأله عن حالِه. فأخبره أنه محتاجٌ يُريدُ شَيْئًا في حبّ اللّه. فاغتمّ ذلك الرّجلُ غَمًّا شديدًا ـ وقال يا سُبحانَ اللّه! أنا موجودٌ فى هذهِ البلدةِ وأنت جائعٌ. ثمّ وعد أخى بخيرٍ وطيّب خاطِرَه وصاح على الخَدَمِ بأن يأتُوا بِطشتٍ وإبريقٍ.

فلمّا حضر الطشتُ والإبريقُ ـ قال لأخي تقدّمْ واغسِلْ يدَك. فقام أخى ليغسلَ يدَه ـ فما رأى طشتًا ولا إبريقًا. فمدّ يده كأنّه يغلسها ـ ثم صاحَ الرجلُ يا غِلمانُ قَدِّموا المائدةَ ـ فلم يَرَ أخي شَيْئًا. ثمّ قال لأخي تفضّلْ كُلْ مِن هـذا الطّعامِ ولا تستحي بحياتى عليك. فمدَّ أخى يدهُ وجعـل نفسـه كـأنّـه يـأكُلُ. فقال الرجلُ لأخي ـ باللّه كُلْ واشبعْ بطنك ـ لانّك جائـعٌ وانظر إلى حسنِ هَذا الخُبْزِ وبياضِه. فقال له أخي ما رأيتُ أحسنَ من هذا الطعام ولا ألذَّ

مِنْ كِتَابِ أَلْفِ لَيْلَةٍ وَلَيْلَةٍ

مـن هَـذا الـخُبـزِ. وقـال أخـي فـى نفسِهِ الظَّاهر أنَّ هذا رجلٌ يـحـبُّ الـلَّهوَ والمزاحَ. ثمَّ قال له الرَّجلُ انَّ هذا الخبزَ خبزتْهُ جـاريةٌ اشتـريتُهـا بـخـمـس مائة دينارٍ. ثمَّ صاح بأعلى صوتِهِ وقال ـ يا غلامُ قدِّم الهريسةَ وصُبَّ عليها دهنًا كثيرًا. والتفَتَ إلـى أخـي وقـال لـه ـ باللّٰه عليك يا ضيفي هَلْ أكَلْتَ أطْيَبَ من هَذه الهريسةِ؟ فقال لا ولا أظنُّ السلطانُ أكل مثلَها.

فقال لأخي كُلْ ولا تستحي. وكان أخي يُحرِّكُ فمَه ويـمـضـغُ مـن غيـر شَيْءٍ. والرَّجلُ يطلب نوعًا بعد نوعٍ وما هُناك شيْءٌ. ويأمُر أخى بالأكلِ وهو لا يَرَى شيئًا ـ واستولَى عـلـى قُـواه الضَّـعـفُ مِـن شِـدَّةِ الـجـوعِ. ثم قال لـه أخي قد اكتـفـيـتُ يـا سيِّدي مِنَ الطَّعـامِ. فَصاحَ الرَّجلُ شِيلوا هذا وقَـدِّمـوا الـحلاوات. ثمَّ قال لأخى كُلْ من هَذا لوزينج ومن هـذه القطائف ومن هذه الكُنافةِ. فقال له أخي ما أطيبَ هذه الـحـلاوات ومـا أحسنَها ـ وهو يُحرِّك فمَه وأشْداقَهُ. ثمَّ قال لـه أخى قـد اكتفيتُ يا سيِّدي وامتلأَ بطنى أنعم اللّٰهُ عليك كـمـا أنعمتَ عليَّ. فقال له الرَّجلُ تُريدُ ان تشربَ؟ قال أخي

نعم. ثمّ قال أخي في نفسِه لأعملنَّ معه عملاً يُتَوِّبُه عن هَذِهِ الأفعال. ثمّ قال الرّجلُ ـ قَدِّموا الشّرابَ. فمدَّ أخي يدَه كانّه يتناولُ قدحًا وقرَّبَ يدَه إلَى فِمِه كانّه يشربُه. فقالَ له الرّجلُ هنيئًا مريئًا. فقال له أخي هنَّاك اللّهُ بالعافيةِ. ثمّ أنّه جعل نفسَه سُكرانَ وشرع في العَربدةِ. ثمّ شال يده ولطم الرّجلُ لطمةً دوَّخَتْ رأسَه واَلحقه بالثّانية. فقال الرّجل ما هَذا يا سفلة؟ فقال أخي يا سيّدي هذا من بخار طعامك اللذيذ وشرابك المُفرِّح. فلمّا سمع الرّجلُ كلامَ أخي ضحك ضحكًا شديدًا وقالَ واللّه ما رأيتُ مثلك مسخرةً وها أنا قد عفوتُ فكُنْ نديمي ولا تُفارقني أبدًا. ثمَّ أنَّه أمر له بالطَّعامِ والشّرابِ فأكَلَ أخي وشَرِبَ واستراحَ.

قَصّةُ التّاجِرِ مع زوجتِهِ ـ وَهِيَ مَأْخُوذَةٌ مِن كِتابِ الفِ لَيلةٍ وَلَيلةٍ

قيل انّه كان تاجرٌ غَنيٌّ وله مالٌ ورجالٌ ومواشي وجِمالٌ. وله زوجةٌ وَ أولادٌ وكان مسكنُه في البرّيّةِ وهو

مِنْ كِتَابِ أَلْفِ لَيْلَةٍ وَ لَيْلَةٍ

ممتحنٌ في الزَّرْعِ. وكان يفهم لُغةَ البهائمِ والحيواناتِ. وإذا أفْشَى لِأَحدٍ سِرَّهُ ماتَ ـ وكان لايُظهرُ لأحدٍ سِرَّهُ خوفًا من المَوتِ. وكان عنده فى الرَّبضِ ثورٌ وحمارٌ وكُلٌّ منهما مربوطٌ في مَعلِفِه. وكانا مُتقارِبَيْنِ أحدهما بجنبِ الآخرِ. فيومًا من الأيَّامِ بينما التَّاجرُ جالِسٌ إلى جانِبِهِما وَ أولادُه يلعبون قدَّامه ـ سَمِعَ الثورَ يقولُ لِلحمارِ ـ يا أبا اليَقْظان هنيًّا لك! فيما أنت فيه من الرَّاحةِ ـ اَلْخِدْمَةُ لك والكَنْسُ والرَّشُّ تحتَك ومَأْكلُك الشَّعيرُ المُغَرْبَلُ وشُرْبُك الماءُ البارِدُ. وأمَّا أنا فيا لِتَعَبي لِأَنَّهُم يأخذونى من نصفِ اللَّيْلِ ويُشغِلونى بالحرثِ ويُركِّبون على رقبتى الفِدَّانَ والمِحراثَ وأبْدأ أعملُ من أوَّلِ النَّهارِ الى آخرِ النَّهارِ بشَقِّ الأرضِ ـ ثمَّ اُكَلَّفُ ما لا طاقَةَ لى بهِ وأُقاسِي أنواعَ الإهانةِ مثل الضَّربِ والزَّجرِ من الزُّرَّاعِ القاسي وقد تَهَرَّتْ أجفاني وانسلختْ رقبتي وسيقاني وفي آخرِ النَّهارِ يحبسوني في الدَّارِ ويطرحون لى التِّبْنَ والفُوْلَ وأبيتُ طولَ اللَّيلِ في النجاسةِ والروائحِ الدَّنِسَةِ. وأنت لم تزَلْ في المكانِ المكنوسِ المرشوشِ ـ وفي

المَعْلَفِ النَّظيفِ الملآن من التِّبنِ النَّاعِم واقفًا مستريحًا ـ وفى النَّادر يعرضُ لصاحبك التَّاجر حاجةٌ ضروريَّةٌ حتَّى أنَّه يركبك ويعود بك سريعًا ـ وفيما عدا ذلك من الأوقاتِ أنت مستريحٌ وأنا تعبانُ وأنت نائمٌ وأنا يقظانُ وأنت معزَّزٌ وأنا مُهانٌ.

فلمَّا إنتهى كلامُ الثورِ قال له الحمارُ يا أفطَحُ صَدَقَ الَّذي سَمَّاك ثورًا لأنَّك بليدٌ إلى الغاية ـ وليس عندك مكرٌ ولا حيلةٌ ولا خُبثٌ ـ بل انَّك تُبْدِي النُّصح وتبذل المجهود قُدّامَ صاحبك وتَشْقى وتقتُلُ نفسَك في راحة غيرك. أمَا سمعتَ الشَّاعر يقول ـ

أُكَـلِّفُ نـفسـي كُـلَّ يومٍ وليـلةٍ
هُـمـومًـا عـلى مـن لا أفوزُ بخيرِهِ
كـما سـوَّدَ القَصَّارُ بالشَّمسِ وجهَهُ
حريصـاً عـلى تبييضِ أثوابِ غيرهِ

ويُـقـالُ فى المثلِ ـ مَنْ عَدِمَ التوفيقَ ضَلَّ عن الطَّريقِ. وأنت تخرج من صلاةِ الصُّبحِ ـ وما تُعاودُ إلَّا المغربَ ـ

وتُقاسي نهارَك كله أصنافَ العذابِ تارةً بالضَّربِ وتارةً بالـحَرْثِ وتارةً بالنَّهْرِ. وعند مجيئِك يربطُك الزرَّاعُ على المَعْلَفِ المُنتنِ الرَّائحةِ. فتبقي تُخَبِّطُ وتمرحُ وتنطحُ بقرنِك وتلبطُ برجليك ويظنّ بك أنّك فرحان وتصيحُ كثيرًا ـ وما تُصدِّق متى يُلقوا لك العلَف ـ فتسرعُ في أكلِهِ بحرصٍ ـ وتشحنُ بطنَك منه ـ فلو أنّك تنبطحُ عند مجيئِك على قَفَاك ــ وإذا قَدَّمُوا لك العلَفَ لا تأكلُ منه ـ وتجعل نفسَك ميِّتًا كان أوفق لك وكنتَ تلقي من الرَّاحةِ أضعافَ ما أنا فيه. فلمّا سمع الثورُ كلامَ الحِمارِ وما أبدي له من النـصيـحـةِ شكره كثيرًا بلسانِ حالِهِ ـ ودَعَا له وجازاهُ خيرًا ـ وتيقَّنَ أنّه ناصِحٌ له وقال له نِعْمَ الرَّأيُ يا أبا اليقظانِ! هَذا كُلُّهُ يجري والتاجرُ يسمعه كَوْنَه يعرفُ لغةَ الحيواناتِ.

فلمّا كان ثاني يـوم جاء خادمُ التاجرِ وأخذ الثورَ وركَّب عليه المِحراثَ واستعمله كالعادةِ. فبَدَأ الثورُ يُقصِّرُ في العـمـلِ والـحرثِ فضربه الزُّرَّاعُ ضربًا مُوْجعًا ـ فكسر المـحراثَ وهربَ لأنّه قَبِلَ وصِيَّةَ الحمارِ. فلحقه الزرَّاعُ

وضربه كثيرًا حتّى أنّه أيِسَ من الحياة ـ فلم يَزَلْ الثورُ يقوم ويقع إلى أن صار المساء. فجاءَ به الزُّرّاعُ إلى الدّارِ وربطَهُ على المَعْلَفِ فبطَّلَ الثورُ الصُّراخَ والمرحَ واللَّبطَ بالرِّجْلَيْنِ ثُمَّ انَّه تباعَدَ عن العلفِ ـ فتعجَّبَ الزُّرّاعُ من ذلك. ثم أنّ الزرّاعَ أتَاه بالفولِ والعلفِ فشَمَّهُ وتأخَّرَ عنه ونامَ بعيدًا منه وبات بغيرِ أكلٍ إلى الصّباحِ. فلمّا جاء الزرّاعُ ووجدَ العلفَ والفُولَ والتِّبنَ مكانَهُ ولم ينقُصْ منه شيءٌ ورأى الثورَ قد انتفخَ بطنه وتكسَّفَتْ أحوالُهُ ومدَّ رجليه حَزِنَ عليه وقال في نفسِهِ ـ واللهِ لقد كان مستضعفًا بالأمسِ فلأجلِ ذلك كان مقصِّرًا بالعملِ.

ثمّ انّ الزرّاعَ جاءَ إلى التّاجرِ وقال له ـ يا مولاي ـ انّ الثورَ لم يأكُلْ العلفَ في هذهِ المُدَّةِ من يومَيْنِ ـ ولا ذاق منه شيئًا. فعرِفَ التّاجرُ الأمرَ بتمامِهِ كوْنه قد سمع ما قاله الحمارُ كما مرَّ سابقًا. ثمّ قال للزرّاع اِذْهَبْ إلى الحمارِ المكَّارِ وشُدَّ عليه المحراثَ واجتهدْ في استعمالِهِ حتّى أنّه يحرث مكانَ الثّورِ. فأخذه الزرّاعُ وشَدَّ عليه المحراثَ واجْتَهَدَ به وكَلَّفَهُ

ما لا يُطيقُ حتّى أنّه حرثَ مكانَ الثَّورِ ـ ولم يَزَلْ الحمارُ يأكلُ الضَّربَ حتى انسلخَ جلدُه وتَهَرَّأَتْ أضلاعُه ورقبتُه. فلمّا كان المساءُ جاءَ بالحمارِ إلى الدّارِ وهو لا يقدرُ على أن يجرَّ يدَيْه ولا رِجليه. وامّا الثورُ فانّه كان ذَلك النهار كلّه نائمًا مستريحًا ـ وقد أكل علفَه كلّه بالهناً والسُّرورِ والرَّاحةِ ـ وهو طولَ نهارِهِ يدعُو للحمار ولم يدْرِ ما أصابَ الحمارَ من أجلِه. فلمّا أقبَلَ اللَّيلُ دخل الحمارُ على الثَّورِ ـ فنهض له الثورُ قائمًا وقال له ـ بُشِّرْتَ بالخيرِ يا أبا اليقظانِ! لانك أَرَحْتَني في هذا اليوم وهَنَّأْتَنِي بطعامى. فما ردَّ عليه الحمارُ جوابًا من غيظِهِ وتعبِهِ ومن الضَّربِ الذي أَكَلَهُ ـ إلّا أنّه قال في نفسِه ـ كُلُّ هَذا جَرَى عَلَيَّ من سُوءِ تدبيري ونصيحتي لغيري ـ كما قيل في المثل ـ كنت قاعِدًا بطُولي ما خَلّانى فُضُولِي. ولٰكن إذا لم أَعْمَلْ له حيلةً وأرُدُّهُ إلَى ما كان فيه هلكتُ. ثُمَّ انّ الحمارَ راح إلى معلفِهِ والثورُ يُخَوِّرُ ويدعُو له.

فلمّا جرى للحمارِ مع الثَّورِ ما جرى خرجَ التاجرُ هو وزوجتُه على السّطحِ ليلةً مُقمِرةً ـ والقمَرُ مُبدِرٌ. فاشرَفَ على

مِنْ كِتَابِ أَلْفِ لَيْلَةٍ وَلَيْلَةٍ

الثور والحمار من السّطح ـ فسمعَ الحمارَ يقول للثّورِ ـ أخبِرْني يا أبا الثِّيران! ما الّذي تَصنَعُهُ غداً. فقال له الثورُ وما الّذي أصنعه غير الّذي أشرْتَ به عليَّ ـ وهذا الثَّورُ في غايةِ الحُسنِ وفيه راحةٌ كُلِّيَّةٌ ـ وما بقيتُ أفارقُهُ مطلقًا ـ وإذا قُدِّمَ العَلَفُ امكرْ فاتمارَضْ وَانْفُخْ بطني. فقال له الحمارُ إيّاكَ أن تفعلَ ذَلِكَ! فقال له لِماذا؟ فقال له ـ سمعتُ صاحبَنا يقولُ لِلزَّرَّاعِ ـ إنْ كان الثورُ لم يأكُلْ علفه ولم ينهَضْ قائمًا فادْعُ الجَزَّارَ حتّى يذبحَهُ ـ وتصدَّقْ بلحمه واجعلْ جلدَه نِطعًا ـ وأنا خائفٌ عليك من ذَلك. ولكن اقبلْ نُصحي قبلَ أن يُصيبَك هذا المصابُ ـ فاذا قدّموا لك العَلَفَ فكُلْهُ وانْهَضْ وارفُسْ برجليك الارضَ. وإذا لم تفعل ذلك فانَّ صاحبَنا يذبحُك. فنهض الثّورُ وصاح. فلمّا سمع التّاجرُ هذا المقالَ نهض على حَيلِه وضحك ضحكًا عاليًا. فقالت له زوجتُه وما هو الّذي جرى حتّى انّك ضحكْتَ هَذا الضحكَ الكثيرَ؟ لعلَّك تهزأُ بي. فقال لها كَلّا. فقالت له ان كنتَ لم تهزأ بى قُلْ لي ما سببُ ضِحْكِكَ. قال لها ـ لستُ أقدر على

ذلك ـ وأخاف اذا بُحْتُ بالسِّرِّ اموتُ. فقالت له زوجته ـ والله انّك تكذب ـ وإنما أردتَ إخفاءَ الكلامِ عني. ولكن وحَقِّ رَبِّ السَّماءِ! إذا لم تقُلْ لي ما سببُ ضحِكِك ما أقعُدُ عندك من الآن. وجَلَسَتْ تبكي. فقال لها زوجها التاجرُ ويْلَكِ ما لَكِ تبكين اتّقي اللهَ وعدّي عن سُؤالك ودَعينا من هذا الكلام. فقالت لا بُدَّ من أن تقولَ لي ما سببُ ضحكك. فقال إنّني سألتُ ربّي أن يُعَلِّمَنِي لُغَةَ الحيواناتِ فعَلَّمَنِي ـ ثمّ إنّي عاهدتُه أن لا أُعلمَ بذلك أحدًا ـ وإنْ أفشيتُ سِرّي فأمُتُ. فقالت لا بُدَّ من أن تقولَ لي ما سمعتَ من الثورِ والحمارِ. ودَعْكَ تموت هذه السّاعةَ. فقال لها ادعي أهلَكِ فدعَتْهم. ثمّ أتَوا بعضَ الجيرانِ ـ فأعلمهم التّاجرُ بأنّه قد حضرته الوفاةُ. فجلسوا يبكون عليه ـ ثمّ بكوا عليه أولادُه الصِّغارُ والكِبارُ والزّرّاعُ والغِلمانُ والخُدّامُ وسائرُ مَنْ يلوذُبه ـ وصار عنده في الدارِ عزاءٌ عظيمٌ.

ثمّ انّه دعا بالشّهودِ ـ فلمّا حضروا أوْفَى زوجتَه حقَّها وجعل وصيًّا على أولادِه ـــ وأعتق جواريَه وودّع أقرباءَهُ

وأهلَه فتباكوا كلُّهم. ثمّ بكتِ الشُّهودُ وأقبلوا على المرأةِ يقولون لها ـ ارجعي عن غيِّكِ واعدلي عن هذا الأمرِ ـ ولو لم يتيقَّنْ أنّه إذا باح بالسِّر يموتُ ـ ما كان فعل هذه الفعال وكان أخْبَركِ به. فقالت لهم ـ واللّٰه لم أرجع عنه إذا لم يخبرني به. فبكى الحاضرون بُكاءً شديدًا.

وكان عنده فى البيتِ خمسُون طيرًا من الدَّجاج ومعها دِيْكٌ. فبينما هو يُودّع أهلَه وعبيدَه سَمِعَ كلبًا من الكلابِ يقـول للدِّيك بلُغَته ـ ما أقلّ عقلك أيّها الدّيكُ! واللّٰهِ لقد خاب مِنْ ربّاك أفي مثل هذا الوقتِ تطيرُ من ظهر هـذه إلى ظهر هذه خيّبك اللّٰهُ تعالى؟ فلمّا سمع التاجرُ هذا الكلامَ سَكَتَ ولم يتكلَّمْ ـ وبقى يسمعُ ما يقول الكلبُ والدّيكُ. فقال الدّيك وما فى هذا اليوم أيّها الكلبُ؟ فقال ـ أما علمتَ أن سيدي اليوم متهيّأً للموت لأنّ زوجتَه تُريدُ أن يبـوح لها بالسِّرِّ الذي علَّمه اللّٰهُ به؟ وإذا باح لها بذلك مات من ساعتِه ـ وها نحن في حُزْنٍ عليه وأنت تُصفِّقُ وتصحيح ما تستحي على نفسك. فلمّا سمع الدِيكُ كلامَ الكلب

قال له إذا كان سيّدُنا قليلَ العقلِ عديمَ التّدبيرِ ـ ما يقدر على تدبيرِ أمرِه مع زوجةٍ واحدةٍ ـ فما لبقاءِ حياتِهِ فائدة.

فقال الكلبُ وماذا يصنعُ سيّدُنا؟ فقا له الدّيكُ ـ أنا عندي خمسون إمرأة ـ أُغضبُ هذه وأُرضي هذه وأُطعم هذه وأُجوّعُ هذه بحسنِ تدبيري ـ وكُلّهنّ تحت طاعتي. وسيّدُنا يدّعي العقلَ والكمالَ ـ وعنده إمرأةٌ واحدةٌ ـ ما عرَفَ تدبيرَ أمرِه معَها. فقال الكلبُ أيّها الدّيكُ اَفِدْنا كيف يصنعُ سيّدُنا حتّى يخلص من هذا الأمر؟

فقال الدّيكُ ـ يقوم في هذه السّاعة ـ ويأخذ عصًا بيده ــ ويدخل بها إلى بعضِ المخازن ـ ويغلق البابَ ويضربها حتّى يكسرَ أضلاعَها وظهرَها وأرجُلَها ـ ويقول لها أنتِ تسألين عن شيءٍ ما لَكِ فيه غرضٌ حتّى تقولَ أتوبُ يا سيّدي ـ لا أسئلُك عن شيءٍ طُولَ عمري ـ توبةً يا مولايَ. فيوجعها ضربًا شديدًا ـ فإذا فعَل هذا استراحَ من الهمِّ وعاشَ. ولكن ما عنده عقلٌ ولا فهمٌ. فلمّا سمعَ التاجرُ هذا الكلامَ من الدّيكِ قامَ مُسرعاً ـ وأخذَ الخيزران ـ ودخلَ الخزانة

وأمرها بالدُّخول معه. فدخلت وهي فرحانةً فقام مسرعًا وغلَق البابَ ونزل بالخيزران على كَتِفَيْها وظهرِها وأضلاعها وأيديها وأرجلها. وهى تُعيّط وترتعد وتنتفض ـ وهو يضربها ويقول لها ـ تسألِيني عن شَيْءٍ ما لكِ فيه حاجةٌ؟ فتقول له أنا واللهِ من التَّائبين ـ ولا أسألُك عن شيءٍ ـ وقد ثبتُ توبةً نَصُوحًا. فبعد ذلك فتح لها الباب ـ وخرجتْ وهي تائبةٌ. ففرح الشُّهودُ والجيرانُ ـــ وأمُّها وأبوها ـ وانقلبَ العزاءُ بالفرحِ والسّرورِ. وتعلَّم التاجرُ حُسْنَ التّدبيرِ من الدِّيْكِ.

✯✯✯

SECTION V

Extracts from the Ikhwānu-ṣ-Ṣafā.

فِي بَيَانِ بَدْءِ العَدَاوَةِ بَيْنَ الجانِّ وبَنِي آدَمَ وَهُوَ مَأْخُوذٌ مِنْ رِسَالةِ إِخْوانِ الصّفا

قال الحكيمُ إنّ فى قديم الأيّام والأزمان قبل خَلْقِ أبي البُشَرِ كان سُكَّانُ الأرضِ بني الجانِّ وقاطِنُوها. وكانوا قد أَطْبَقُوا الأرضَ بَحرًا وبَرًّا سهلًا وجَبَلًا. فطالَتْ أعمارُهم وكثرتِ النعمةُ عندهم ـ وكان فيهم المُلْكُ والنُّبوَّةُ والدِّينُ والشَّريعةُ. فَطَغَتْ وبَغَتْ وتركَتْ وصيّةَ أنبيائِها وأكثرَتْ في الأرضِ الفسادَ ـ فضجَّتِ الأرضُ ومَنْ عليها من جورِهم. فلمَّا انقضَى الدَّورُ واستأنَفَ القَرْنُ أرسلَ اللّهُ جُنْدًا من الملائكةِ نزلَتْ من السَّماء فسكنَتْ في الأرضِ وطردَتْ بَني

الـجانّ إلى أطرافِ الارضِ مُنهَزِمةً. وأخَذَتْ سَبايا كثيرةً منها ــ وكـان فيـمَـنْ أُخِـذَ أسيراً عزازيلُ ابليسُ اللّعينُ فرعونُ آدم وحَوّاء ــ وهو إذ ذاك صَبِيٌّ لم يُدرِكْ. فلمّا نَشأ مع الملائكةِ تَـعـلَّـمَ مِـن عِـلْمها وتشبَّهَ بها في ظاهرِ الأمرِ ورسمهُ وجوهرُهُ غيـرُ رُسُـومِها وجوهرِها. فلما تطاولتِ الأيّامُ صار رَئيساً فيها آمِرًا ناهيًا مَتبوعًا حِينًا ودَهراً من الزّمان.

فـلـمّـا انـقـضَـى الـدَّورُ واستـأنف القرنُ أَوْحَى اللهُ إلى أولـئِك الـمـلائكةِ الّذين كانوا في الأرضِ فقال لهم ــ إِنِّي جَاعِلٌ فِي الأرْضِ خَـلِـيـفَـةً مِـنْ غَيرِكُم وأَرْفَعُكُم إِلَى السَّمَاءِ. فكرِهَتِ الملائكةُ الذين كانوا في الأرضِ مفارقةَ الوَطنِ المألوفِ وقالت فـى مـراجعةِ الـجـواب ــ أَتَجْعَلُ فِيهَا مَنْ يُفْسِدُ فِيهَا ويَسْفِكُ الـدِّمـاء كَـمـا كَـانَتْ بَنُو الجانّ ونحنُ نُسَبِّحُ بِحَمْدِكَ ونُقَدِّسُ لَكَ؟ قال إِنِّي أَعْـلَـمُ مَا لَا تَعْلَمُون لأنّي آلَيْتُ على نَفْسي أن لا أترُكُ آخرَ الأمرِ بعد انقضاءِ دولةِ آدمَ وذُرِّيّته على وجهِ الأرضِ أحدًا مـن الـمـلائكةِ ولا مِن الجنِّ ولا من الإنسِ ولا من سائر الحيواناتِ ولهذه اليمين سِرٌّ قد بَيَّنَاهُ فى موضع آخر.

مِنْ رِسالَةِ إِخْوانِ الصَّفا

فلـمّا خلق آدم فسوّاه ونفخ فيه من رُوْحِهِ وخلق منه زوجتَه حَوّاءَ أَمَرَ الملائكةَ الذين كانوا فى الأرضِ بالسّجودِ له والطّاعةِ. فانقادَتْ له الملائكةُ بأجمعِهم غير عَزازيلَ - فإنّه أَنِفَ وتكبّر وأخذَتْـهُ حَمِيّـةُ الجاهليّةِ والحسدُ لمّا رأى أن رِئاستَهُ قد زالَتْ واحتاج أن يكون تابعًا بعد أَنْ كانَ مَتبوعًا ومرؤُسًا بعد أَنْ كـان رئيسًا. وأَمَرَ أُولئك الملائكةَ أن اصعَدُوا بآدم إلى السّماءِ فأَدْخِلُوه الجنّةَ. ثمّ أَوْحى اللّه تعالى إلى آدَمَ (علـيـه السّـلام) وقال - يا آدَمُ اسكُنْ أَنْتَ وزَوجُكَ الـجنّةَ وكُلا مِنها رَغَدًا حَيْثُ شِئتُما وَلا تَقْرَبا هذِهِ الشَّجَرَةَ فَتَكُونا مِنَ الظّالِمِين.

وهذه الجنّةُ بُستانٌ بالمشرقِ على رأسِ جبلِ الياقوتِ الذي لا يقدرُ أحدٌ من البشرِ أن يصعَدَ إلى هُناك - وهى طيّبةُ التربةِ معتدلُ الهواءِ صَيفًا وشتاءً وليلًا ونهارًا - كثيرةُ الأنهارِ مُـخْضَرَّةُ الأشجارِ مُفنّنةُ الفواكهِ والثّمارِ والرياضِ والرياحينِ والأزهارِ كثيرةُ الـحيوانـاتِ الغيرِ المؤذيةِ والطيورِ الطيّبةِ الأصـواتِ الـلـذيذةِ الإلحانِ والنَّغَماتِ. وكان على رأسِ آدمَ

وحَوَّاءَ شعرٌ طويلٌ مُدَلَّى كَاحْسَنِ ما يكون على الجواري الأبْكارِ ويَبْلُغُ قَدَمَيْهِـما ويَسْتُرُ عَوْرَتَيْهِما وكان دِثارًا لهما وسِتْرًا وزِيْنَـةً وجَمـالًا. وكـان يـمشيانِ على حافّاتِ تلك الأنهارِ بيـن الـرياحينِ والأشجارِ ـ ويأكلان من ألوانِ تلك الثمـارـ ويشربانِ من مياهِ تلك الأنهارِ بلا تَعَبٍ من الأبدانِ ولا عنـاءٍ مـن النّـفـوسِ. ولا شَقـاءٍ من كَدِّ الحَرْثِ والزَرْع والسَّقيِ والحصدِ والدِّياسةِ والطَحْنِ والعَجْنِ والخُبْزِ والغَزْلِ والـنَسـجِ والغَسْل كما في هذه الأيَّامِ أوْلادُهما مُبْتَلُونَ به من شقاوةِ أسبابِ المعاشِ في هذه الدنيا.

وكـان حُكْمُـهـمـا فـي تـلك الـجـنّـةِ كحُكْمِ أَحَدِ الحيـوانـاتِ التى هناك مستودَعَيْنِ مُسْتَمْتِعَيْنِ مستريحين متـلـذّذيـن ـ وكـان الـلـه تعـالى أَلْهَمَ إلى آدمَ أسماءَ تلك الأشجارِ والثمارِ والرَّياحينِ وأسماءَ تلك الحيواناتِ التى هناك فلمّا نطق سأَلَ الملائكةَ عنها فلم يكن عندها جوابٌ ـ فـقـعـد عـنـد ذلك آدمُ مُعلِّمًا يُعرِّفُها أسماءَ ها ومنافعها ومضارَّهـا ـ فانقادتِ الملائكةُ لأمرِه ونهيِهِ لِما تبيَّنَ لها من

فضلِهِ عليها. ولمّا رأى عزازيلُ ذلك ازداد حسدًا وبُغْضًا فاحْتال لهما المكرَ والخديعةَ والحِيلَ غدًا وعِشاءً. ثم أتاهُما بصورةِ النّاصحِ فقال لهما ـ لقد فضّلكما اللهُ بما أنْعَم عليكما به من الفصاحةِ والبيانِ ـ ولو أكَلْتُما من هَذه الشَّجرةِ لا زدَدْتُّما عِلْمًا ويقينًا وبَقِيْتُما ههنا خالدَيْن آمنَيْن لاتمـوتانِ أبدًا. فاغترًّا بقولِهِ لَمّا حلَفَ لهما ـ إنِّي لَكُمَا لَمِنَ النّاصِحِين. وحَمَلَهُمـا الحرصُ فتسابَقا وتناوَلا ما كانا مَنْهِيَّيْنِ عنه.

فلمّـا أكلا منها طارتْ عنهما ألْبِسَةُ الجنّةِ وحُلَلُها وحُلِيّها ـ فبدَتْ لهُمَا سَوْآتُهما ـ وطَفِقا يخْصِفانِ من ورقِ الجنّـة. ثم تناثَرَتْ شعورُهما وانكشفتْ عوراتُهما وبَقِيَا عُريانَيْن ـ وأصابهما حرُّ الشمسِ واسودَّتْ أبدانُهما وتغيَّرتْ ألوانُ وجوهِهِمـا. ورأتِ الحيواناتُ حالَهما فأنكرَتْهما ونفـرَتْ منهمـا واستوحشَتْ من سوءِ حالِهما. فأمَرَ اللهُ الملائكَةَ أن اخْرِجُوْهما من هُناك وازْمُوا بهما إلى أسفلِ الجبلِ. فوقعا في بَرٍّ قَفْرٍ لا نَبْتَ فيها ولا ثمرَ وبقيا هناك

زماناً طويلاً يبكيانِ ويَنوحانِ حزناً وأسفًا على ما فاتهما نادِمَيْنِ على ما كان منهما. ثمَّ إنَّ رحمة اللَّه تدارَكَتْهما فتاب اللَّهُ عليهما ـ وأرسلَ مَلَكًا يُعَلِّمُهما الحرثَ والزرعَ والحصادَ والدِّياسةَ والطَّحْنَ والخُبْزَ والغزلَ والنَّسجَ والخياطةَ واِتخاذَ اللِّباسِ. ولمَّا تَوالَدُوا وكثرتْ ذُرِّيَّتُهما خالطهم أولادُ بني الجانّ وعَلَّموهم الصنائعَ والحرثَ والغرسَ والبنيانَ والمنافعَ والمضارَّ وصادقُوْهُـم وتَوَدَّدوا إليهم وعَاشَرُوهم مدّةً من الزمان بالحُسنى.

ولكن كلَّما ذَكَرَ بنو آدم ما جرى على أبيهم من كيدِ عَـزازيلَ ابليس اللعينِ وعداوتِه لهم امتلأتْ قلوبُ بنى آدم غيظًا وبُغْضًا وحَنَقًا عَلَى أولاد بني الجانّ. فلمَّا قَتَلَ قابيلُ هابيلَ اعتقدَ أولادُ هابيلَ أنَّ ذلك كان من تعليم بني الجانّ ـ فازدادوا غيظًا وبغضًا وحنقًا على أولاد بني الجانّ ـ وطلبوهم كلَّ مطلبٍ ـ واحتالُوْا لَهُمْ بكلِّ حيلةٍ من العزائم والرّقي والمَنادِلِ والحَبْسِ في القواريرِ والعذابِ بألْوانِ الأدْخِنَةِ والبَخُوراتِ المُؤذِيةِ لأوْلادِ الجانِّ الْمُنَفِّرَةِ لهم

المُمِثَّةِ لأمرهم. وكان ذلك دأبهم إلى أَنْ بعث اللَّهُ تعالى ادريسَ النبيَّ (على نبيّنا وعليه السلام) فأصلحَ بين بني الجانّ وبني آدم بالدّين والشّريعةِ والإسلام والملَّةِ. وتراجعتْ بنو الجانِّ إلى ديارِ بني آدَمَ وخالطوهم وعاشوا معهم بخير إلى أيَّامِ الطوفانِ الثاني ـ وبعدها إلى أيَّامِ إبراهيمَ خليلِ الرّحمٰن (على نبيّنا وعليه السّلام). فلمّا طُرِحَ في النارِ اِعْتقدَ بنو آدم بأنّ تعليمَ المنجنيق كان من بني الجانّ لنمرود الجَبّارِ. ولمّا طَرَحَ إخْوةُ يوسُفَ أخاهم في البئرِ نُسِبَ ذلك أيضًا إلى نزغات الشيطان من أولادِ الجانِّ. فلمّا بُعِثَ موسىً أصلَح بين بني الجانّ وبني إسرائيلَ بالدّين والشريعةِ ـ ودخل كثيرٌ من الجنّ في دين موسىً. فلمّا كان أيّامُ سُلَيمَانَ بنِ داؤد (عليهما السلام) وشَيَّد اللَّهُ مُلْكه وسَخَّر له الجنَّ والشياطينَ وغلب سليمانُ على مُلوكِ الأرضِ افتخرتِ الجنُّ على الإنسِ بأنّ ذلك من مُعاونةِ الجنِّ لسليمانَ ـ وقالت لو لا معاونةُ الجنِّ لسليمان لكان حكمهُ حكم أحدِ ملوكِ بني آدم ـ وكانتِ الجنُّ توهِمُ الإنسَ أنّها تَعلمُ الغيبَ.

ولمّا مات سليمانُ والجنّ كانوا في العذابِ المُهينِ ولم يشعروا بموتِه ـ فتبيّن للانسِ أنّها لو كانت تَعْلَمُ الغيبَ ما لَبِثَتْ في العذابِ المُهينِ. وأيضًا لمّا جاء الهُدْهُدُ بخبر بِلقيسِ ـ وقال سليمانُ لِمَلَاءِ الجنّ والإنسِ أيَّكم ياتيني بعرشِها قبل اَن يأتوني مسلمين افتخرت الجنُّ ـ وقال عفريتٌ منها أنا آتيك به قبل أن تقوم من مقامك أي من مجلس الحكم وهو اصطوس بن الايوان. قال سليمان أُريدُ أَسْرَعَ من ذلك. فقال الذي عنده علمٌ من الكتاب وهو آصَفُ بنُ بَرْخِيا ـ أنا آتيك به قبل أن يرتدّ إليك طرفُك. فلمّا رآه مُسْتَقِرًّا عنده خَرَّ سليمانُ ساجدًا لله حين تَبَيَّنَ فَضْلُ الإنسِ على الجنّ ـ وانقضى المجلسُ وانصرفتِ الجنّ من هناك خَجِلِينَ مُنَكِّسِينَ رُوُوسهم وغَوْغاءُ الإنسِ يُطَقْطِقُون في أَثَرِهم ـ ويُصَفِّقُونَ خَلْفَهم شامِتِينَ بهم.

فلمّا جرى ما ذكرتُ هربَتْ طائفةٌ من الجنّ من سليمانَ ـ وخرج عليه خارجيٌّ منهم. فوجَّهَ سليمانُ في طلبه من جُنوده ـــ وعَلَّمَهُمْ كيف يأخذونَهم بالرّقي والعزائمِ

والكلماتِ والآياتِ المُنْزَلات — وكيف يحبسونهم بالمناديل. وَعَمِلَ لذالك كتابًا وُجِدَ فى خزانتِه بعد موتِه۔ وأَشْغَلَ سليمانُ طغاةَ الجنِّ بالاعمال الشاقَّة إلى أنْ ماتَ. ولمَّا اَنْ بُعِثَ المسيحُ ودعا الخلقَ من الجنِّ والإنسِ إلى اللهِ تعالى ورغَّبَهم في لقائه وبيَّن لهم طريقَ الهُدَى وعَلَّمهم كيفَ الصَّعودُ إلى ملكوتِ السَّمواتِ. فدخل فى دينه طوائفُ من الجنِّ وتَرَهَّبَتْ وارتقتْ إلى هُناك۔ وسمعَتْ من الملاء الأعلى الأخبارَ وأَلْقَتْ إلى الكَهَنَةِ. فلمَّا بَعثَ اللهُ محمَّدًا (صلى الله عليه وآله وسلَّم) مُنِعَتْ من استراقِ السَّمْعِ فقالَتْ لا نَدْرِي أَشَرٌّ أُرِيْدَ بِمَنْ في الأرضِ أَمْ أَرادَ بِهِمْ رَبُّهُمْ رَشَدًا. ودخلَتْ قبائلُ من الجنِّ فى دينِه ۔ وحَسُنَ إسلامُها وصَلُحَ الأمرُ بين الجانِّ وبين المسلمين من أولادِ آدمَ إلى يومِنا هذا.

★★★

SECTION VI

Historical Extracts

وَاقِعَةُ رِحْلَةِ رَسُولِ اللّٰهِ ﷺ عَلَىٰ مَا ذَكَرَ أَبُو الفِداءِ

لـمّـا قدم رسولُ اللّٰه من حجةِ الوداع أقام بالمدينةِ حتى خرجت سنة عشر والمحرم من سنة إحدى عشرة ومعظم صفر وابتدى برسول الله مرضه في أواخِر صفر وقيل لليلتين بقيتا منه وهو في بيت زينب بنت جحش وكان يدورُ على نسائِهِ حتّى اشتدَّ مرضُه وهو في بيت ميمونة بنت الحارث فجمع نساءه واستأذنهنّ في أن يمرض في بيت إحداهنّ فأذنّ له أن يمرض في بيت عائشةَ فانتقل إليها وكان قد جهّز جيشًا مع مولاه أسامة بن زيد وأكّد فى مسيره في

مِنْ كُتُبِ التَّوَارِيخِ

مرضه وروي عن عائشةَ رضي الله عنها أنها قالت جاء رسولُ الله وبى صداعٌ وأنا أقول وا راساه فقال بل أنا والله يا عائشة اقول وا راساه ثم قال ما ضرّك لو متّ قبلي فقمت عليك وكفنتك وصلّيت عليك ودفنتك قالت فقلت كاني بك والله لو فعلت ذلك ورجعت إلى بيتي وتعزيت ببعض نسائك فتبسّم صلعم.

وفي أثناءِ مرضِه (وهو فى بيت عائشة) خرج بين الفضل بن العباس وعليّ بن أبي طالب حتى جلس على المنبرِ فحمد الله ثم قال أيها الناس من كنت جلدتُ له ظهرًا فهذا ظهري فليستقد منّي ومن كنت شتمت له عِرْضًا فهذا عرضي فليستقد منه ومن أخذت له مالًا فهذا مالي فلياخذ منه ولا يخشى الشحناء من قبلي فانها ليست من شاني ثم نزل وصلّى الظهرَ ثم رجع إلى المنبرِ فعاد إلى مقالتِه فادّعى عليه رجل ثلاثة دراهمَ فاعطاه عوضها ثم قال الا انّ فضوح الدنيا اَمْوَن من فضوح الآخرة ثم صلّى على أصحاب أُحُدٍ واستغفر لهم ثم قال إنّ عبدًا خيّره الله بين الدنيا وبين ما

عنده فاختار ما عنده فبكى أبوبكر ثم قال فديناك بأنفسنا ثم أوصى بالأنصار.

فلما اشتدّ به وجعُه قال ايتونى بدواة وبيضاء فاكتب لكم كتابًا لا تضلّون بعدي أبدًا فتنازعوا فقال قوموا عنى لا ينبغي عند نبي تنازع فقالوا انّ رسول الله يهجر فذهبوا يعيدون عليه فقال دعوني فما أنا فيه خير مما تدعونني إليه وكان فى أيام مرضه يصلّي بالناس وانّما انقطع بثلاثة أيام فلما أوذنَ بالصلوةِ أول ما انقطع فقال مروا أبا بكرٍ فليصلّي بالناس وتزايد به مرضه حتى توفّي يوم الاثنين ضحوة النهار وقيل نصف النهار قالت عائشة رأيتُ رسول الله وهو يموتُ وعنده قدحٌ فيه ماء يُدْخِل يده في القدح ثم يمسح وجهَه بالماء ثم يقول اللهمّ اعنّي على سكراتِ الموتِ قالت وثقل في حجري فذهبت أنظر فى وجهه وإذا بصره قد شخص وهو يقول بل الرفيق الأعلى.

مِنْ كُتُبِ التَّوَارِيخِ

فِي بَيَانِ خِلَافَةِ هَارُونَ الرَّشِيدِ وإِنْقِضَاءِ الْبَرَامِكَةِ
من تَارِيخِ أَبِي الْفَرَج

لمّا توفّي الهادي بويع الرشيد هارون بالخلافة في الليلةِ التي مات فيها الهادي وكان عمره حين ولي اثنتين وعشرين سنة وامّه الخيزران ولمّا مات الهادي خرج الرشيدُ فصلّى عليه بعيساباد ولمّا عاد الرشيد إلى بغداد وبلغ الجسر دعا الغوّاصين وقال كان أبي قد وهب لي خاتماً شراه مأة ألف دينار فأتاني رسولُ الهادي أخي يطلب الخاتم وأنا ههنا فألقيته في الماءِ فغاصوا عليه وأخرجوه فسرَّ به ولمّا مات الهادي هجم خزيمة بن حازم تلك الليلة على جعفر بن الهادي فأخذه من فراشِه وقال له لتخلعنها أو لاضربنّ عنقك فأجاب إلى الخلع واشهد الناس عليه فحظي بها خزيمة.

وقيل لمّا مات الهادي جاء يحيى بن خالد البرمكي إلى الرشيد فأعلمه بموتِه فبينا هو يكلّمُه إذ أتاه رسول آخر يبشّره بمولود فسمّاه عبد الله وهو المامون فقيل في ليلة

مات خليفة وقام خليفة وولد خليفة وفي هذه السنة ولد الامين واسمه محمّد في شوال وكان المامون أكبر منه ولمّا ولي الرشيد استوزر يحيى البرمكي وفى سنة اثنتين وسبعين ومأة بايع الرشيد لعبد الله المامون بولاية العهد بعد الامين وولّاه خراسان وما يتّصل بها إلى همدان ولقبه المامون وسلّمه إلى جعفر بن يحيى البرمكي وفيها حملت بنت حاقان الخزر إلى الفضل بن يحيى البرمكي فماتت ببرذعة فرجع من معها إلى أبيها فاخبروه أنّها قتلت غيلة فتجهّز إلى بلادِ الاسلام وفيها سملت الروم عيني ملكهم قسطنطين بن لاون واقرّوا امّه ايريني وغزى المسلمون الصائفة فبلغوا افسوس مدينة أصحاب الكهف.

وفي سنة ثلث وثمانين ومأة خرج الخزر بسبب ابنة خاقان من باب الأبواب فاوقعوا بالمسلمين وأهل الذمّة وسبوا أكثر من مأة الف راس وانتهكوا أمرًا عظيمًا لم يسمع بمثله في الأرض وفي سنة ست وثمانين ومأة أخذ الرشيدُ البيعـة لقاسم ابنه بولاية العهد بعد المامون وسمّاه المؤتمن

مِنْ كُتُبِ التَّوَارِيخِ

وفي سنة سبع وثمانين ومأة خلعت الروم ايريني الملكة وملّكت نيقيفور وهو من أولاد جبلة فكتب إلى الرشيد من نيقيفور ملك الروم إلى هارون ملك العرب أمّا بعد فانّ الملكة ايريني حملت إليك من أموالها ما كانت حقيقًا تحمل اضعافه إليها لكن ذلك ضعف النساء وحمقهنّ فاذا قرأت كتابي هذا فاردد ما أخذت وإلّا فالسيف بيننا وبينك.

فلمّا قرأ الرشيد الكتابَ استفزّه الغضبُ وكتب في ظهر الكتاب من هارون أمير المومنين إلى نيقيفور زعيم الروم قد قرأت كتابك والجواب ما تراه دون ما تسمعه ثمّ سار من يومه حتى نزل على حرقلة فاحرق ورجع وفى هذه السنة اوقع الرشيد بالبرامكة وقتل جعفر بن يحيى البرمكي وكان سبب ذلك أن الرشيد كان لا يصبر عن جعفر وعن اخته عباسة بنت المهدي وكان يحضرهما إذا جلس للشرب فقال لجعفر ازوّجكها ليحلّ لك النظر إليها ولا تقربها فأجابه إلى ذلك فزوّجها منه وكانا يحضران معه ثمّ يقوم عنهما وهما شابّان فجامعها جعفر فحملت منه وولدته

توأمين فعلم ذلك الرشيد فغضب وأمر بضرب عنق جعفر بن يحيى وحبس أخاه الفضل وأباه يحيى بالزقة حتى ماتا وكتب إلى العمّال في جميع النواحي بالقبض على البرامكه واستصفى أموالهم.

ثمّ أمر بعبّاسة فجعلت في صندوق وتدلت في بئر وهى حيّة وأمر بابنيها فنظر إليهما مليّاً وكانا كلولوتين فبكى ثم رمى بهما إلى البئر وطمّها عليهما وفى سنة تسعين ومأة ظهر رافع بن الليث بماورا النهر مخالفًا للرشيد بسمرقند وفي سنة اثنتين وتسعين ومأة سار الرشيد من الرقة إلى بغداد يريد خراسان لحرب رافع ولمّا صار ببعض الطريق ابتدأت به العلّةُ ولما بلغ جرجان في صفر اشتد مرضُه وكان معه ابنه المامون فسيّره إلى مرو ومعه جماعةٌ من القوّاد وسار الرشيدُ إلى طوس واشتدّ به المرضُ حتى ضعف عن الحركةِ ووصل إليه هناك بشير بن الليث أخو رافع أسيرًا فقال له الرشيد والله لو لم يبق من أجلي إلا أن أحرك شفتي بكلمة لقلت اقتلوه ثم دعا بقصّاب فأمر به ففصل أعضاه

مِنْ كُتُبِ التَّوَارِيخِ

فلمّا فرغ منه اغمى عليه ثم مات ودفن بطوس سنة ثلث وتسعين ومأة وكانت خلافته ثلثًا وعشرين سنة وكان عمره سبعًا وأربعين سنة وكانا جميلًا وسيمًا أبيض جعدًا قد وخطه الشيب وكان بعهده ثلثة الامين وأمّه زبيدة بنت جعفر بن المنصور ثم المامون وأمّه أمّ ولد اسمها مراجل ثم المؤتمن وأمّه أمّ ولد قيل وكان الرشيد يصلّي كل يوم مأة ركعة إلى أن فارق الدنيا الامن مرض وكان يتصدّق من صلب ماله كل يوم بألف درهم بعد زكاتها.

قيل ان الرشيد فى بدو خلافته سنة إحدى وسبعين ومأة مرض من صداع لحقه فقال ليحيى بن خالد بن برمك هاولا الاطبّا ليسوا يفهمون شيًا وينبغي أن تطلب لي طبيبًا ماهرًا فقال له عن بختيشوع بن جيورجيس فأرسل البريد فى حمله من نيسابور ولمّا كان بعد أيّام ورد ودخل على الرشيدِ فأكرمه وخلع عليه خلعة سنية ووهب له مالًا وافرًا وجعله رئيس الأطبّا ولمّا كان في سنة خمس وسبعين ومأة مرض جعفر بن يحيى بن خالد بن برمك فتقدّم الرشيد إلى

بختيشوع أن يخدمه ولمّا أفاق جعفر من مرضه قال لبختيشوع أريد أن تختار لي طبيبًا ماهرًا اكرمه واحسن اليه قال له بختيشوع لست أعرف في ها ولا الأطبّاء احذق من ابني جبريل فقال له جعفر احضرنيه فلمّا أحضره شكا إليه مرضًا كان يخفيه فدبّره في مدة ثلاثة أيام وبرا فأحبّه جعفر مثل نفسه.

وفي بعض الأيّام تمطَّت حظية الرشيد ورفعت يدها فبقيت مبسوطة لا يمكنها ردّها والأطبّاء يعالجونها بالتمريخ والأدهان فلا ينفعُ ذلك شيئًا فقال له جعفر عن جبريل ومهارته فأحضره وشرح له حال الصبيّة فقال جبريل ان لم يسخط امير المومنين عليَّ فلها عندي حيلة قال له الرشيد ما هي قال تخرج الجارية إلى هاهنا بحضرة الجمع حتى أعمل ما أريد وتمتهل عليَّ ولا تسخط عاجلا فأمر الرشيد فخرجت وحين رأها جبريل أسرع إليها ونكس راسها وأمسك ذيلها كانّه يريد أن يكشفها فانزعجت الجاريةُ ومن شدّة الحياء والانزعاج استرسلت أعضاؤها وبسطت يدها

مِنْ كُتُبِ التَّوَارِيخِ

إلى أسفل وأمسكت ذيلَها فقال جبريل لقد برأت يا أمير المومنين فقال الرشيد للجارية ابسطي يدك يمنة ويسرة ففعلت فعجب الرشيد وكُلّ من حضر وأمر لجبريل فى الوقت بخمس مأة ألف درهم وأحبّه.

☆☆☆

SECTION VII

Selection from the Qur'an

سِتُّ سُوَرٍ مِنَ الْقُرآنِ

سُورَةُ الْفَاتِحَةِ

بِسْمِ اللهِ الرَّحْمَٰنِ الرَّحِيمِ ۝ الْحَمْدُ لِلَّهِ رَبِّ الْعَالَمِينَ ۝ الرَّحْمَٰنِ الرَّحِيمِ ۝ مَالِكِ يَوْمِ الدِّينِ ۝ إِيَّاكَ نَعْبُدُ وَإِيَّاكَ نَسْتَعِينُ ۝ اهْدِنَا الصِّرَاطَ الْمُسْتَقِيمَ ۝ صِرَاطَ الَّذِينَ أَنْعَمْتَ عَلَيْهِمْ غَيْرِ الْمَغْضُوبِ عَلَيْهِمْ وَلَا الضَّالِّينَ ۝

سُورَةُ التَّغَابُنِ

بِسْمِ اللهِ الرَّحْمَٰنِ الرَّحِيمِ

يُسَبِّحُ لِلَّهِ مَا فِي السَّمَاوَاتِ وَمَا فِي الْأَرْضِ لَهُ الْمُلْكُ وَلَهُ الْحَمْدُ وَهُوَ عَلَىٰ كُلِّ شَيْءٍ قَدِيرٌ ۝ هُوَ الَّذِي خَلَقَكُمْ فَمِنكُمْ كَافِرٌ وَمِنكُم مُّؤْمِنٌ وَاللَّهُ بِمَا تَعْمَلُونَ بَصِيرٌ ۝ خَلَقَ السَّمَاوَاتِ وَالْأَرْضَ بِالْحَقِّ وَصَوَّرَكُمْ فَأَحْسَنَ صُوَرَكُمْ وَإِلَيْهِ الْمَصِيرُ ۝ يَعْلَمُ مَا فِي السَّمَاوَاتِ وَالْأَرْضِ وَيَعْلَمُ مَا تُسِرُّونَ وَمَا تُعْلِنُونَ وَاللَّهُ

سُورَةُ التَّغَابُنِ

عَلِيمٌ بِذَاتِ ٱلصُّدُورِ ۝ أَلَمْ يَأْتِكُمْ نَبَؤُا۟ ٱلَّذِينَ كَفَرُوا۟ مِن قَبْلُ فَذَاقُوا۟ وَبَالَ أَمْرِهِمْ وَلَهُمْ عَذَابٌ أَلِيمٌ ۝ ذَٰلِكَ بِأَنَّهُۥ كَانَت تَّأْتِيهِمْ رُسُلُهُم بِٱلْبَيِّنَٰتِ فَقَالُوٓا۟ أَبَشَرٌ يَهْدُونَنَا فَكَفَرُوا۟ وَتَوَلَّوا۟ وَّٱسْتَغْنَى ٱللَّهُ وَٱللَّهُ غَنِىٌّ حَمِيدٌ ۝ زَعَمَ ٱلَّذِينَ كَفَرُوٓا۟ أَن لَّن يُبْعَثُوا۟ قُلْ بَلَىٰ وَرَبِّى لَتُبْعَثُنَّ ثُمَّ لَتُنَبَّؤُنَّ بِمَا عَمِلْتُمْ وَذَٰلِكَ عَلَى ٱللَّهِ يَسِيرٌ ۝ فَـَٔامِنُوا۟ بِٱللَّهِ وَرَسُولِهِۦ وَٱلنُّورِ ٱلَّذِىٓ أَنزَلْنَا وَٱللَّهُ بِمَا تَعْمَلُونَ خَبِيرٌ ۝ يَوْمَ يَجْمَعُكُمْ لِيَوْمِ ٱلْجَمْعِ ذَٰلِكَ يَوْمُ ٱلتَّغَابُنِ وَمَن يُؤْمِنۢ بِٱللَّهِ وَيَعْمَلْ صَٰلِحًا يُكَفِّرْ عَنْهُ سَيِّـَٔاتِهِۦ وَيُدْخِلْهُ جَنَّٰتٍ تَجْرِى مِن تَحْتِهَا ٱلْأَنْهَٰرُ خَٰلِدِينَ فِيهَآ أَبَدًا ذَٰلِكَ ٱلْفَوْزُ ٱلْعَظِيمُ ۝ وَٱلَّذِينَ كَفَرُوا۟ وَكَذَّبُوا۟ بِـَٔايَٰتِنَآ أُو۟لَٰٓئِكَ أَصْحَٰبُ ٱلنَّارِ خَٰلِدِينَ فِيهَا وَبِئْسَ ٱلْمَصِيرُ ۝ مَآ أَصَابَ مِن مُّصِيبَةٍ إِلَّا بِإِذْنِ ٱللَّهِ وَمَن يُؤْمِنۢ بِٱللَّهِ يَهْدِ قَلْبَهُۥ وَٱللَّهُ بِكُلِّ شَىْءٍ عَلِيمٌ ۝ وَأَطِيعُوا۟ ٱللَّهَ وَأَطِيعُوا۟ ٱلرَّسُولَ فَإِن تَوَلَّيْتُمْ فَإِنَّمَا عَلَىٰ رَسُولِنَا ٱلْبَلَٰغُ ٱلْمُبِينُ ۝ ٱللَّهُ لَآ إِلَٰهَ إِلَّا هُوَ وَعَلَى ٱللَّهِ فَلْيَتَوَكَّلِ ٱلْمُؤْمِنُونَ ۝ يَٰٓأَيُّهَا ٱلَّذِينَ ءَامَنُوٓا۟ إِنَّ مِنْ أَزْوَٰجِكُمْ وَأَوْلَٰدِكُمْ عَدُوًّا

سُورَةُ الإنْسَان

لَكُمْ فَاحْذَرُوهُمْ وَإِن تَعْفُوا وَتَصْفَحُوا وَتَغْفِرُوا فَإِنَّ ٱللَّهَ غَفُورٌ رَّحِيمٌ ۝ إِنَّمَآ أَمْوَٰلُكُمْ وَأَوْلَٰدُكُمْ فِتْنَةٌ وَٱللَّهُ عِندَهُۥٓ أَجْرٌ عَظِيمٌ ۝ فَٱتَّقُوا ٱللَّهَ مَا ٱسْتَطَعْتُمْ وَٱسْمَعُوا وَأَطِيعُوا وَأَنفِقُوا خَيْرًا لِّأَنفُسِكُمْ وَمَن يُوقَ شُحَّ نَفْسِهِۦ فَأُو۟لَٰٓئِكَ هُمُ ٱلْمُفْلِحُونَ ۝ إِن تُقْرِضُوا ٱللَّهَ قَرْضًا حَسَنًا يُضَٰعِفْهُ لَكُمْ وَيَغْفِرْ لَكُمْ وَٱللَّهُ شَكُورٌ حَلِيمٌ ۝ عَٰلِمُ ٱلْغَيْبِ وَٱلشَّهَٰدَةِ ٱلْعَزِيزُ ٱلْحَكِيمُ ۝

سُورَةُ الإنْسَان

بِسْمِ ٱللَّهِ ٱلرَّحْمَٰنِ ٱلرَّحِيمِ

هَلْ أَتَىٰ عَلَى ٱلْإِنسَٰنِ حِينٌ مِّنَ ٱلدَّهْرِ لَمْ يَكُن شَيْـًٔا مَّذْكُورًا ۝ إِنَّا خَلَقْنَا ٱلْإِنسَٰنَ مِن نُّطْفَةٍ أَمْشَاجٍ نَّبْتَلِيهِ فَجَعَلْنَٰهُ سَمِيعًۢا بَصِيرًا ۝ إِنَّا هَدَيْنَٰهُ ٱلسَّبِيلَ إِمَّا شَاكِرًا وَإِمَّا كَفُورًا ۝ إِنَّآ أَعْتَدْنَا لِلْكَٰفِرِينَ سَلَٰسِلَا۟ وَأَغْلَٰلًا وَسَعِيرًا ۝ إِنَّ ٱلْأَبْرَارَ يَشْرَبُونَ مِن كَأْسٍ كَانَ مِزَاجُهَا كَافُورًا ۝ عَيْنًا يَشْرَبُ بِهَا عِبَادُ ٱللَّهِ يُفَجِّرُونَهَا تَفْجِيرًا ۝ يُوفُونَ بِٱلنَّذْرِ وَيَخَافُونَ يَوْمًا كَانَ شَرُّهُۥ مُسْتَطِيرًا ۝ وَيُطْعِمُونَ ٱلطَّعَامَ عَلَىٰ حُبِّهِۦ مِسْكِينًا

سُورَةُ الإِنْسَانِ

وَيَتِيمًا وَأَسِيرًا ۝ إِنَّمَا نُطْعِمُكُمْ لِوَجْهِ اللَّهِ لَا نُرِيدُ مِنكُمْ جَزَاءً وَلَا شُكُورًا ۝ إِنَّا نَخَافُ مِن رَّبِّنَا يَوْمًا عَبُوسًا قَمْطَرِيرًا ۝ فَوَقَىٰهُمُ اللَّهُ شَرَّ ذَٰلِكَ الْيَوْمِ وَلَقَّىٰهُمْ نَضْرَةً وَسُرُورًا ۝ وَجَزَىٰهُم بِمَا صَبَرُوا جَنَّةً وَحَرِيرًا ۝ مُّتَّكِئِينَ فِيهَا عَلَى الْأَرَائِكِ ۖ لَا يَرَوْنَ فِيهَا شَمْسًا وَلَا زَمْهَرِيرًا ۝ وَدَانِيَةً عَلَيْهِمْ ظِلَالُهَا وَذُلِّلَتْ قُطُوفُهَا تَذْلِيلًا ۝ وَيُطَافُ عَلَيْهِم بِآنِيَةٍ مِّن فِضَّةٍ وَأَكْوَابٍ كَانَتْ قَوَارِيرَا۠ ۝ قَوَارِيرَا۠ مِن فِضَّةٍ قَدَّرُوهَا تَقْدِيرًا ۝ وَيُسْقَوْنَ فِيهَا كَأْسًا كَانَ مِزَاجُهَا زَنجَبِيلًا ۝ عَيْنًا فِيهَا تُسَمَّىٰ سَلْسَبِيلًا ۝ وَيَطُوفُ عَلَيْهِمْ وِلْدَانٌ مُّخَلَّدُونَ إِذَا رَأَيْتَهُمْ حَسِبْتَهُمْ لُؤْلُؤًا مَّنثُورًا ۝ وَإِذَا رَأَيْتَ ثَمَّ رَأَيْتَ نَعِيمًا وَمُلْكًا كَبِيرًا ۝ عَالِيَهُمْ ثِيَابُ سُندُسٍ خُضْرٌ وَإِسْتَبْرَقٌ ۖ وَحُلُّوا أَسَاوِرَ مِن فِضَّةٍ وَسَقَاهُمْ رَبُّهُمْ شَرَابًا طَهُورًا ۝ إِنَّ هَٰذَا كَانَ لَكُمْ جَزَاءً وَكَانَ سَعْيُكُم مَّشْكُورًا ۝ إِنَّا نَحْنُ نَزَّلْنَا عَلَيْكَ الْقُرْآنَ تَنزِيلًا ۝ فَاصْبِرْ لِحُكْمِ رَبِّكَ وَلَا تُطِعْ مِنْهُمْ آثِمًا أَوْ كَفُورًا ۝ وَاذْكُرِ اسْمَ رَبِّكَ بُكْرَةً وَأَصِيلًا ۝ وَمِنَ اللَّيْلِ فَاسْجُدْ لَهُ وَسَبِّحْهُ لَيْلًا طَوِيلًا ۝ إِنَّ هَٰؤُلَاءِ يُحِبُّونَ الْعَاجِلَةَ وَيَذَرُونَ وَرَاءَهُمْ يَوْمًا ثَقِيلًا ۝ نَّحْنُ خَلَقْنَاهُمْ وَشَدَدْنَا أَسْرَهُمْ ۖ وَإِذَا شِئْنَا بَدَّلْنَا أَمْثَالَهُم تَبْدِيلًا ۝ إِنَّ هَٰذِهِ تَذْكِرَةٌ ۖ فَمَن شَاءَ اتَّخَذَ إِلَىٰ رَبِّهِ سَبِيلًا ۝

سُورَةُ الصَّفّ

وَمَا تَشَاءُونَ إِلَّا أَن يَشَاءَ ٱللَّهُ إِنَّ ٱللَّهَ كَانَ عَلِيمًا حَكِيمًا ۝ يُدْخِلُ مَن يَشَاءُ فِى رَحْمَتِهِۦ وَٱلظَّٰلِمِينَ أَعَدَّ لَهُمْ عَذَابًا أَلِيمًۢا ۝

سُورَةُ الصَّفّ

بِسْمِ ٱللَّهِ ٱلرَّحْمَٰنِ ٱلرَّحِيمِ

سَبَّحَ لِلَّهِ مَا فِى ٱلسَّمَٰوَٰتِ وَمَا فِى ٱلْأَرْضِ وَهُوَ ٱلْعَزِيزُ ٱلْحَكِيمُ ۝ يَٰٓأَيُّهَا ٱلَّذِينَ ءَامَنُوا۟ لِمَ تَقُولُونَ مَا لَا تَفْعَلُونَ ۝ كَبُرَ مَقْتًا عِندَ ٱللَّهِ أَن تَقُولُوا۟ مَا لَا تَفْعَلُونَ ۝ إِنَّ ٱللَّهَ يُحِبُّ ٱلَّذِينَ يُقَٰتِلُونَ فِى سَبِيلِهِۦ صَفًّا كَأَنَّهُم بُنْيَٰنٌ مَّرْصُوصٌ ۝ وَإِذْ قَالَ مُوسَىٰ لِقَوْمِهِۦ يَٰقَوْمِ لِمَ تُؤْذُونَنِى وَقَد تَّعْلَمُونَ أَنِّى رَسُولُ ٱللَّهِ إِلَيْكُمْ فَلَمَّا زَاغُوٓا۟ أَزَاغَ ٱللَّهُ قُلُوبَهُمْ وَٱللَّهُ لَا يَهْدِى ٱلْقَوْمَ ٱلْفَٰسِقِينَ ۝ وَإِذْ قَالَ عِيسَى ٱبْنُ مَرْيَمَ يَٰبَنِىٓ إِسْرَٰٓءِيلَ إِنِّى رَسُولُ ٱللَّهِ إِلَيْكُم مُّصَدِّقًا لِّمَا بَيْنَ يَدَىَّ مِنَ ٱلتَّوْرَىٰةِ وَمُبَشِّرًۢا بِرَسُولٍ يَأْتِى مِنۢ بَعْدِى ٱسْمُهُۥٓ أَحْمَدُ فَلَمَّا جَآءَهُم بِٱلْبَيِّنَٰتِ قَالُوا۟ هَٰذَا سِحْرٌ مُّبِينٌ ۝ وَمَنْ أَظْلَمُ مِمَّنِ ٱفْتَرَىٰ عَلَى ٱللَّهِ ٱلْكَذِبَ وَهُوَ يُدْعَىٰٓ إِلَى ٱلْإِسْلَٰمِ وَٱللَّهُ لَا يَهْدِى ٱلْقَوْمَ ٱلظَّٰلِمِينَ ۝ يُرِيدُونَ لِيُطْفِـُٔوا۟ نُورَ ٱللَّهِ بِأَفْوَٰهِهِمْ وَٱللَّهُ مُتِمُّ نُورِهِۦ وَلَوْ كَرِهَ

ٱلْكَٰفِرُونَ ۝ هُوَ ٱلَّذِىٓ أَرْسَلَ رَسُولَهُۥ بِٱلْهُدَىٰ وَدِينِ ٱلْحَقِّ لِيُظْهِرَهُۥ عَلَى ٱلدِّينِ كُلِّهِۦ وَلَوْ كَرِهَ ٱلْمُشْرِكُونَ ۝ يَٰٓأَيُّهَا ٱلَّذِينَ ءَامَنُوا۟ هَلْ أَدُلُّكُمْ عَلَىٰ تِجَٰرَةٍ تُنجِيكُم مِّنْ عَذَابٍ أَلِيمٍ ۝ تُؤْمِنُونَ بِٱللَّهِ وَرَسُولِهِۦ وَتُجَٰهِدُونَ فِى سَبِيلِ ٱللَّهِ بِأَمْوَٰلِكُمْ وَأَنفُسِكُمْ ذَٰلِكُمْ خَيْرٌ لَّكُمْ إِن كُنتُمْ تَعْلَمُونَ ۝ يَغْفِرْ لَكُمْ ذُنُوبَكُمْ وَيُدْخِلْكُمْ جَنَّٰتٍ تَجْرِى مِن تَحْتِهَا ٱلْأَنْهَٰرُ وَمَسَٰكِنَ طَيِّبَةً فِى جَنَّٰتِ عَدْنٍ ذَٰلِكَ ٱلْفَوْزُ ٱلْعَظِيمُ ۝ وَأُخْرَىٰ تُحِبُّونَهَا نَصْرٌ مِّنَ ٱللَّهِ وَفَتْحٌ قَرِيبٌ وَبَشِّرِ ٱلْمُؤْمِنِينَ ۝ يَٰٓأَيُّهَا ٱلَّذِينَ ءَامَنُوا۟ كُونُوٓا۟ أَنصَارَ ٱللَّهِ كَمَا قَالَ عِيسَى ٱبْنُ مَرْيَمَ لِلْحَوَارِيِّـۧنَ مَنْ أَنصَارِىٓ إِلَى ٱللَّهِ قَالَ ٱلْحَوَارِيُّونَ نَحْنُ أَنصَارُ ٱللَّهِ فَـَٔامَنَت طَّآئِفَةٌ مِّنۢ بَنِىٓ إِسْرَٰٓءِيلَ وَكَفَرَت طَّآئِفَةٌ فَأَيَّدْنَا ٱلَّذِينَ ءَامَنُوا۟ عَلَىٰ عَدُوِّهِمْ فَأَصْبَحُوا۟ ظَٰهِرِينَ ۝

سُورَةُ لُقْمَان

بِسْمِ ٱللَّهِ ٱلرَّحْمَٰنِ ٱلرَّحِيمِ

الٓمٓ ۝ تِلْكَ ءَايَٰتُ ٱلْكِتَٰبِ ٱلْحَكِيمِ ۝ هُدًى وَرَحْمَةً لِّلْمُحْسِنِينَ ۝ ٱلَّذِينَ يُقِيمُونَ ٱلصَّلَوٰةَ وَيُؤْتُونَ ٱلزَّكَوٰةَ وَهُم بِٱلْءَاخِرَةِ هُمْ يُوقِنُونَ ۝ أُو۟لَٰٓئِكَ عَلَىٰ هُدًى مِّن رَّبِّهِمْ وَأُو۟لَٰٓئِكَ هُمُ ٱلْمُفْلِحُونَ ۝ وَمِنَ ٱلنَّاسِ مَن يَشْتَرِى لَهْوَ ٱلْحَدِيثِ

سُورَةُ لُقْمَان

لِيُضِلَّ عَن سَبِيلِ ٱللَّهِ بِغَيْرِ عِلْمٍ وَيَتَّخِذَهَا هُزُوًا أُوْلَٰٓئِكَ لَهُمْ عَذَابٌ مُّهِينٌ ۝ وَإِذَا تُتْلَىٰ عَلَيْهِ ءَايَٰتُنَا وَلَّىٰ مُسْتَكْبِرًا كَأَن لَّمْ يَسْمَعْهَا كَأَنَّ فِىٓ أُذُنَيْهِ وَقْرًا فَبَشِّرْهُ بِعَذَابٍ أَلِيمٍ ۝ إِنَّ ٱلَّذِينَ ءَامَنُواْ وَعَمِلُواْ ٱلصَّٰلِحَٰتِ لَهُمْ جَنَّٰتُ ٱلنَّعِيمِ ۝ خَٰلِدِينَ فِيهَا وَعْدَ ٱللَّهِ حَقًّا وَهُوَ ٱلْعَزِيزُ ٱلْحَكِيمُ ۝ خَلَقَ ٱلسَّمَٰوَٰتِ بِغَيْرِ عَمَدٍ تَرَوْنَهَا وَأَلْقَىٰ فِى ٱلْأَرْضِ رَوَٰسِىَ أَن تَمِيدَ بِكُمْ وَبَثَّ فِيهَا مِن كُلِّ دَآبَّةٍ وَأَنزَلْنَا مِنَ ٱلسَّمَآءِ مَآءً فَأَنبَتْنَا فِيهَا مِن كُلِّ زَوْجٍ كَرِيمٍ ۝ هَٰذَا خَلْقُ ٱللَّهِ فَأَرُونِى مَاذَا خَلَقَ ٱلَّذِينَ مِن دُونِهِۦ بَلِ ٱلظَّٰلِمُونَ فِى ضَلَٰلٍ مُّبِينٍ ۝ وَلَقَدْ ءَاتَيْنَا لُقْمَٰنَ ٱلْحِكْمَةَ أَنِ ٱشْكُرْ لِلَّهِ وَمَن يَشْكُرْ فَإِنَّمَا يَشْكُرُ لِنَفْسِهِۦ وَمَن كَفَرَ فَإِنَّ ٱللَّهَ غَنِىٌّ حَمِيدٌ ۝ وَإِذْ قَالَ لُقْمَٰنُ لِٱبْنِهِۦ وَهُوَ يَعِظُهُۥ يَٰبُنَىَّ لَا تُشْرِكْ بِٱللَّهِ إِنَّ ٱلشِّرْكَ لَظُلْمٌ عَظِيمٌ ۝ وَوَصَّيْنَا ٱلْإِنسَٰنَ بِوَٰلِدَيْهِ حَمَلَتْهُ أُمُّهُۥ وَهْنًا عَلَىٰ وَهْنٍ وَفِصَٰلُهُۥ فِى عَامَيْنِ أَنِ ٱشْكُرْ لِى وَلِوَٰلِدَيْكَ إِلَىَّ ٱلْمَصِيرُ ۝ وَإِن جَٰهَدَاكَ عَلَىٰٓ أَن تُشْرِكَ بِى مَا لَيْسَ لَكَ بِهِۦ عِلْمٌ فَلَا تُطِعْهُمَا وَصَاحِبْهُمَا فِى ٱلدُّنْيَا مَعْرُوفًا

سُورَةُ لُقْمَانَ

وَٱتَّبِعْ سَبِيلَ مَنْ أَنَابَ إِلَيَّ ثُمَّ إِلَيَّ مَرْجِعُكُمْ فَأُنَبِّئُكُم بِمَا كُنتُمْ تَعْمَلُونَ ۝ يَٰبُنَيَّ إِنَّهَآ إِن تَكُ مِثْقَالَ حَبَّةٍ مِّنْ خَرْدَلٍ فَتَكُن فِى صَخْرَةٍ أَوْ فِى ٱلسَّمَٰوَٰتِ أَوْ فِى ٱلْأَرْضِ يَأْتِ بِهَا ٱللَّهُ إِنَّ ٱللَّهَ لَطِيفٌ خَبِيرٌ ۝ يَٰبُنَيَّ أَقِمِ ٱلصَّلَوٰةَ وَأْمُرْ بِٱلْمَعْرُوفِ وَٱنْهَ عَنِ ٱلْمُنكَرِ وَٱصْبِرْ عَلَىٰ مَآ أَصَابَكَ إِنَّ ذَٰلِكَ مِنْ عَزْمِ ٱلْأُمُورِ ۝ وَلَا تُصَعِّرْ خَدَّكَ لِلنَّاسِ وَلَا تَمْشِ فِى ٱلْأَرْضِ مَرَحًا إِنَّ ٱللَّهَ لَا يُحِبُّ كُلَّ مُخْتَالٍ فَخُورٍ ۝ وَٱقْصِدْ فِى مَشْيِكَ وَٱغْضُضْ مِن صَوْتِكَ إِنَّ أَنكَرَ ٱلْأَصْوَٰتِ لَصَوْتُ ٱلْحَمِيرِ ۝ أَلَمْ تَرَوْا۟ أَنَّ ٱللَّهَ سَخَّرَ لَكُم مَّا فِى ٱلسَّمَٰوَٰتِ وَمَا فِى ٱلْأَرْضِ وَأَسْبَغَ عَلَيْكُمْ نِعَمَهُۥ ظَٰهِرَةً وَبَاطِنَةً وَمِنَ ٱلنَّاسِ مَن يُجَٰدِلُ فِى ٱللَّهِ بِغَيْرِ عِلْمٍ وَلَا هُدًى وَلَا كِتَٰبٍ مُّنِيرٍ ۝ وَإِذَا قِيلَ لَهُمُ ٱتَّبِعُوا۟ مَآ أَنزَلَ ٱللَّهُ قَالُوا۟ بَلْ نَتَّبِعُ مَا وَجَدْنَا عَلَيْهِ ءَابَآءَنَآ أَوَلَوْ كَانَ ٱلشَّيْطَٰنُ يَدْعُوهُمْ إِلَىٰ عَذَابِ ٱلسَّعِيرِ ۝ ۞ وَمَن يُسْلِمْ وَجْهَهُۥٓ إِلَى ٱللَّهِ وَهُوَ مُحْسِنٌ فَقَدِ ٱسْتَمْسَكَ بِٱلْعُرْوَةِ ٱلْوُثْقَىٰ وَإِلَى ٱللَّهِ عَٰقِبَةُ ٱلْأُمُورِ ۝ وَمَن كَفَرَ فَلَا يَحْزُنكَ كُفْرُهُۥٓ إِلَيْنَا مَرْجِعُهُمْ فَنُنَبِّئُهُم بِمَا عَمِلُوٓا۟ إِنَّ ٱللَّهَ عَلِيمٌۢ بِذَاتِ ٱلصُّدُورِ

سُورَةُ لُقْمَانَ

﴿٢٣﴾ نُمَتِّعُهُمْ قَلِيلًا ثُمَّ نَضْطَرُّهُمْ إِلَىٰ عَذَابٍ غَلِيظٍ ﴿٢٤﴾ وَلَئِن سَأَلْتَهُم مَّنْ خَلَقَ السَّمَاوَاتِ وَالْأَرْضَ لَيَقُولُنَّ اللَّهُ قُلِ الْحَمْدُ لِلَّهِ بَلْ أَكْثَرُهُمْ لَا يَعْلَمُونَ ﴿٢٥﴾ لِلَّهِ مَا فِي السَّمَاوَاتِ وَالْأَرْضِ إِنَّ اللَّهَ هُوَ الْغَنِيُّ الْحَمِيدُ ﴿٢٦﴾ وَلَوْ أَنَّمَا فِي الْأَرْضِ مِن شَجَرَةٍ أَقْلَامٌ وَالْبَحْرُ يَمُدُّهُ مِن بَعْدِهِ سَبْعَةُ أَبْحُرٍ مَّا نَفِدَتْ كَلِمَاتُ اللَّهِ إِنَّ اللَّهَ عَزِيزٌ حَكِيمٌ ﴿٢٧﴾ مَّا خَلْقُكُمْ وَلَا بَعْثُكُمْ إِلَّا كَنَفْسٍ وَاحِدَةٍ إِنَّ اللَّهَ سَمِيعٌ بَصِيرٌ ﴿٢٨﴾ أَلَمْ تَرَ أَنَّ اللَّهَ يُولِجُ اللَّيْلَ فِي النَّهَارِ وَيُولِجُ النَّهَارَ فِي اللَّيْلِ وَسَخَّرَ الشَّمْسَ وَالْقَمَرَ كُلٌّ يَجْرِي إِلَىٰ أَجَلٍ مُّسَمًّى وَأَنَّ اللَّهَ بِمَا تَعْمَلُونَ خَبِيرٌ ﴿٢٩﴾ ذَٰلِكَ بِأَنَّ اللَّهَ هُوَ الْحَقُّ وَأَنَّ مَا يَدْعُونَ مِن دُونِهِ الْبَاطِلُ وَأَنَّ اللَّهَ هُوَ الْعَلِيُّ الْكَبِيرُ ﴿٣٠﴾ أَلَمْ تَرَ أَنَّ الْفُلْكَ تَجْرِي فِي الْبَحْرِ بِنِعْمَتِ اللَّهِ لِيُرِيَكُم مِّنْ آيَاتِهِ إِنَّ فِي ذَٰلِكَ لَآيَاتٍ لِّكُلِّ صَبَّارٍ شَكُورٍ ﴿٣١﴾ وَإِذَا غَشِيَهُم مَّوْجٌ كَالظُّلَلِ دَعَوُا اللَّهَ مُخْلِصِينَ لَهُ الدِّينَ فَلَمَّا نَجَّاهُمْ إِلَى الْبَرِّ فَمِنْهُم مُّقْتَصِدٌ وَمَا يَجْحَدُ بِآيَاتِنَا إِلَّا كُلُّ خَتَّارٍ كَفُورٍ ﴿٣٢﴾ يَا أَيُّهَا النَّاسُ اتَّقُوا رَبَّكُمْ وَاخْشَوْا يَوْمًا لَا يَجْزِي وَالِدٌ

عَن وَلَدِهِۦ وَلَا مَوْلُودٌ هُوَ جَازٍ عَن وَالِدِهِۦ شَيْـًٔا ۚ إِنَّ وَعْدَ ٱللَّهِ حَقٌّ ۖ فَلَا تَغُرَّنَّكُمُ ٱلْحَيَوٰةُ ٱلدُّنْيَا وَلَا يَغُرَّنَّكُم بِٱللَّهِ ٱلْغَرُورُ ۝ إِنَّ ٱللَّهَ عِندَهُۥ عِلْمُ ٱلسَّاعَةِ وَيُنَزِّلُ ٱلْغَيْثَ وَيَعْلَمُ مَا فِى ٱلْأَرْحَامِ ۖ وَمَا تَدْرِى نَفْسٌ مَّاذَا تَكْسِبُ غَدًا ۖ وَمَا تَدْرِى نَفْسٌۢ بِأَىِّ أَرْضٍ تَمُوتُ ۚ إِنَّ ٱللَّهَ عَلِيمٌ خَبِيرٌۢ ۝

سُورَةُ يُوسُفَ

بِسْمِ ٱللَّهِ ٱلرَّحْمَٰنِ ٱلرَّحِيمِ

الٓر ۚ تِلْكَ ءَايَٰتُ ٱلْكِتَٰبِ ٱلْمُبِينِ ۝ إِنَّآ أَنزَلْنَٰهُ قُرْءَٰنًا عَرَبِيًّا لَّعَلَّكُمْ تَعْقِلُونَ ۝ نَحْنُ نَقُصُّ عَلَيْكَ أَحْسَنَ ٱلْقَصَصِ بِمَآ أَوْحَيْنَآ إِلَيْكَ هَٰذَا ٱلْقُرْءَانَ وَإِن كُنتَ مِن قَبْلِهِۦ لَمِنَ ٱلْغَٰفِلِينَ ۝ إِذْ قَالَ يُوسُفُ لِأَبِيهِ يَٰٓأَبَتِ إِنِّى رَأَيْتُ أَحَدَ عَشَرَ كَوْكَبًا وَٱلشَّمْسَ وَٱلْقَمَرَ رَأَيْتُهُمْ لِى سَٰجِدِينَ ۝ قَالَ يَٰبُنَىَّ لَا تَقْصُصْ رُءْيَاكَ عَلَىٰٓ إِخْوَتِكَ فَيَكِيدُوا۟ لَكَ كَيْدًا ۖ إِنَّ ٱلشَّيْطَٰنَ لِلْإِنسَٰنِ عَدُوٌّ مُّبِينٌ ۝ وَكَذَٰلِكَ يَجْتَبِيكَ رَبُّكَ وَيُعَلِّمُكَ مِن تَأْوِيلِ ٱلْأَحَادِيثِ وَيُتِمُّ نِعْمَتَهُۥ عَلَيْكَ وَعَلَىٰٓ ءَالِ يَعْقُوبَ كَمَآ أَتَمَّهَا عَلَىٰٓ أَبَوَيْكَ مِن قَبْلُ إِبْرَٰهِيمَ وَإِسْحَٰقَ ۚ

سُورَةُ يُوسُفَ

إِنَّ رَبَّكَ عَلِيمٌ حَكِيمٌ ۝ ۞ لَقَدْ كَانَ فِي يُوسُفَ وَإِخْوَتِهِ ءَايَٰتٌ لِّلسَّآئِلِينَ ۝ إِذْ قَالُواْ لَيُوسُفُ وَأَخُوهُ أَحَبُّ إِلَىٰ أَبِينَا مِنَّا وَنَحْنُ عُصْبَةٌ إِنَّ أَبَانَا لَفِى ضَلَٰلٍ مُّبِينٍ ۝ ٱقْتُلُواْ يُوسُفَ أَوِ ٱطْرَحُوهُ أَرْضًا يَخْلُ لَكُمْ وَجْهُ أَبِيكُمْ وَتَكُونُواْ مِنْ بَعْدِهِۦ قَوْمًا صَٰلِحِينَ ۝ قَالَ قَآئِلٌ مِّنْهُمْ لَا تَقْتُلُواْ يُوسُفَ وَأَلْقُوهُ فِى غَيَٰبَتِ ٱلْجُبِّ يَلْتَقِطْهُ بَعْضُ ٱلسَّيَّارَةِ إِن كُنتُمْ فَٰعِلِينَ ۝ قَالُواْ يَٰٓأَبَانَا مَا لَكَ لَا تَأْمَنَّا عَلَىٰ يُوسُفَ وَإِنَّا لَهُۥ لَنَٰصِحُونَ ۝ أَرْسِلْهُ مَعَنَا غَدًا يَرْتَعْ وَيَلْعَبْ وَإِنَّا لَهُۥ لَحَٰفِظُونَ ۝ قَالَ إِنِّى لَيَحْزُنُنِىٓ أَن تَذْهَبُواْ بِهِۦ وَأَخَافُ أَن يَأْكُلَهُ ٱلذِّئْبُ وَأَنتُمْ عَنْهُ غَٰفِلُونَ ۝ قَالُواْ لَئِنْ أَكَلَهُ ٱلذِّئْبُ وَنَحْنُ عُصْبَةٌ إِنَّآ إِذًا لَّخَٰسِرُونَ ۝ فَلَمَّا ذَهَبُواْ بِهِۦ وَأَجْمَعُوٓاْ أَن يَجْعَلُوهُ فِى غَيَٰبَتِ ٱلْجُبِّ وَأَوْحَيْنَآ إِلَيْهِ لَتُنَبِّئَنَّهُم بِأَمْرِهِمْ هَٰذَا وَهُمْ لَا يَشْعُرُونَ ۝ وَجَآءُوٓ أَبَاهُمْ عِشَآءً يَبْكُونَ ۝ قَالُواْ يَٰٓأَبَانَآ إِنَّا ذَهَبْنَا نَسْتَبِقُ وَتَرَكْنَا يُوسُفَ عِندَ مَتَٰعِنَا فَأَكَلَهُ ٱلذِّئْبُ وَمَآ أَنتَ بِمُؤْمِنٍ لَّنَا وَلَوْ كُنَّا صَٰدِقِينَ ۝ وَجَآءُو عَلَىٰ قَمِيصِهِۦ بِدَمٍ كَذِبٍ قَالَ بَلْ سَوَّلَتْ لَكُمْ أَنفُسُكُمْ أَمْرًا فَصَبْرٌ جَمِيلٌ

سُورَةُ يُوسُفَ

وَٱللَّهُ ٱلْمُسْتَعَانُ عَلَىٰ مَا تَصِفُونَ ۝ وَجَآءَتْ سَيَّارَةٌ فَأَرْسَلُوا۟ وَارِدَهُمْ فَأَدْلَىٰ دَلْوَهُۥ ۖ قَالَ يَٰبُشْرَىٰ هَٰذَا غُلَٰمٌ ۚ وَأَسَرُّوهُ بِضَٰعَةً ۚ وَٱللَّهُ عَلِيمٌۢ بِمَا يَعْمَلُونَ ۝ وَشَرَوْهُ بِثَمَنٍۭ بَخْسٍ دَرَٰهِمَ مَعْدُودَةٍ وَكَانُوا۟ فِيهِ مِنَ ٱلزَّٰهِدِينَ ۝ وَقَالَ ٱلَّذِى ٱشْتَرَىٰهُ مِن مِّصْرَ لِٱمْرَأَتِهِۦٓ أَكْرِمِى مَثْوَىٰهُ عَسَىٰٓ أَن يَنفَعَنَآ أَوْ نَتَّخِذَهُۥ وَلَدًا ۚ وَكَذَٰلِكَ مَكَّنَّا لِيُوسُفَ فِى ٱلْأَرْضِ وَلِنُعَلِّمَهُۥ مِن تَأْوِيلِ ٱلْأَحَادِيثِ ۚ وَٱللَّهُ غَالِبٌ عَلَىٰٓ أَمْرِهِۦ وَلَٰكِنَّ أَكْثَرَ ٱلنَّاسِ لَا يَعْلَمُونَ ۝ وَلَمَّا بَلَغَ أَشُدَّهُۥٓ ءَاتَيْنَٰهُ حُكْمًا وَعِلْمًا ۚ وَكَذَٰلِكَ نَجْزِى ٱلْمُحْسِنِينَ ۝ وَرَٰوَدَتْهُ ٱلَّتِى هُوَ فِى بَيْتِهَا عَن نَّفْسِهِۦ وَغَلَّقَتِ ٱلْأَبْوَٰبَ وَقَالَتْ هَيْتَ لَكَ ۚ قَالَ مَعَاذَ ٱللَّهِ ۖ إِنَّهُۥ رَبِّىٓ أَحْسَنَ مَثْوَاىَ ۖ إِنَّهُۥ لَا يُفْلِحُ ٱلظَّٰلِمُونَ ۝ وَلَقَدْ هَمَّتْ بِهِۦ ۖ وَهَمَّ بِهَا لَوْلَآ أَن رَّءَا بُرْهَٰنَ رَبِّهِۦ ۚ كَذَٰلِكَ لِنَصْرِفَ عَنْهُ ٱلسُّوٓءَ وَٱلْفَحْشَآءَ ۚ إِنَّهُۥ مِنْ عِبَادِنَا ٱلْمُخْلَصِينَ ۝ وَٱسْتَبَقَا ٱلْبَابَ وَقَدَّتْ قَمِيصَهُۥ مِن دُبُرٍ وَأَلْفَيَا سَيِّدَهَا لَدَا ٱلْبَابِ ۚ قَالَتْ مَا جَزَآءُ مَنْ أَرَادَ بِأَهْلِكَ سُوٓءًا إِلَّآ أَن يُسْجَنَ أَوْ عَذَابٌ

سُورَةُ يُوسُفَ

أَلِيمٌ ۝ قَالَ هِيَ رَاوَدَتْنِي عَن نَّفْسِي ۚ وَشَهِدَ شَاهِدٌ مِّنْ أَهْلِهَا إِن كَانَ قَمِيصُهُ قُدَّ مِن قُبُلٍ فَصَدَقَتْ وَهُوَ مِنَ ٱلْكَـٰذِبِينَ ۝ وَإِن كَانَ قَمِيصُهُ قُدَّ مِن دُبُرٍ فَكَذَبَتْ وَهُوَ مِنَ ٱلصَّـٰدِقِينَ ۝ فَلَمَّا رَءَا قَمِيصَهُ قُدَّ مِن دُبُرٍ قَالَ إِنَّهُ مِن كَيْدِكُنَّ ۖ إِنَّ كَيْدَكُنَّ عَظِيمٌ ۝ يُوسُفُ أَعْرِضْ عَنْ هَـٰذَا ۚ وَٱسْتَغْفِرِي لِذَنۢبِكِ ۖ إِنَّكِ كُنتِ مِنَ ٱلْخَاطِـِٔينَ ۝ ۞ وَقَالَ نِسْوَةٌ فِى ٱلْمَدِينَةِ ٱمْرَأَتُ ٱلْعَزِيزِ تُرَٰوِدُ فَتَىٰهَا عَن نَّفْسِهِ ۖ قَدْ شَغَفَهَا حُبًّا ۖ إِنَّا لَنَرَىٰهَا فِى ضَلَـٰلٍ مُّبِينٍ ۝ فَلَمَّا سَمِعَتْ بِمَكْرِهِنَّ أَرْسَلَتْ إِلَيْهِنَّ وَأَعْتَدَتْ لَهُنَّ مُتَّكَـًٔا وَءَاتَتْ كُلَّ وَٰحِدَةٍ مِّنْهُنَّ سِكِّينًا وَقَالَتِ ٱخْرُجْ عَلَيْهِنَّ ۖ فَلَمَّا رَأَيْنَهُۥٓ أَكْبَرْنَهُۥ وَقَطَّعْنَ أَيْدِيَهُنَّ وَقُلْنَ حَـٰشَ لِلَّهِ مَا هَـٰذَا بَشَرًا إِنْ هَـٰذَآ إِلَّا مَلَكٌ كَرِيمٌ ۝ قَالَتْ فَذَٰلِكُنَّ ٱلَّذِى لُمْتُنَّنِى فِيهِ ۖ وَلَقَدْ رَٰوَدتُّهُۥ عَن نَّفْسِهِۦ فَٱسْتَعْصَمَ ۖ وَلَئِن لَّمْ يَفْعَلْ مَآ ءَامُرُهُۥ لَيُسْجَنَنَّ وَلَيَكُونًا مِّنَ ٱلصَّـٰغِرِينَ ۝ قَالَ رَبِّ ٱلسِّجْنُ أَحَبُّ إِلَىَّ مِمَّا يَدْعُونَنِى إِلَيْهِ ۖ وَإِلَّا تَصْرِفْ عَنِّى كَيْدَهُنَّ أَصْبُ إِلَيْهِنَّ وَأَكُن مِّنَ ٱلْجَـٰهِلِينَ ۝ فَٱسْتَجَابَ لَهُۥ رَبُّهُۥ فَصَرَفَ عَنْهُ كَيْدَهُنَّ ۚ إِنَّهُۥ هُوَ ٱلسَّمِيعُ

سُورَةُ يُوسُفَ

ٱلۡعَلِيمُ ۝ ثُمَّ بَدَا لَهُم مِّنۢ بَعۡدِ مَا رَأَوُاْ ٱلۡءَايَٰتِ لَيَسۡجُنُنَّهُۥ حَتَّىٰ حِينٍ ۝ وَدَخَلَ مَعَهُ ٱلسِّجۡنَ فَتَيَانِۖ قَالَ أَحَدُهُمَآ إِنِّيٓ أَرَىٰنِيٓ أَعۡصِرُ خَمۡرٗاۖ وَقَالَ ٱلۡءَاخَرُ إِنِّيٓ أَرَىٰنِيٓ أَحۡمِلُ فَوۡقَ رَأۡسِي خُبۡزٗا تَأۡكُلُ ٱلطَّيۡرُ مِنۡهُۖ نَبِّئۡنَا بِتَأۡوِيلِهِۦٓۖ إِنَّا نَرَىٰكَ مِنَ ٱلۡمُحۡسِنِينَ ۝ قَالَ لَا يَأۡتِيكُمَا طَعَامٞ تُرۡزَقَانِهِۦٓ إِلَّا نَبَّأۡتُكُمَا بِتَأۡوِيلِهِۦ قَبۡلَ أَن يَأۡتِيَكُمَاۚ ذَٰلِكُمَا مِمَّا عَلَّمَنِي رَبِّيٓۚ إِنِّي تَرَكۡتُ مِلَّةَ قَوۡمٖ لَّا يُؤۡمِنُونَ بِٱللَّهِ وَهُم بِٱلۡءَاخِرَةِ هُمۡ كَٰفِرُونَ ۝ وَٱتَّبَعۡتُ مِلَّةَ ءَابَآءِيٓ إِبۡرَٰهِيمَ وَإِسۡحَٰقَ وَيَعۡقُوبَۚ مَا كَانَ لَنَآ أَن نُّشۡرِكَ بِٱللَّهِ مِن شَيۡءٖۚ ذَٰلِكَ مِن فَضۡلِ ٱللَّهِ عَلَيۡنَا وَعَلَى ٱلنَّاسِ وَلَٰكِنَّ أَكۡثَرَ ٱلنَّاسِ لَا يَشۡكُرُونَ ۝ يَٰصَٰحِبَيِ ٱلسِّجۡنِ ءَأَرۡبَابٞ مُّتَفَرِّقُونَ خَيۡرٌ أَمِ ٱللَّهُ ٱلۡوَٰحِدُ ٱلۡقَهَّارُ ۝ مَا تَعۡبُدُونَ مِن دُونِهِۦٓ إِلَّآ أَسۡمَآءٗ سَمَّيۡتُمُوهَآ أَنتُمۡ وَءَابَآؤُكُم مَّآ أَنزَلَ ٱللَّهُ بِهَا مِن سُلۡطَٰنٍۚ إِنِ ٱلۡحُكۡمُ إِلَّا لِلَّهِ أَمَرَ أَلَّا تَعۡبُدُوٓاْ إِلَّآ إِيَّاهُۚ ذَٰلِكَ ٱلدِّينُ ٱلۡقَيِّمُ وَلَٰكِنَّ أَكۡثَرَ ٱلنَّاسِ لَا يَعۡلَمُونَ ۝ يَٰصَٰحِبَيِ ٱلسِّجۡنِ أَمَّآ أَحَدُكُمَا فَيَسۡقِي رَبَّهُۥ خَمۡرٗاۖ وَأَمَّا ٱلۡءَاخَرُ فَيُصۡلَبُ فَتَأۡكُلُ ٱلطَّيۡرُ

سُورَةُ يُوسُف

مِن رَّأْسِهِۦ قُضِيَ ٱلْأَمْرُ ٱلَّذِى فِيهِ تَسْتَفْتِيَانِ ۝ وَقَالَ لِلَّذِى ظَنَّ أَنَّهُۥ نَاجٍ مِّنْهُمَا ٱذْكُرْنِى عِندَ رَبِّكَ فَأَنسَىٰهُ ٱلشَّيْطَٰنُ ذِكْرَ رَبِّهِۦ فَلَبِثَ فِى ٱلسِّجْنِ بِضْعَ سِنِينَ ۝ وَقَالَ ٱلْمَلِكُ إِنِّى أَرَىٰ سَبْعَ بَقَرَٰتٍ سِمَانٍ يَأْكُلُهُنَّ سَبْعٌ عِجَافٌ وَسَبْعَ سُنۢبُلَٰتٍ خُضْرٍ وَأُخَرَ يَابِسَٰتٍ يَٰٓأَيُّهَا ٱلْمَلَأُ أَفْتُونِى فِى رُءْيَٰىَ إِن كُنتُمْ لِلرُّءْيَا تَعْبُرُونَ ۝ قَالُوٓا۟ أَضْغَٰثُ أَحْلَٰمٍ وَمَا نَحْنُ بِتَأْوِيلِ ٱلْأَحْلَٰمِ بِعَٰلِمِينَ ۝ وَقَالَ ٱلَّذِى نَجَا مِنْهُمَا وَٱدَّكَرَ بَعْدَ أُمَّةٍ أَنَا۠ أُنَبِّئُكُم بِتَأْوِيلِهِۦ فَأَرْسِلُونِ ۝ يُوسُفُ أَيُّهَا ٱلصِّدِّيقُ أَفْتِنَا فِى سَبْعِ بَقَرَٰتٍ سِمَانٍ يَأْكُلُهُنَّ سَبْعٌ عِجَافٌ وَسَبْعِ سُنۢبُلَٰتٍ خُضْرٍ وَأُخَرَ يَابِسَٰتٍ لَّعَلِّىٓ أَرْجِعُ إِلَى ٱلنَّاسِ لَعَلَّهُمْ يَعْلَمُونَ ۝ قَالَ تَزْرَعُونَ سَبْعَ سِنِينَ دَأَبًا فَمَا حَصَدتُّمْ فَذَرُوهُ فِى سُنۢبُلِهِۦٓ إِلَّا قَلِيلًا مِّمَّا تَأْكُلُونَ ۝ ثُمَّ يَأْتِى مِنۢ بَعْدِ ذَٰلِكَ سَبْعٌ شِدَادٌ يَأْكُلْنَ مَا قَدَّمْتُمْ لَهُنَّ إِلَّا قَلِيلًا مِّمَّا تُحْصِنُونَ ۝ ثُمَّ يَأْتِى مِنۢ بَعْدِ ذَٰلِكَ عَامٌ فِيهِ يُغَاثُ ٱلنَّاسُ وَفِيهِ يَعْصِرُونَ ۝ وَقَالَ ٱلْمَلِكُ ٱئْتُونِى بِهِۦ فَلَمَّا جَآءَهُ ٱلرَّسُولُ قَالَ ٱرْجِعْ إِلَىٰ رَبِّكَ فَسْـَٔلْهُ مَا بَالُ

ٱلنِّسْوَةِ ٱلَّٰتِى قَطَّعْنَ أَيْدِيَهُنَّ إِنَّ رَبِّى بِكَيْدِهِنَّ عَلِيمٌ ۞ قَالَ مَا خَطْبُكُنَّ إِذْ رَٰوَدتُّنَّ يُوسُفَ عَن نَّفْسِهِۦ قُلْنَ حَٰشَ لِلَّهِ مَا عَلِمْنَا عَلَيْهِ مِن سُوٓءٍ قَالَتِ ٱمْرَأَتُ ٱلْعَزِيزِ ٱلْـَٰٔنَ حَصْحَصَ ٱلْحَقُّ أَنَا۠ رَٰوَدتُّهُۥ عَن نَّفْسِهِۦ وَإِنَّهُۥ لَمِنَ ٱلصَّٰدِقِينَ ۞ ذَٰلِكَ لِيَعْلَمَ أَنِّى لَمْ أَخُنْهُ بِٱلْغَيْبِ وَأَنَّ ٱللَّهَ لَا يَهْدِى كَيْدَ ٱلْخَآئِنِينَ ۞ ۞ وَمَآ أُبَرِّئُ نَفْسِىٓ إِنَّ ٱلنَّفْسَ لَأَمَّارَةٌۢ بِٱلسُّوٓءِ إِلَّا مَا رَحِمَ رَبِّىٓ إِنَّ رَبِّى غَفُورٌ رَّحِيمٌ ۞ وَقَالَ ٱلْمَلِكُ ٱئْتُونِى بِهِۦٓ أَسْتَخْلِصْهُ لِنَفْسِى فَلَمَّا كَلَّمَهُۥ قَالَ إِنَّكَ ٱلْيَوْمَ لَدَيْنَا مَكِينٌ أَمِينٌ ۞ قَالَ ٱجْعَلْنِى عَلَىٰ خَزَآئِنِ ٱلْأَرْضِ إِنِّى حَفِيظٌ عَلِيمٌ ۞ وَكَذَٰلِكَ مَكَّنَّا لِيُوسُفَ فِى ٱلْأَرْضِ يَتَبَوَّأُ مِنْهَا حَيْثُ يَشَآءُ نُصِيبُ بِرَحْمَتِنَا مَن نَّشَآءُ وَلَا نُضِيعُ أَجْرَ ٱلْمُحْسِنِينَ ۞ وَلَأَجْرُ ٱلْـَٔاخِرَةِ خَيْرٌ لِّلَّذِينَ ءَامَنُوا۟ وَكَانُوا۟ يَتَّقُونَ ۞ وَجَآءَ إِخْوَةُ يُوسُفَ فَدَخَلُوا۟ عَلَيْهِ فَعَرَفَهُمْ وَهُمْ لَهُۥ مُنكِرُونَ ۞ وَلَمَّا جَهَّزَهُم بِجَهَازِهِمْ قَالَ ٱئْتُونِى بِأَخٍ لَّكُم مِّنْ أَبِيكُمْ أَلَا تَرَوْنَ أَنِّىٓ أُوفِى ٱلْكَيْلَ وَأَنَا۠ خَيْرُ ٱلْمُنزِلِينَ ۞ فَإِن لَّمْ تَأْتُونِى بِهِۦ فَلَا كَيْلَ لَكُمْ عِندِى وَلَا تَقْرَبُونِ ۞ قَالُوا۟ سَنُرَٰوِدُ عَنْهُ أَبَاهُ

سُورَةُ يُوسُفَ

وَإِنَّا لَفَاعِلُونَ ۝ وَقَالَ لِفِتْيَانِهِ اجْعَلُوا بِضَاعَتَهُمْ فِي رِحَالِهِمْ لَعَلَّهُمْ يَعْرِفُونَهَا إِذَا انقَلَبُوا إِلَىٰ أَهْلِهِمْ لَعَلَّهُمْ يَرْجِعُونَ ۝ فَلَمَّا رَجَعُوا إِلَىٰ أَبِيهِمْ قَالُوا يَا أَبَانَا مُنِعَ مِنَّا الْكَيْلُ فَأَرْسِلْ مَعَنَا أَخَانَا نَكْتَلْ وَإِنَّا لَهُ لَحَافِظُونَ ۝ قَالَ هَلْ آمَنُكُمْ عَلَيْهِ إِلَّا كَمَا أَمِنْتُكُمْ عَلَىٰ أَخِيهِ مِن قَبْلُ فَاللَّهُ خَيْرٌ حَافِظًا ۖ وَهُوَ أَرْحَمُ الرَّاحِمِينَ ۝ وَلَمَّا فَتَحُوا مَتَاعَهُمْ وَجَدُوا بِضَاعَتَهُمْ رُدَّتْ إِلَيْهِمْ ۖ قَالُوا يَا أَبَانَا مَا نَبْغِي ۖ هَـٰذِهِ بِضَاعَتُنَا رُدَّتْ إِلَيْنَا ۖ وَنَمِيرُ أَهْلَنَا وَنَحْفَظُ أَخَانَا وَنَزْدَادُ كَيْلَ بَعِيرٍ ۖ ذَٰلِكَ كَيْلٌ يَسِيرٌ ۝ قَالَ لَنْ أُرْسِلَهُ مَعَكُمْ حَتَّىٰ تُؤْتُونِ مَوْثِقًا مِّنَ اللَّهِ لَتَأْتُنَّنِي بِهِ إِلَّا أَن يُحَاطَ بِكُمْ ۖ فَلَمَّا آتَوْهُ مَوْثِقَهُمْ قَالَ اللَّهُ عَلَىٰ مَا نَقُولُ وَكِيلٌ ۝ وَقَالَ يَا بَنِيَّ لَا تَدْخُلُوا مِن بَابٍ وَاحِدٍ وَادْخُلُوا مِنْ أَبْوَابٍ مُّتَفَرِّقَةٍ ۖ وَمَا أُغْنِي عَنكُم مِّنَ اللَّهِ مِن شَيْءٍ ۖ إِنِ الْحُكْمُ إِلَّا لِلَّهِ ۖ عَلَيْهِ تَوَكَّلْتُ ۖ وَعَلَيْهِ فَلْيَتَوَكَّلِ الْمُتَوَكِّلُونَ ۝ وَلَمَّا دَخَلُوا مِنْ حَيْثُ أَمَرَهُمْ أَبُوهُم مَّا كَانَ يُغْنِي عَنْهُم مِّنَ اللَّهِ مِن شَيْءٍ إِلَّا حَاجَةً فِي نَفْسِ يَعْقُوبَ قَضَاهَا ۚ وَإِنَّهُ

سُورَةُ يُوسُف

لَذُو عِلْمٍ لِّمَا عَلَّمْنَهُ وَلَكِنَّ أَكْثَرَ ٱلنَّاسِ لَا يَعْلَمُونَ ۝ وَلَمَّا دَخَلُوا۟ عَلَىٰ يُوسُفَ ءَاوَىٰٓ إِلَيْهِ أَخَاهُ قَالَ إِنِّىٓ أَنَا۠ أَخُوكَ فَلَا تَبْتَئِسْ بِمَا كَانُوا۟ يَعْمَلُونَ ۝ فَلَمَّا جَهَّزَهُم بِجَهَازِهِمْ جَعَلَ ٱلسِّقَايَةَ فِى رَحْلِ أَخِيهِ ثُمَّ أَذَّنَ مُؤَذِّنٌ أَيَّتُهَا ٱلْعِيرُ إِنَّكُمْ لَسَٰرِقُونَ ۝ قَالُوا۟ وَأَقْبَلُوا۟ عَلَيْهِم مَّاذَا تَفْقِدُونَ ۝ قَالُوا۟ نَفْقِدُ صُوَاعَ ٱلْمَلِكِ وَلِمَن جَآءَ بِهِۦ حِمْلُ بَعِيرٍ وَأَنَا۠ بِهِۦ زَعِيمٌ ۝ قَالُوا۟ تَٱللَّهِ لَقَدْ عَلِمْتُم مَّا جِئْنَا لِنُفْسِدَ فِى ٱلْأَرْضِ وَمَا كُنَّا سَٰرِقِينَ ۝ قَالُوا۟ فَمَا جَزَٰٓؤُهُۥٓ إِن كُنتُمْ كَٰذِبِينَ ۝ قَالُوا۟ جَزَٰٓؤُهُۥ مَن وُجِدَ فِى رَحْلِهِۦ فَهُوَ جَزَٰٓؤُهُۥ كَذَٰلِكَ نَجْزِى ٱلظَّٰلِمِينَ ۝ فَبَدَأَ بِأَوْعِيَتِهِمْ قَبْلَ وِعَآءِ أَخِيهِ ثُمَّ ٱسْتَخْرَجَهَا مِن وِعَآءِ أَخِيهِ كَذَٰلِكَ كِدْنَا لِيُوسُفَ مَا كَانَ لِيَأْخُذَ أَخَاهُ فِى دِينِ ٱلْمَلِكِ إِلَّآ أَن يَشَآءَ ٱللَّهُ نَرْفَعُ دَرَجَٰتٍ مَّن نَّشَآءُ وَفَوْقَ كُلِّ ذِى عِلْمٍ عَلِيمٌ ۝ قَالُوٓا۟ إِن يَسْرِقْ فَقَدْ سَرَقَ أَخٌ لَّهُۥ مِن قَبْلُ فَأَسَرَّهَا يُوسُفُ فِى نَفْسِهِۦ وَلَمْ يُبْدِهَا لَهُمْ قَالَ أَنتُمْ شَرٌّ مَّكَانًا وَٱللَّهُ أَعْلَمُ بِمَا

سُورَةُ يُوسُفَ

تَصِفُونَ ۝ قَالُوا۟ يَـٰٓأَيُّهَا ٱلْعَزِيزُ إِنَّ لَهُۥٓ أَبًا شَيْخًا كَبِيرًا فَخُذْ أَحَدَنَا مَكَانَهُۥٓ إِنَّا نَرَىٰكَ مِنَ ٱلْمُحْسِنِينَ ۝ قَالَ مَعَاذَ ٱللَّهِ أَن نَّأْخُذَ إِلَّا مَن وَجَدْنَا مَتَـٰعَنَا عِندَهُۥٓ إِنَّآ إِذًا لَّظَـٰلِمُونَ ۝ فَلَمَّا ٱسْتَيْـَٔسُوا۟ مِنْهُ خَلَصُوا۟ نَجِيًّا ۖ قَالَ كَبِيرُهُمْ أَلَمْ تَعْلَمُوٓا۟ أَنَّ أَبَاكُمْ قَدْ أَخَذَ عَلَيْكُم مَّوْثِقًا مِّنَ ٱللَّهِ وَمِن قَبْلُ مَا فَرَّطتُمْ فِى يُوسُفَ ۖ فَلَنْ أَبْرَحَ ٱلْأَرْضَ حَتَّىٰ يَأْذَنَ لِىٓ أَبِىٓ أَوْ يَحْكُمَ ٱللَّهُ لِى ۖ وَهُوَ خَيْرُ ٱلْحَـٰكِمِينَ ۝ ٱرْجِعُوٓا۟ إِلَىٰٓ أَبِيكُمْ فَقُولُوا۟ يَـٰٓأَبَانَآ إِنَّ ٱبْنَكَ سَرَقَ وَمَا شَهِدْنَآ إِلَّا بِمَا عَلِمْنَا وَمَا كُنَّا لِلْغَيْبِ حَـٰفِظِينَ ۝ وَسْـَٔلِ ٱلْقَرْيَةَ ٱلَّتِى كُنَّا فِيهَا وَٱلْعِيرَ ٱلَّتِىٓ أَقْبَلْنَا فِيهَا ۖ وَإِنَّا لَصَـٰدِقُونَ ۝ قَالَ بَلْ سَوَّلَتْ لَكُمْ أَنفُسُكُمْ أَمْرًا ۖ فَصَبْرٌ جَمِيلٌ ۖ عَسَى ٱللَّهُ أَن يَأْتِيَنِى بِهِمْ جَمِيعًا ۚ إِنَّهُۥ هُوَ ٱلْعَلِيمُ ٱلْحَكِيمُ ۝ وَتَوَلَّىٰ عَنْهُمْ وَقَالَ يَـٰٓأَسَفَىٰ عَلَىٰ يُوسُفَ وَٱبْيَضَّتْ عَيْنَاهُ مِنَ ٱلْحُزْنِ فَهُوَ كَظِيمٌ ۝ قَالُوا۟ تَٱللَّهِ تَفْتَؤُا۟ تَذْكُرُ يُوسُفَ حَتَّىٰ تَكُونَ حَرَضًا أَوْ تَكُونَ مِنَ ٱلْهَـٰلِكِينَ ۝ قَالَ إِنَّمَآ أَشْكُوا۟ بَثِّى وَحُزْنِىٓ إِلَى ٱللَّهِ وَأَعْلَمُ مِنَ ٱللَّهِ مَا لَا تَعْلَمُونَ ۝

سُورَةُ يُوسُفَ

يَٰبَنِىَّ ٱذْهَبُوا۟ فَتَحَسَّسُوا۟ مِن يُوسُفَ وَأَخِيهِ وَلَا تَا۟يْـَٔسُوا۟ مِن رَّوْحِ ٱللَّهِ إِنَّهُۥ لَا يَا۟يْـَٔسُ مِن رَّوْحِ ٱللَّهِ إِلَّا ٱلْقَوْمُ ٱلْكَٰفِرُونَ ۝٨٧ فَلَمَّا دَخَلُوا۟ عَلَيْهِ قَالُوا۟ يَٰٓأَيُّهَا ٱلْعَزِيزُ مَسَّنَا وَأَهْلَنَا ٱلضُّرُّ وَجِئْنَا بِبِضَٰعَةٍ مُّزْجَىٰةٍ فَأَوْفِ لَنَا ٱلْكَيْلَ وَتَصَدَّقْ عَلَيْنَآ إِنَّ ٱللَّهَ يَجْزِى ٱلْمُتَصَدِّقِينَ ۝٨٨ قَالَ هَلْ عَلِمْتُم مَّا فَعَلْتُم بِيُوسُفَ وَأَخِيهِ إِذْ أَنتُمْ جَٰهِلُونَ ۝٨٩ قَالُوٓا۟ أَءِنَّكَ لَأَنتَ يُوسُفُ قَالَ أَنَا۠ يُوسُفُ وَهَٰذَآ أَخِى قَدْ مَنَّ ٱللَّهُ عَلَيْنَآ إِنَّهُۥ مَن يَتَّقِ وَيَصْبِرْ فَإِنَّ ٱللَّهَ لَا يُضِيعُ أَجْرَ ٱلْمُحْسِنِينَ ۝٩٠ قَالُوا۟ تَٱللَّهِ لَقَدْ ءَاثَرَكَ ٱللَّهُ عَلَيْنَا وَإِن كُنَّا لَخَٰطِـِٔينَ ۝٩١ قَالَ لَا تَثْرِيبَ عَلَيْكُمُ ٱلْيَوْمَ يَغْفِرُ ٱللَّهُ لَكُمْ وَهُوَ أَرْحَمُ ٱلرَّٰحِمِينَ ۝٩٢ ٱذْهَبُوا۟ بِقَمِيصِى هَٰذَا فَأَلْقُوهُ عَلَىٰ وَجْهِ أَبِى يَأْتِ بَصِيرًا وَأْتُونِى بِأَهْلِكُمْ أَجْمَعِينَ ۝٩٣ وَلَمَّا فَصَلَتِ ٱلْعِيرُ قَالَ أَبُوهُمْ إِنِّى لَأَجِدُ رِيحَ يُوسُفَ لَوْلَآ أَن تُفَنِّدُونِ ۝٩٤ قَالُوا۟ تَٱللَّهِ إِنَّكَ لَفِى ضَلَٰلِكَ ٱلْقَدِيمِ ۝٩٥ فَلَمَّآ أَن جَآءَ ٱلْبَشِيرُ أَلْقَىٰهُ عَلَىٰ وَجْهِهِۦ فَٱرْتَدَّ بَصِيرًا قَالَ

سُورَةُ يُوسُفَ

أَلَمْ أَقُل لَّكُمْ إِنِّي أَعْلَمُ مِنَ ٱللَّهِ مَا لَا تَعْلَمُونَ ۞ قَالُوا۟ يَـٰٓأَبَانَا ٱسْتَغْفِرْ لَنَا ذُنُوبَنَآ إِنَّا كُنَّا خَـٰطِـِٔينَ ۞ قَالَ سَوْفَ أَسْتَغْفِرُ لَكُمْ رَبِّىٓ إِنَّهُۥ هُوَ ٱلْغَفُورُ ٱلرَّحِيمُ ۞ فَلَمَّا دَخَلُوا۟ عَلَىٰ يُوسُفَ ءَاوَىٰٓ إِلَيْهِ أَبَوَيْهِ وَقَالَ ٱدْخُلُوا۟ مِصْرَ إِن شَآءَ ٱللَّهُ ءَامِنِينَ ۞ وَرَفَعَ أَبَوَيْهِ عَلَى ٱلْعَرْشِ وَخَرُّوا۟ لَهُۥ سُجَّدًا وَقَالَ يَـٰٓأَبَتِ هَـٰذَا تَأْوِيلُ رُءْيَـٰىَ مِن قَبْلُ قَدْ جَعَلَهَا رَبِّى حَقًّا وَقَدْ أَحْسَنَ بِىٓ إِذْ أَخْرَجَنِى مِنَ ٱلسِّجْنِ وَجَآءَ بِكُم مِّنَ ٱلْبَدْوِ مِنۢ بَعْدِ أَن نَّزَغَ ٱلشَّيْطَـٰنُ بَيْنِى وَبَيْنَ إِخْوَتِىٓ إِنَّ رَبِّى لَطِيفٌ لِّمَا يَشَآءُ إِنَّهُۥ هُوَ ٱلْعَلِيمُ ٱلْحَكِيمُ ۞ رَبِّ قَدْ ءَاتَيْتَنِى مِنَ ٱلْمُلْكِ وَعَلَّمْتَنِى مِن تَأْوِيلِ ٱلْأَحَادِيثِ فَاطِرَ ٱلسَّمَـٰوَٰتِ وَٱلْأَرْضِ أَنتَ وَلِىِّۦ فِى ٱلدُّنْيَا وَٱلْـَٔاخِرَةِ تَوَفَّنِى مُسْلِمًا وَأَلْحِقْنِى بِٱلصَّـٰلِحِينَ ۞ ذَٰلِكَ مِنْ أَنۢبَآءِ ٱلْغَيْبِ نُوحِيهِ إِلَيْكَ وَمَا كُنتَ لَدَيْهِمْ إِذْ أَجْمَعُوٓا۟ أَمْرَهُمْ وَهُمْ يَمْكُرُونَ ۞ وَمَآ أَكْثَرُ ٱلنَّاسِ وَلَوْ حَرَصْتَ بِمُؤْمِنِينَ ۞ وَمَا تَسْـَٔلُهُمْ عَلَيْهِ مِنْ أَجْرٍ إِنْ هُوَ إِلَّا ذِكْرٌ لِّلْعَـٰلَمِينَ ۞ وَكَأَيِّن مِّنْ ءَايَةٍ فِى ٱلسَّمَـٰوَٰتِ وَٱلْأَرْضِ يَمُرُّونَ عَلَيْهَا

سورة يوسف

وَهُم عَنْهَا مُعْرِضُونَ ۝ وَمَا يُؤْمِنُ أَكْثَرُهُم بِٱللَّهِ إِلَّا وَهُم مُّشْرِكُونَ ۝ أَفَأَمِنُوٓا۟ أَن تَأْتِيَهُمْ غَٰشِيَةٌ مِّنْ عَذَابِ ٱللَّهِ أَوْ تَأْتِيَهُمُ ٱلسَّاعَةُ بَغْتَةً وَهُمْ لَا يَشْعُرُونَ ۝ قُلْ هَٰذِهِۦ سَبِيلِىٓ أَدْعُوٓا۟ إِلَى ٱللَّهِ عَلَىٰ بَصِيرَةٍ أَنَا۠ وَمَنِ ٱتَّبَعَنِى وَسُبْحَٰنَ ٱللَّهِ وَمَآ أَنَا۠ مِنَ ٱلْمُشْرِكِينَ ۝ وَمَآ أَرْسَلْنَا مِن قَبْلِكَ إِلَّا رِجَالًا نُّوحِىٓ إِلَيْهِم مِّنْ أَهْلِ ٱلْقُرَىٰٓ أَفَلَمْ يَسِيرُوا۟ فِى ٱلْأَرْضِ فَيَنظُرُوا۟ كَيْفَ كَانَ عَٰقِبَةُ ٱلَّذِينَ مِن قَبْلِهِمْ وَلَدَارُ ٱلْءَاخِرَةِ خَيْرٌ لِّلَّذِينَ ٱتَّقَوْا۟ أَفَلَا تَعْقِلُونَ ۝ حَتَّىٰٓ إِذَا ٱسْتَيْـَٔسَ ٱلرُّسُلُ وَظَنُّوٓا۟ أَنَّهُمْ قَدْ كُذِبُوا۟ جَآءَهُمْ نَصْرُنَا فَنُجِّىَ مَن نَّشَآءُ وَلَا يُرَدُّ بَأْسُنَا عَنِ ٱلْقَوْمِ ٱلْمُجْرِمِينَ ۝ لَقَدْ كَانَ فِى قَصَصِهِمْ عِبْرَةٌ لِّأُو۟لِى ٱلْأَلْبَٰبِ مَا كَانَ حَدِيثًا يُفْتَرَىٰ وَلَٰكِن تَصْدِيقَ ٱلَّذِى بَيْنَ يَدَيْهِ وَتَفْصِيلَ كُلِّ شَىْءٍ وَهُدًى وَرَحْمَةً لِّقَوْمٍ يُؤْمِنُونَ ۝